Ecclesiological Investigations

Series Editor

Gerard Mannion

Volume 1

Receiving 'The Nature and Mission of the Church'

Forthcoming titles in the series:

Receiving 'The Nature and Mission of the Church'

ECCLESIAL REALITY AND ECUMENICAL HORIZONS
FOR THE TWENTY-FIRST CENTURY

Edited by

Paul M. Collins
Michael A. Fahey

t&t clark

Published by T&T Clark
A Continuum imprint
The Tower Building, 11 York Road, London SE1 7NX
80 Maiden Lane, Suite 704, New York, NY 10038

www.continuumbooks.com

British Library Cataloguing-in-Publication Data
A catalogue record for this book is available from the British Library.

Typeset by Data Standards Ltd, Frome, Somerset
Printed and bound in Great Britain by Biddles Ltd, King's Lynn, Norfolk

ISBN-10: HB: 0-567-03243-4
ISBN-13: HB: 978-0-567-03243-0

CONTENTS

The Open Church Re-envisioned: Ecclesiological Investigations – a New International Research Network

Gerard Mannion

The Church emerged out of a world of flux and change in first-century Palestine and quickly spread throughout the Hellenistic world of what we today call the Middle East and beyond. Within just a few centuries the message of the gospel of love, justice and righteousness had spread to much of the then known world. Why did this way of being-in-community have such an impact and so soon? Some might well say, because it eventually became the official religion of the Roman Empire, but that happened long after Christianity had spread far from its roots in Palestine. Perhaps one of the key reasons why people wished to hear this 'good news' and to join these new communities was because of *what* was being said in the proclamation of this news and because of how these people lived their lives.

First-century Palestine was an occupied land where many cultures interacted with one another. There were numerous charismatic leaders and would-be prophets and new religious movements jostling for converts alongside one other and in the midst of the older more established forms of the Jewish faith as well. Why today do we still have one of these movements, which emerged out of the teaching of one such charismatic leader, Jesus of Nazareth, whose followers came to understand him as 'the Christ', the Messiah or 'Anointed One' of God, indeed as God become human – 'God among us'?

The Church emerged out of those Jewish communities that wished to offer a renewed way of relating to God and hearing and responding to God's message and thus a renewed way of living in the world. Jesus had led the way. They felt this was the best way to respond to the challenges of those times. The very earliest Christians rejected alternative ways available at the time such as violent insurrection, retreat into an overt emphasis upon certain fundamentals of religion, or ways of being religious where a privileged few prospered at the expense of the many, or of departing from the faith altogether. They rejected a community with distinct membership criteria and with fixed boundaries. Everyone, from Roman officials and soldiers to the despised and marginalized of society – the tax collectors, prostitutes and those who were seen as insane and those with diseases such as leprosy – none was turned away. It did not matter if one was poor (or wealthy) – all were welcome.

So the Church flourished and grew because, from the outset, it recognized that, in the midst of a very pluralistic society, perhaps God was trying to indicate how people should live alongside one another. The early Church grew and spread because it was not exclusive but rather inclusive. This is not to say that some Christians, from early times, did not clash with those of other faiths, of no faith, and even with each other, but, by and large, the evidence suggests that the gospel of love, justice and righteousness entailed a commitment that such love and openness should be extended to all persons.

Today our societies, indeed our globalized world, mirror that world of first-century Palestine in many ways. There are divisions, there are clashes among people and among faiths, there are those who are despised and marginalized in our societies, there is mass poverty. For the Church today then, as in its earliest days, the way forward, the way to follow the gospel and the Church's mission, is not simply to recognize the pluralistic reality in the midst of which we live, but to affirm and to celebrate it. The Church must be inclusive as opposed to building artificial barriers to the love of God. The gospel calls us to heal divisions, to build bridges, to love all persons – even our 'enemies'.

It was with such sentiments in mind that theologians and activists from four different continents and from many different churches gathered one year ago to discuss the issues and themes of greatest importance to the Church of today and of the future, including explorations concerning the nature and role of the Church. Their discussions took place between 12 and 15 January 2007, in Wales, at St Deiniol's Library, founded by the 'Grand Old Man', the Victorian statesman Sir William Gladstone. The event marked the first conference of the recently established Ecclesiological Investigations International Research Network.

This conference was a landmark event for the new Network and follows another initiative exploring the nature and role of the Church that has proved very successful indeed, namely, the establishment of the new Ecclesiological Investigations Group of the American Academy of Religion, which staged its first sessions in Washington, DC, toward the end of November 2006 – and whose presentations are published in this present volume.[1]

The Mission of the Ecclesiological Investigations Research Network

The embryonic mission statement of this new Network states that it seeks to serve as a hub for national and international collaboration in ecclesiology, drawing together other groups and networks, initiating research ventures, and providing both administrative support as well as funding to support conversations, research, and education in this field. The abiding ethos of the Network will be that the Church must be inclusive in order to be relevant and truly to fulfil its mission. Finally, the task of this international Network is to facilitate open and pluralistic conversation and collaboration.

The Network's Five Fundamental Aims

The aims of the Network are:

1. The establishment of partnerships between scholars, research projects and research centres across the world.
2. The development of virtual, textual and actual conversation between the many persons and groups involved in research and debate about ecclesiology.
3. Organizing and sharing in colloquia, symposia and conferences.
4. Encouraging joint teaching, exchanges of postgraduate students and faculty.
5. Publishing this new and ongoing series of volumes on Ecclesiological Investigations.

Some Background

The Network has emerged from small beginnings. In 2002, questions concerning the nature, role, and contemporary life of the Church led four scholars to begin a series of meetings to discuss a series of papers on a wide variety of ecclesiological themes. Hence there emerged a three-year research initiative and series of conversations involving Paul Collins, Gerard Mannion, Gareth Powell, and Kenneth Wilson. They initially met under the auspices of Chichester University and hence the group took as their name 'The Chichester Group', which brought together an Anglican, a Roman Catholic, and two Methodists. A volume from these discussions (*Christian Community Now: Ecclesiological Investigations*) will be published shortly.

In the summer of 2005, invitations were sent out to persons in the United Kingdom to form a small steering group to help establish a broader network of people and institutions involved in the field of ecclesiology. The group's chief aims included the intention to focus upon ecclesiology from the standpoint of different Christian denominations and from differing international and cultural perspectives (ecumenical and comparative intentions). The group was to share an openness to and celebration of the pluralistic reality in the midst of which the churches today find themselves living (pluralistic intentions). The work of the group would deal with the challenges facing churches today (praxis-oriented intentions). A major new publication series formed a key part of the new group's intentions, along with the establishment of study days and teaching initiatives pertaining to the Church (educational intentions). A limited amount of funding was raised for the initial meetings of this group. Members from a wide variety of church and organizational backgrounds agreed to join the steering group.

The outcome was the establishment of a partnership involving five institutions in which the Centre for the Study of the Contemporary Ecclesiology (originally located at Liverpool Hope University) has played a leading role. Links were established with numerous other centres and institutions pursuing similar aims across the international community. In addition to this research centre, the four initial partners in the United Kingdom were thus the Department of Theology at Chichester University; Durham University's Research Centre for Contemporary Catholic Studies; Heythrop College, London; and Ripon College, Cuddesdon, Oxford. Further international partner institutions have since been added to their number, including from Canada (St Michael's College, Toronto), the USA (Boston College), Belgium (Catholic University of Leuven), and three from India (Old Orthodox Seminary, Kottayam, the University of Calicut, and the Tamil Nadu Theological Seminary, Madurai). Most recently the Queen's Ecumenical Foundation, Birmingham, and the Milltown Institute, Dublin, have also joined this expanding group. From this there has emerged the Ecclesiological Investigations Research Network.

In November 2005, at Old Saint Joseph's Parish Hall, Philadelphia, a reception was held to launch the proposed New Ecclesiology Program Unit of the American Academy of Religion, sponsored by Liverpool Hope University and organized by Paul Collins, Michael Fahey and Gerard Mannion, and with much support from elsewhere. In December of that year the Academy approved the proposals. The new group also took the title Ecclesiological Investigations and aims to provide a ready platform and further opportunities for dialogue for those involved in the field of the study of the Church in its numerous forms.

From such beginnings, the American Academy of Religion Group has progressed from strength to strength. In November 2007, its sessions held in San Diego explored 'Communion and Otherness: Contemporary Challenges of "Impaired Communion"' and 'The Church and Its Many Asian Faces/ Perspectives on Transnational Communion'. Thus the Network's significant and swift progress in helping to raise the profile of the study of ecclesiology to date.

Network Initiatives to Date

The Network has already made significant progress which has brought new attention to the importance of the study of ecclesiology for our times. In addition to the popular new program unit of the American Academy of Religion, a new seminar of the United Kingdom's Society for the Study of Theology, also focusing upon ecclesiology, was established at last year's conference at Girton College, Cambridge University, and a twice-yearly series of 'Study Days in Ecclesiology' for research students and other interested parties in the field, has taken take place. The first three were held in the United Kingdom and the next is planned for Dublin in 2008. Analogous study-oriented events are planned in other countries. Successful negotiations with T&T Clark International led to the launch of this new series of publications for the Network, with the first four volumes announced for 2008.[2]

This series seeks to help fulfil the broader aims and objectives of the Network and involves collaboration among a wide range of international scholars, research centres, and projects across the field of ecclesiological inquiry. This includes work in historical, collaborative, denominational, methodological, ecumenical, inter-faith, conceptual, thematic, and interdisciplinary forms of ecclesiological inquiry, as well as studies of particular traditions, developments, and debates pertinent to the wider field.

Not only does the series seek to publish the very best of research presented to the Network's various meetings, conferences and colloquia, it also seeks to be a visibly identifiable publication outlet for quality research in ecclesiology worldwide, tapping into a truly global network of research groups, projects, church organizations and practitioners, experts and scholars in the field. The series also aims to encourage and indeed commission collaborative volumes and 'cutting edge' monographs in the field, as well as textbooks that will further enhance knowledge, understanding, and dialogue in the field. The series also seeks to offer a home to thematic collections of essays and conferences proceedings from numerous additional groups and research centres in the field. Thus, in particular, the series seeks to incorporate the best of the scholarly papers presented at the American Academy of Religion Program Group sessions, the annual Ecclesiological Investigations International Conference, the Society for the Study of Theology, the European Society of Catholic Theologians, the Catholic Theological Society of America, and similar gatherings. It will also seek to reflect the wider debates generated in relation to such papers and meetings.

The Network and Series alike are in partnership with the journal *Ecclesiology*, edited by Paul Avis, which the Network endorses as a further worthy and fruitful outlet for ongoing ecclesiological inquiry.

Catholicity in Action: The St Deiniol's First International Conference

This conference arose from a shared concern that the future of the Church is of crucial importance for the well-being of all human society, not just to those who happen to call themselves Christians. Delegates came from India, Pakistan, the United States, Australia, Belgium, Canada, Germany, the Netherlands, Ireland, Italy, Scotland, Wales, and England. The number of denominations represented ran well into double figures.

The concern of the gathering at St Deiniol's was to be clear sighted about the present situation of the Church, to think through appropriate methodologies, and to plan the future work of the Network. Those attending came in their personal capacities and not as representatives of churches or academic institutions. They were united by a passion for the subject and conviction of its importance. They hoped that the freedom of the conversation that took place would, in turn, characterize the future work of this initiative.

This first conference was not a 'private conference' to which only the great and the good were invited. Far from it. Its organizers tried to make it as inclusive of all churches, perspectives, and geographical representation as they possibly could. They invited various people from across the globe and from different churches and perspectives and with differing experiences. The organizers felt that the quality and productivity of the conversation would be greatly enhanced by the fact that nobody was there to peddle an official or party line – all discussion would be open in character.

The participants thus gathered to identify and discern key issues, topics, and themes of concern and importance for the Church and for ecclesiological research and collaboration for the Church in our times. Members of the Network steering group were keen to invite and welcome further suggestions and collaboration, while emphasizing that no one issue or interest group (or ecclesial perspective, of course), should be allowed to dominate the work of the Network itself.

The term 'inclusive' as employed in the Network's literature is meant in an ecclesiologically broader sense than purely being welcoming to minority groups and persons that the Church has treated shamefully in various ways in the past and present alike – although of course it is meant in that sense in a very real and vivid fashion. It also means 'inclusive' as opposed to 'exclusivist' and 'superior' (in contrast to certain ecclesiologies afoot in many churches today) whereby the Church turns inwards from postmodernity and retreats into 'fundamentals', perceiving itself to be superior to 'the world' and needing to stay aloof from being 'infected' by the trends of modernity and now postmodernity. In other words, the preference for an open and pluralistic and dialogical ecclesiology is represented by the phrase 'the Church must be inclusive if it is to be relevant'.

So inclusivity is about much more than any single issue or any particular ecclesial community or group. The conference had no dominant theme other than to foster open and honest ecclesiological dialogue toward the end of enhancing that wider ecumenism within and without the Church that our age requires.

We did not start with a list of organizations and groups; instead we started with contexts, the work people have been engaged in, and the potential perspectives they could bring to the conversation.

The themes touched upon by the various conference sessions and papers included developments in ecclesiology within different ecclesial traditions since 1965, recent ecumenical horizons and developments, including the idea of 'receptive ecumenism', the notion of partial communion, minority churches in Muslim countries, experimental, emerging and house church movements, inclusivity and the Church itself, the Anglican Church today, perspectives on the current situation *vis-à-vis* homosexuals across numerous churches, a Dalit liberation theology perspective, Christian–Muslim dialogue, Black Christianity in Britain, countering prejudice within church communities, interreligious dialogue in general, postmodern approaches and challenges, fostering greater ecclesial dialogue and trends and prospects for research, as well as the need to publish in the field today. Perspectives on the Church were offered from different national, continental, denominational, and contextual perspectives.

The organizers knew that an atmosphere of openness and courtesy to all were essential to the conference's success. And so it proved to be: the event was a gathering of committed people and an extremely positive atmosphere prevailed throughout. It was a special, constructive and moving weekend in many ways and participants stressed afterwards that they have no doubt that much good will come out of it for the Church, for ecumenical discussions, and for ecclesiology in general. The Open Church – a community where all are welcomed – was mirrored in that gathering.

All in all, the enduring hope was manifestly expressed that the outcomes of this conference would help inform, develop and enhance the fundamental aims of the proposed Network, namely, fostering and developing academic collaboration, building international understanding and interchanges among academics, sharing ideas and experiences between many diverse institutions, and the creation and development of a truly effective international Network.

Developing the International Network

Thus the Ecclesiological Investigations Network has been established to gather people together regularly to discuss issues and themes of interest and concern in contemporary ecclesiology. The plan is to spread the work of this group wider to embrace other partners in the international scene further afield. The Network hopes to dovetail its work with the efforts of the American Academy of Religion program unit in order to continue to establish broader and inclusive conversations and networks in ecclesiology and to further raise the profile of the sub-discipline.

To date, each partner institution involved in the Network brings considerable and diverse gifts and expertise. The international partners are institutions of the highest quality in which groundbreaking study and research in ecclesiology have been pursued for many years now. The geographical and social contexts in which their work is carried out, as well as the demonstrative societal benefits of such work, will surely inform and enhance the work of institutions elsewhere and the Network in general. Furthermore, the initial conference sought to help mechanisms to be developed that will ensure that the experiences and insights of all international partners gain exposure, scrutiny, and a wider hearing than might otherwise be possible.

The rapid progress made in this initial work in building the foundations for this Network demonstrates that it is very much needed, can serve the requisite communities and scholars alike in a wide variety of ways, and will not simply enhance the standing of the discipline in the academic community across the globe, but might also, through bringing people and communities together in ongoing conversation and partnership, have a major positive impact on the lives of those communities that form the subject-matter that ecclesiology is studying.

The Network will also be groundbreaking in that in all its activities it seeks to build partnerships, collaboration and understanding, in contrast to the competitive ethos that prevails in much of the contemporary academic world. Collaboration over and against competition will be its guiding principle.

Practical and Public Implications[3]

Ecclesiology is linked in many ways to the contemporary socio-economic and political situation in whatever societies the Christian churches find themselves situated. The Church can and should seek to play a unifying role in any given society, as well as to be an advocate for those who are least well off, for the marginalized, and for those oppressed. Hence the Church should take an active part in the development of a new cohesiveness across our societies.

In a global economy the Church has to find a new way of proclaiming its vision of peace, justice, and equality. However, the real 'business' of the Church is too often shielded from the public eye.

Therefore, a higher-profile platform of initiatives in 'public *ecclesiology*' and indeed '*practical* ecclesiology' may help to assuage such fears and to bring to that pluralist table which reflects the reality of most of our societies today the rich array of communitarian, socially transformative, moral, and cohesive resources that the Church has at its heart. Such initiatives can help ensure the Church really does make a positive difference; that it really does bring 'good news' into practical existence.

There is a basic need, for the well-being of our wider societies and human well-being in general, for a new approach to understanding the essence of the Church, its theological nature, its living reality, and its future role. The Church today needs to renew its self-understanding of its own catholicity and, in the broadest sense, of its ecumenical responsibilities; in other words, its efforts toward dialogue and closer unity with people of all faiths or of no faith. Ecclesiology is the science that can help build resources and fulfil such needs and that can service such bridge-building across our multifarious communities.

Intended and Enduring Collaborative Legacy

Roger Haight, a notable pioneer in the field of comparative ecclesiology, offers persuasive resources upon which to construct the case for the ecclesiological *necessity* of dialogue. Foreshadowing the particular constructive ends of his later comparative project, he asserts that: 'ecumenical theology must consider a variety of authoritative witnesses from many churches. It must also employ various comparative and dialectical procedures to frame a more general statement of the issue than will be reflected in the particular view of only one church.'[4] This analysis leads him to argue that we cannot confine theology to patently ecclesial matters alone, nor can one church alone authorize and dictate the shape and form of theology in our ecumenical age and, as he later writes, this is particularly the case with regard to ecclesiology and ecclesial organization and practice. But far from undermining the need for teaching authority, Haight's analysis instead allows us to appreciate that, in our contemporary world, such magisterium must be shaped by dialogue and ecumenical spirit, as opposed to being driven by fear of dissent and the other, and thus entrenched.[5]

Within the Christian Church, this entails a call to acknowledge even the plurality of teaching authorities, of magisteria at work in the service of the gospel today and hence to dialogue with and learn from each of these. Thus, a further fundamental principle that we see expanded in Haight's later writings:

But the church at the end of the twentieth century as a result of the ecumenical movement is recognized to be the whole or total church, despite its disunity and divisions. This means, negatively, that the church in the sense of a particular communion cannot by itself be a final or exclusive limit or constraint or criterion or norm for Christian theology today. Rather, positively, the many magisteria of various churches are witnesses to Christian truth and sources for data for Christian theology.[6]

The ethos behind the initial mission statement of the Network entails a firm commitment to exploring issues pertaining to pluralism, both religious and otherwise, as well as toward ethical debates of national, international and intercontinental relevance from the outset. Such endeavours offer further scope for the Network's lasting legacy to be positive in numerous ways. The Network seeks to cut across a variety of disciplinary, cultural, religious and geographical boundaries. Finally, it is worth emphasizing that it is also a key aim of the Network to involve particular partners from those regions of the world that have extremely limited access to funding to facilitate their participation in the broader international Network.

In January 2008, the Network's second International Conference, taking the theme 'Church in Pluralist Contexts' was hosted at Old St Joseph's Orthodox Seminary in Kerala, India (thanks to Fr K. M. George) and was enormously successful in launching the work of the Network in earnest in the South Asian continent, with the vast majority of contributors being from the region itself. Of equal significance and success was the linked conference in Trichur at the University of Calicut (thanks to the Chair of Christian Studies, Professor Paul Pulikkan) on Inculturation and Church. Paul M. Collins is owed a great debt of gratitude for his tireless efforts in overseeing the organization of these events.

Making Open Ecclesial Dialogue Possible

What prospects lie ahead for the work of the Network? Here, I am indebted for these closing remarks to two valued, ecumenical and collaborative ecclesiologists who embody the commitment to ecclesial dialogue that we hope this new international Network will contribute toward the twenty-first century. One is a long-deceased Anglican whose words would have escaped my attention but for the work of a living Roman Catholic.

In his excellent new study, *Practices of Dialogue in the Roman Catholic Church: Aims and Obstacles, Lessons and Laments*, Bradford E. Hinze has unearthed some illuminating passages in relation to past ecumenical gatherings, several of which are mentioned here to offer pause for reflection and stimulation toward the future engagement in conversation that the Network might make possible, with all due gratitude to Hinze's engaging study.[7] The first passage is from the Anglican founder of the Society of Sacred Mission, Herbert Kelly, who, as long ago as 1915 (in a paper for the emergent Faith and Order movement), offered the following advice:

The ulterior object of Conferences, as of all sincere thought and discussion, is to ascertain the truth ... Our search should be directed not so much to discovery of agreements, as to appreciation of differences ... A Conference will be helpful if its members honestly desire to receive as well as to give help. At least this far, that they desire to learn what others are thinking, i.e., what their ideas or convictions are, what exactly they mean by them, and how they apply them ... We must be prepared to face new questions, not only in regard to the views of others which we have not studied, but even in regard to our own, however carefully we may have thought them out.[8]

The participants at St Deiniol's attempted to heed these words of advice as have others at conferences and events the Network has organized. Some such events have entailed quite a packed schedule – partly because of the earnest desire to ensure that participants all gain as much as possible from their short time together and partly because of the riches of insight and contextual and ecclesial backgrounds that these events have brought together into one place.

Nonetheless, as an abiding principle, we have tried to build in time for discussion and to avoid formal work in the evenings in order to help foster the quality of conversation. Again, Herbert Kelly's wise words from 1915 are here pertinent. As Hinze observes, Kelly offered three key guidelines for any ecumenical conference to be successful, namely, 'there must be leisurely discussions, abundant time for exchanges, and respite so that participants can develop and modify their views'.[9] And, in a passage that helps encapsulate the warm and collegial atmosphere of the Network's First International Conference, and offers an organizational principle that is perhaps the most important of all, we see that Kelly was convinced that the informal conversations would perhaps be the most important elements of any conference at all – those exchanges, 'in the smoke rooms rather than in full-dress debates'.[10] As Hinze continues, '[Kelly] proposed a small conference so that genuine and honest discussion could take place and papers could, optimally, be circulated beforehand'[11] and he further mooted that *nobody should expect major changes in perspectives overnight* – perhaps one, two, or three generations might have to pass before real change could be witnessed. But, nonetheless, *the seeds for such positive transformation would have been sown* by those positive exchanges at such a small gathering.

No doubt there will be negatives along the way and steps backward as well as forward. But from small beginnings such ecclesiological conversations and investigations can hopefully serve as the 'leaven in the bread', can be like the mustard seed that brings forth a bounteous harvest.

Thus, we hope that we have followed Kelly's advice as closely as possible and, as for the positive ecclesial and ecumenical transformations that might come from our initial gathering in Wales and from subsequent gatherings to follow, let us simply hope and pray time will tell it was very worthwhile all our delegates coming from across the globe to converse in the library of that 'Grand Old Man' of diplomacy and politic.

Let me express my own hopes, this time, through the words of Hinze, who is here reflecting upon the thoughts expressed in the 'Working Paper on Ecumenical

Dialogue' issued in 1967 by the Joint Working Group of the World Council of Churches and the Roman Catholic Church.

> *Anything* can become important in these dialogues. One does not know beforehand what will be the most decisive or the most interesting; this is *revealed in the course of the dialogue.* Because dialogue is a *spiritual endeavour* and not an academic exercise, certain conditions are required: purification of heart, genuine love of others, loyalty to one's own church.[12]

I wish here to express gratitude to all who participated in that first gathering and indeed to those who have been part of all the activities of the Ecclesiological Investigations International Research Network: thank you for your time, energy, friendship, humour, and insight. Above all else, for your *agape* and communion.[13]

The Key to the Future: Major Funding and Support

The next major task for the steering group is to secure the substantial funding necessary so that all the initial faith, hope and charity may come to long-lasting fruition. This will require a coalition of funding organizations, institutions and individuals to help ensure that the open, pluralistic and collaborative vision can bear much ongoing fruit in future.

We invite all institutions, charities, organizations and individuals committed to the life and mission of the Church today and tomorrow, who believe in a Church of churches called into being to bear witness to the gospel and to serve the wider human family through tireless work toward the kingdom ends of justice, peace and righteousness, to join and sponsor the collegial and collaborative work of this new Network.

Pluralism is not an ideology; rather it is first of all a descriptive term for the way things are, for reality. At the same time, it is also the name for the healthiest and most appropriate response to the way things are, as opposed to turning away from and attempting to deny that reality in various modes of self-delusion and community delusion. Pluralism is all around us and inescapable. Why would anyone seek to escape the riches of the diverse gifts that God gives humanity to share? I can think of no better way to close this introductory account of the work of Ecclesiological Investigations than to share this stirring poem from one of the participants in the First International Conference, John O'Brien, a Spiritan priest, specialist in liberation theology and inculturated ecclesiology, currently working among minority Christians in Pakistan.

ST DEINIOL'S

In the library of the grand old man
Who understood Ireland and her ills
An oasis of erudition and exchange.
His twenty-two thousand books
An extended series of footnotes to
The provisionality of all our knowing
Even to defining the unity we seek.
Clarity the garb of vision unsustained
Narratives too neat cannot be complete.
Meeting minds and stretching boundaries
Excited to receive from otherness
Yielding to the never exhausted question
An implicit impossible in each deconstruction.
The torch passed to younger practitioners
Unchained from apologetics and deference.
The strong red wine of friendships forged
By gazing beyond in the same direction.
Humility now the high road to understanding.
A voice raised neither strident nor silent
To retrieve an ecumenical promise in the
Greater catholicity where difference is gift.

Notes

1. Some 130 persons attended the second session on 'Comparative Ecclesiology: Critical Investigations', exploring the nature, scope and promise of this new method in general and the pioneering work of Roger Haight, SJ, in particular.
2. In addition to the present volume, these publications are projected: *Christian Community Now* ed. Paul Collins, Gerard Mannion, Gareth Powell and Kenneth Wilson; *Comparative Ecclesiology: Critical Investigations* ed. Gerard Mannion; *Church and Religious Other* ed. Gerard Mannion.
3. I express my gratitude to Kenneth Wilson for his input to this section.
4. Roger D. Haight, 'The Church as Locus of Theology', *Why Theology? Concilium: Fundamental Theology* 256 (1994): 13–22, at 16–17.
5. Ibid.: 17–18.
6. Ibid.: 18.
7. Bradford Hinze, *Practices of Dialogue in the Roman Catholic Church: Aims and Obstacles, Lessons and Laments* (New York and London: Continuum, 2006).
8. Herbert Kelly, 'The Object and Method of Conference', in *The World Conference for the Consideration of Questions Touching Faith and Order* (Gardiner, Maine: Protestant Episcopal Church, 1915), pp. 9, 10, 11, cited in Hinze, *Practices of Dialogue*, p. 181.
9. Hinze, p. 182.
10. Kelly, p. 27; Hinze, p. 182.
11. Ibid., p. 182.
12. Ibid., p. 192 (my italics).
13. I am grateful to Michael Hayes, editor of *The Pastoral Review*, for permission to utilize some material here that first appeared in a much briefer article, 'Catholicity Today: New Ecclesiological Investigations and the Open Church' (May/June 2007): 42–5.

CONTRIBUTORS

Thomas F. Best, a pastor of the Christian Church (Disciples of Christ), is currently Director of the Faith and Order Commission of the World Council of Churches in Geneva.

Paul M. Collins, a priest of the Church of England, teaches systematic theology at the University of Chichester, West Sussex, United Kingdom. Besides his ecumenical research, he also specializes in the theology and liturgical traditions of South India.

Peter De Mey, Roman Catholic, is Professor of Dogmatic Theology at the Katholieke Universiteit Leuven, Belgium, where he also collaborates in the Centre for Ecumenical Research. He has served as the secretary for the Societas Oecumenica.

Michael A. Fahey is Jesuit Professor of Theology and Ecumenical Studies at Boston College, Chestnut Hill, Massachusetts. Former Editor of the journal *Theological Studies*, he has specialized in Orthodox–Catholic relations.

Kondothra M. George is a priest of the Oriental Orthodox Church, and Professor of Theology at the Orthodox Seminary in Kottayam, Kerala, India.

John W. Hind is Anglican Bishop of Chichester in the United Kingdom. He has served as a member of the drafting committee for the Faith and Order document *The Nature and Mission of the Church*.

Bradford E. Hinze, Roman Catholic, is Professor of Theology at Fordham University, New York City. He is the current President of the International Network of Societies of Catholic Theology.

Gerard Mannion, a Roman Catholic layman and citizen of the Irish Republic, studied at the Universities of Cambridge and Oxford, and has lectured at Church Colleges in Oxford, Leeds, and Liverpool. Director of the Centre for the Study of Contemporary Ecclesiology, Chair of the Ecclesiological Investigations International Research Network, his main interests lie in the fields of ecclesiology, ethics, social justice and philosophy.

Risto Saarinen, Finnish Lutheran, is Professor of Ecumenics at the University of Helsinski and research fellow at the Helsinki Collegium for Advanced Studies. He served as Research Professor at the Institute for Ecumenical Research in Strasbourg.

Wolfgang Vondey, originally from Germany, did his doctoral studies at Marquette University and is now Assistant Professor of Systematic Theology in the School of Divinity at Regent University, Virginia Beach, USA. He organized the ecumenical studies group of the Society of Pentecostal Studies in 2001.

Korinna Zamfir is Professor in the Faculty of Roman Catholic Theology as well as Executive Director of the Centre for Biblical Studies at the Babes-Bolyai University, Cluj-Napoca, Romania.

INTRODUCTION TO THE PRESENT VOLUME

We are pleased to present the first volume in a new series entitled *Ecclesiological Investigations*. We hope that it will be followed over the years by a number of scholarly and ecumenically focused books exploring the nature of the Church.

This collection contains studies on the important document *The Nature and Mission of the Church* (NMC) published by the Faith and Order Commission of the World Council of Churches (WCC) at its ninth General Assembly held in Porto Alegre, Brazil, in February 2006. These analyses, initially delivered in November 2006 at the annual convention of the American Academy of Religion (AAR) held in Washington, DC, were subsequently revised for publication.

This project originated with three persons: Gerard Mannion (Liverpool Hope University, UK), as well as the present editors, Paul M. Collins (University of Chichester, UK) and Michael A. Fahey (Boston College, USA). In 2005 we formally petitioned the governing body of the AAR to approve, for its annual convention, the establishment of a new Program Unit devoted to ecclesiology or theological investigations about the Church. As petitioners we noted the major interest in this theme worldwide, reflected through numerous ecumenical consensus statements written by the WCC, the Vatican, and a host of other church agencies. We were fortunate to receive authorization from the AAR to hold these explorations over a period of five years.

Our first task was to choose a specific topic for the 2006 convention. We quickly settled on a project to analyse and evaluate the NMC text. Through the AAR's website, we then solicited proposals from AAR members from around the world which were subsequently evaluated by a team of specialists. The large number of submissions confirmed our conviction that there was considerable interest in this theme among the membership. From the many applications, we chose seven promising ones that also reflected geographical and confessional diversity.

At the presentations, we were pleased to have in the audience two members of the Faith and Order staff, its Director Thomas F. Best (who contributes a preface to this volume) and his Associate Tamara Grdzelidze. The local programme committee had assigned a small room in anticipation of some fifteen or so people. In fact, nearly one hundred theologians attended so ended up sitting on the floor.

We trust that these well-researched studies will assist the Faith and Order Commission and ecumenists internationally in the work that still remains to be developed.

Paul M. Collins
University of Chichester, UK

Michael A. Fahey
Boston College, USA

Chapter 1

ECCLESIAL REALITY AND ECUMENICAL HORIZONS FOR THE TWENTY-
FIRST CENTURY: *THE NATURE AND MISSION OF THE CHURCH*:
A PREFACE

Thomas F. Best

The Church is one; the churches manifest their unity in manifold ways. Common confession, worship, witness and service are all practised among many churches to a degree that was unthinkable 50 or 100 years ago. Among many, the one baptism into Christ is understood as a fundamental bond of unity, as Christ's claiming each believer for his own, making us one as members of his one body. The ecumenical movement has indeed brought churches together, putting the imperative of Christian unity firmly on the agenda of churches and local congregations alike.

The Church is one; yet the churches are divided. Theological, ecclesiological, historical, social and cultural – a host of factors all too often prevent the churches from making manifest the unity which is theirs in the triune God. Not all churches recognize the baptism of others; all too often it is not possible for Christians from one church to approach the Lord's Table in another church. Divisions within the human community, divisions of race, gender or economic status, seek to impose themselves upon the life of the church and local congregations. And new sources of division within and among churches are arising, as scientific and social developments challenge traditional positions on issues of personal and social ethics.

Striving to make visible their unity, and to overcome their divisions, the churches have pursued dialogues which express their common faith and which confront and seek to overcome issues that divide them. The most significant multilateral dialogue remains *Baptism, Eucharist and Ministry* (BEM), sent in 1982 by the Faith and Order Commission of the World Council of Churches (WCC) to WCC member churches for response 'at the highest appropriate level of authority'.[1] This convergence, which text drew official responses from a very diverse spectrum of some 180 WCC member churches worldwide,[2] has served as the basis for many interchurch agreements, and – now in its 39th printing in English and translated into some 40 languages – continues to serve as a reference today. Meanwhile, and complementary to this, bilateral discussions have tackled issues that have been divisive in specific ecclesial and historical contexts.[3] Many of these have produced important results, the best-known recent example being the seminal Joint Declaration on the Doctrine of Justification by Faith, signed by the

Lutheran World Federation and the Roman Catholic Church in 1999 and affirmed by the World Methodist Council in 2006.[4]

The churches' responses to BEM identified three areas crucial to progress toward visible unity: the issues of scripture and tradition, sacrament and sacramentality, and the nature of the Church itself.[5] Among these divisive issues none is more central to the search for visible unity than ecclesiology, the understanding of the Church itself – its identity, its mission in the world, its structure, its understanding of authority and how it is exercised. Differences in the churches' self-understanding have immediate consequences for their recognition of one another as churches, for their mission and witness in the world.

Since the early 1990s, Faith and Order has tackled the difficult but decisive area of ecclesiology in a focused and, I believe, fruitful way. The initial reference point for this work on ecclesiology was the study document *The Nature and Purpose of the Church* published in 1998. This document sought 'to give expression to what the churches can now say together about the nature and purpose of the Church and within that perspective to state the remaining areas of disagreement'.[6] Critical responses were requested from the churches. Before and following this publication, consultations were held on complex and controversial ecclesiological topics, the nature and exercise of *episkope*,[7] to name but one. Also a consultation on ecclesiology and mission was mounted with the WCC's Commission on World Mission and Evangelism (CWME).[8]

Responses from churches together with the investigations pursued led to a far-reaching revision of the study document, published in 2005 as the new text *The Nature and Mission of the Church*.[9] The new title reflects a more dynamic approach to the understanding of the nature of the Church, and the treatment of mission as an integral dimension of the life of the Church. What is the nature of *The Nature and Mission of the Church*? Not yet a convergence text as was BEM, it nevertheless identifies important areas of ecclesiological agreement in the understanding of the Church.[10] No less important, it seeks to indicate clearly the fundamental issues at stake in the churches' disagreement on issues of understanding and practice, for example, whether the Church has a sacramental nature.[11]

The Nature and Mission of the Church was sent to the churches with four questions, inviting their response as to whether the document accurately reflects their 'common ecclesial convictions', as well as indicating the issues which remain divisive; whether the text reflects an 'emerging convergence' on the nature and mission of the Church; whether there remain significant areas in which the concerns of particular churches 'are not adequately addressed'; whether the text can help churches together take 'concrete steps towards unity'. Finally, the churches are invited to make concrete suggestions 'for the future development of this text';[12] *The Nature and Mission of the Church* is thus still 'underway'. Whether it becomes a convergence text as was BEM – and as hoped – depends how the text is taken forward and that, in turn, depends on the extent and quality of the responses from the churches.

But not only from the churches. Ecclesiological reflection lives also, and equally, from the investigations pursued by ecclesiologists, liturgists and theologians. Therefore, the critical academic analysis of ecclesiological positions, the exploration of possibilities in light of the experience of the history of the Church through the ages, academic reflection on the experience of believers – all these offer a vital resource for further work on the central ecclesiological issues treated in *The Nature and Mission of the Church*, and potentially for the development of that text itself.

Therefore it is of major significance that the 'Ecclesiological Investigations' group chose *The Nature and Mission of the Church* as the theme for its inaugural session, held within the framework of the American Academy of Religion meeting in Washington, DC, in November 2006. The papers gathered in this volume reflect a wide range of confessional perspectives including Oriental Orthodox, Roman Catholic, Anglican, Lutheran and Pentecostal, and something of the regional diversity of the Church worldwide. It is a strong collection, with papers of high quality by critical scholars rooted in their own traditions but with a generous ecumenical spirit. It probes, explores, challenges, and ultimately affirms the ecclesiological enterprise set forth in *The Nature and Mission of the Church*, while suggesting areas where further work is needed.

Faith and Order, and indeed the churches, will learn much from these essays by experienced scholars. This volume will take forward the ecumenical discussion on ecclesiology and contribute in significant ways to the further development of *The Nature and Mission of the Church*. It is a sign of hope for scholars and churches alike, indeed for all those committed to the unity of Christ's Church.

Notes

1. Faith and Order Paper, 111 (Geneva: WCC, 1982).
2. Max Thurian (ed.), *Churches Respond to BEM: Official Responses to the 'Baptism, Eucharist and Ministry' Text*, vols I–VI. Faith and Order Papers, 129, 132, 135, 137, 143, 144 (Geneva: WCC, 1986–88).
3. Most recently collected in Jeffrey Gros, FSC, Thomas F. Best and Lorelei F. Fuchs, SA (eds), *Growth in Agreement III: International Dialogue Texts and Agreed Statements, 1998–2005*. Faith and Order Paper, 204 (Geneva: WCC; Grand Rapids: Eerdmans, 2007).
4. In Jeffrey Gros, FSC, Harding Meyer, and William G. Rusch (eds), *Growth in Agreement II: Reports and Agreed Statements of Ecumenical Conversations on a World Level, 1982–1998 [sic]*. Faith and Order Paper, 187 (Geneva: WCC; Grand Rapids: Eerdmans, 2000), pp. 566–82; for the Methodist affirmation see the pages on Lutheran–Methodist dialogue at www. lutheranworld.org.
5. See *Baptism, Eucharist and Ministry 1982–1990: Report on the Process and Responses*, Faith and Order Paper, 149 (Geneva: WCC, 1990), esp. pp. 131–51.
6. *The Nature and Purpose of the Church: A Stage on the Way to a Common Statement*. Faith and Order Paper, 181 (Geneva: WCC, 1998), no. 4.
7. See Peter C. Bouteneff and Alan D. Falconer (eds), *Episkopé and Episcopacy and the Quest for Visible Unity*. Faith and Order Paper, 193 (Geneva: WCC, 1999).
8. Documents from the consultation are found in *International Review of Mission* XC, 358 (July 2001) and 359 (October 2001).
9. *The Nature and Mission of the Church*. Faith and Order Paper, 198 (Geneva: WCC, 2005). The document is available from WCC Publications and online through the Faith and Order pages on the WCC Website, www.wcc-coe.org.
10. Ibid., nos. 34–47.
11. Ibid., shaded text following no. 48.
12. Ibid., no. 8.

Chapter 2

Reflections on the Porto Alegre Text: *Called to Be the One Church*

Kondothra M. George

All ecclesiological documents and studies of the Faith and Order Commission of the World Council of Churches (WCC) have a singular goal, namely, 'to serve the churches in their search for the manifestation of the unity of the Church of Jesus Christ'.[1] More specifically, it is the mandate of the WCC to seek the goal of 'visible unity in one faith and in one Eucharistic fellowship expressed in worship and in common life in Christ'.[2]

The Faith and Order methodology has evolved from comparative ecclesiology in Lausanne (1927) to convergence and consensus ecclesiology in Kuala Lumpur (2004).[3] This is certainly a significant development. From conflict and competition the ecumenical movement has led the churches to cooperative and consensual efforts in their understanding of the nature and calling of the Christian Church. The ecclesiology text, *Called to Be the One Church*, prepared by the Faith and Order Commission as a companion piece to *The Nature and Mission of the Church* and adopted by the Ninth General Assembly of the WCC in Porto Alegre in February 2006, is in tune with this process of promoting consensus and mutual accountability of the churches to the point of real oneness. It is offered as 'an invitation to the churches to renew their commitment to search for unity and to deepen their dialogue'.

Ever since the WCC General Assembly at New Delhi in 1961, it has become customary for the assemblies to adopt a statement on ecclesiology for study, reflection and possible action on the part of the member churches. Adoption of a statement at every assembly every seven years is a reminder that the visible unity of the Church is the central concern and the very rationale of the existence of the WCC. Every new statement is expected to build on previous work done by the Faith and Order Commission in the framework of the WCC and to advance a bit more the frontier of research and reflection, consensus, and common action.

A hermeneutic of coherence is proposed to interpret texts, symbols, gestures and other endeavours of the WCC.[4] It seeks to manifest the integral unity of the Christian faith and community. As a hermeneutic for unity it should:

- 'aim at greater coherence in the interpretation of faith and in the community of all believers as their voices unite in common praise of God;

- make possible a mutually recognizable (re)appropriation of the sources of the Christian faith; and
- prepare ways of confession and prayer in spirit and truth'.[5]

In this regard the Church acts as a *hermeneutical community* with a commitment to explore and interpret the given texts, symbols and gestures in order to overcome misunderstandings and divisions, to identify dangers, and to resolve conflicts.

The Porto Alegre text on ecclesiology refers to the following 13 themes and issues as both a reminder of what is already accomplished and as an invitation to further the cause of dialogue and unity:[6]

a) Reaffirmation of the commitment to visible unity in one faith and one eucharistic fellowship as the basis of the fellowship of churches in the WCC. Christian divisions are wounds in the Body of Christ, and defeat the Church's witness and mission in the world. Confessing Jesus Christ as God and Savior requires that the churches seek to fulfill their common calling to the glory of one God, Father, Son, and Holy Spirit.

b) Unity is a gift and calling as well as a *koinonia*. The one baptism is a unique door to the common sacramental life celebrated together in the one eucharist. Mutually recognized and reconciled ministries are fundamental. Expression of *koinonia* in each place, the meaning of one baptism, conciliarity, and catholicity all need to be further understood and deepened.

c) The common confession of the one, holy, catholic, and apostolic Church in the Nicene-Constantinopolitan creed. The oneness of the Church and the rich diversity of the gifts and expressions of the one Holy Spirit.

d) The Church is created by the Word and the Holy Spirit (*creatura Verbi et Spiritus*). The process of growing into a holy temple.

e) Differences in formulations of faith, ecclesiological starting points and approaches need to be reviewed in the light of God's plan for the fullness of time to gather up all in God's self and to reconcile human divisions. Healing and inclusivity are integral to this.

f) The 'part and whole' logic is to be overcome in ecclesiology. Each church is the Church Catholic and not simply a part of it. Each church is the Church Catholic, but not the whole of it. The most visible expressions of catholicity are eucharistic sharing and mutually reconciled and recognized ministry.

g) Mutual giving and receiving as well as mutual accountability as aspects of catholicity in spite of the fact that eucharistic sharing is not yet permitted everywhere.

h) Significance of one baptism as expression of our mutual belonging. The affirmation of churches in the Toronto Declaration of the WCC, namely that membership of the Church of Christ is more inclusive than the membership of their own church body must motivate them to enter into living contact with those not in full communion.

i) Church is mystery, sign, and instrument of God's kingdom. It implies the Church's participation in the reconciling ministry of Christ, affirming the image of God in humanity and working along with all those whose human dignity has been denied.

j) Mission to proclaim the gospel is intertwined with the call to dialogue and collaboration with people of other living faiths and ideologies in the search for peace, justice, and fullness of human life.

k) Call to churches for deep conversations among them since the churches appear not to acknowledge *mutual responsibility* despite their bilateral and multilateral dialogues.

l) The churches are to journey together in conversation and common action in the hope of receiving deeper meaning as the disciples received radically new insight and inspiration on the road to Emmaus.

m) Several pointed questions arising from the above themes and issues are to be raised by churches for honest and concrete answers in the hope that their positive response will take us further and transform our struggles for unity into the fruits of communion.

In light of these themes and issues in the ecclesiology text, I would argue that the following methodological observations are in order:

1) This text comes in the form of 'an invitation' to the churches and not in fact as a statement. However, it recapitulates a good number of ecclesiological affirmations and statements made by the Faith and Order Commission over the past seven decades, in its preoccupation with questions of unity. The language of this 'invitation' displays humility in its approach probably in light of the failure of our common affirmations and statements in the past to realize the desired unity. This is clearly borne out by bilateral dialogues between the major traditions, for example, the Roman Catholic/Orthodox, Roman Catholic/Oriental Orthodox, Orthodox/Oriental Orthodox, etc. Arriving at agreement on the crucial theological issues that historically divided these ecclesial traditions does not automatically restore unity and communion between them. To the disappointment of enthusiastic ecumenists, this phenomenon casts serious doubts on the role of doctrinal agreements as the key to church unity. The key seems to lie elsewhere.

2) Both the WCC as a whole and the Faith and Order Commission have invested much sanguine trust and optimism in the potential of agreed statements and formulations in bringing about unity. This attitude may have been produced by the historical background of the two main partners in the WCC, namely, the confessionally inclined Protestant churches and the doctrinally oriented Orthodox churches. The Protestant confessional positions were clearly *stated* in theological propositions to which assent was required from the faithful. For the Orthodox churches, the essential doctrines of the Church were clearly *stated* in creeds and theological formulae in the early 'undivided Tradition'. The Nicene-Constantinopolitan Creed which is recognized by the churches in the WCC fellowship as a fundamental and quintessential statement of Christian faith is held by these churches in their separate existence. The best of patristic tradition believed that a better statement of faith was not possible and that another statement was not necessary for the unity of the Church. Yet the churches were and continue to be divided endlessly despite this common declaration of one faith. Can we now hope to produce a better and more effective statement for unity?

3) The major effort of the Faith and Order Commission in its mandatory concern for unity was to produce consensus documents. The case of *Baptism, Eucharist and Ministry* (BEM) has become a classic example. A whole generation of theologians and ecumenists laboured to produce the text, only to come to the recognition, from the voluminous response of the churches, that the crux of the matter was not in the common text on BEM, but in the ecclesiologies implicit in the responses. So was the case with the celebrated Lima Liturgy based on the BEM text. Well-meaning ecumenists believed that a well-balanced liturgical text and ritual, evolved by the joint efforts of Catholic, Orthodox and Protestant theologians and specialists on liturgy for the celebration of a common Eucharist, would contribute to unity. But it did not.

4) The ten 'questions to be addressed continually by the churches', as formulated in the Porto Alegre document, will probably be answered by the churches, some positively, some negatively, some in a grey zone. But these answers of themselves will not in all likelihood solve the basic question of visible unity. They will still be 'confessional' answers going over the same ground again and again.

5) The document ends with trust in the risen Lord that in the course of our journey together, further steps would be revealed. The invitational tone goes well with this hope. It indirectly acknowledges the present uncertainty and helplessness, probably reflecting the actual situation of the WCC and the Faith and Order commission. This is perhaps a spiritual moment to begin the search for a new paradigm.

6) Every year the WCC receives applications for membership by newly constituted churches. These new churches are mostly the result of division. The mechanism of division and the formation of churches today will probably shed light, to some extent, on the real obstacles to unity in the case of historic divisions in older churches. Factors such as cultural and political questions of identity, power, authority and personal ego clashes are at play under the veneer of theological issues. This makes one suspect that it was not strictly theological or ecclesiological factors that were decisive in fomenting division. This could be illustrated from a political-cultural reading of the ancient schisms and divisions between the East and the West, as well as the divisions within the East and the West. If this is the case, the methodology of Faith and Order will require a serious review. What would be needed is a new hermeneutic to deal with identity, power, and hegemony as keys to division and unity in the Christian churches along with the conventional ecclesiological method to arrive at agreed and consensus documents.

Notes

1. Günther Gassmann (ed.), *Documentary History of the Faith and Order 1963–1993.* Faith and Order Paper, 159 (Geneva: WCC, 1993), p. 20.
2. Constitution of the World Council of Churches, 1.1.

3. Tamara Grdzelidze (ed.), *One, Holy, Catholic and Apostolic: Ecumenical Reflections on the Church*. Faith and Order Paper, 197 (Geneva: WCC, 2005), pp. 1–2.

4. *A Treasure in Earthen Vessels: An Instrument for an Ecumenical Reflection on Hermeneutics*. Faith and Order Paper, 182 (Geneva: WCC, 1998), p. 9.

5. Ibid.

6. For a listing of the theological and ecclesiological issues in the draft document, see also Gennadios of Sassima, 'The Statement on Ecclesiology for the Ninth Assembly of the World Council of Churches', in Thomas F. Best (ed.), *Faith and Order at the Crossroads: Kuala Lumpur 2004*; Faith and Order Paper, 196 (Geneva: WCC, 2005), pp. 379–82.

Chapter 3

UNITY, CATHOLICITY AND IDENTITY: THE UNITY STATEMENTS OF
THE WORLD COUNCIL OF CHURCHES AND THEIR RECEPTION IN *THE
NATURE AND MISSION OF THE CHURCH*

Risto Saarinen

In its statement on church unity, *Called to Be the One Church*, the assembly of the
World Council of Churches (WCC), meeting in Porto Alegre in February 2006,
urged the member churches to give priority to the ecclesiological issues of unity
and catholicity. These issues also play a significant role in the new WCC text on
ecclesiology, *The Nature and Mission of the Church* (NMC). I will proceed in this
study in three steps. First, I will discuss the so-called unity statements of the WCC
and their reception in NMC, by focusing on the issue of *catholicity*. Second, I will
argue that these statements, as well as NMC, reflect certain tensions present in the
models of *unity* employed in ecumenism. Third, I will briefly describe some
contemporary Protestant positions, with a view on how the more recent concept of
identity relates to the classical marks of unity and catholicity.

Catholicity

The WCC has adopted four unity statements that aim to spell out the nature of
the unity sought in the ecumenical movement. The first and probably most
important of these is the New Delhi 1961 statement:

> We believe that the unity which is both God's will and his gift to his Church is being
> made visible as all in each place who are baptized into Jesus Christ and confess him as
> Lord and Savior are brought by the Holy Spirit into one fully committed fellowship,
> holding the one apostolic faith, preaching the one Gospel, breaking the one bread,
> joining in common prayer, and having a corporate life reaching out in witness and
> service to all and who at the same time are united with the whole Christian fellowship
> in all places and all ages in such wise that ministry and members are accepted by all,
> and that all can act and speak together as occasion requires for the tasks to which God
> calls his people.[1]

The New Delhi statement connects unity and catholicity with the help of the
concept of place. A lived communion is presupposed in 'each place'. The different
places need not be identical with one another, but they are nevertheless united 'in

such wise that ministry and members are accepted by all'. Thus a fellowship emerges which comprises 'all places and all ages'. Catholicity in the sense of universality and commonality is thus embedded in the unity statement of New Delhi, although the actual model is set out in terms of the concept of place.

At the same time, the concept of place may pose problems for this unity statement. The New Delhi statement presupposes a territorial concept of one church at one place. Differences can be tolerated if other churches remain in another territory and under another jurisdiction. This model, let us label it as 'catholicity among places', may be helpful for the Orthodox churches as well as for some territorial churches of European Protestantism. For some other churches. the model is, however, both too easy and too difficult at the same time. The easy option can be seen in the case of the so-called Porvoo Communion. In Porvoo, Scandinavian Lutherans and British Anglicans are in communion and thus participate in the same catholicity in different places. In fact, however, because of geographical distance both continue to preserve their status quo. This solution is too easy for the problem of unity.

The difficulty can be exemplified with the relationship of Finnish Lutheran and Finnish Orthodox churches. We have peaceful coexistence and good cooperation in my home country. But, according to New Delhi, the Finnish Orthodox should actually join the Lutheran church in order to obtain the 'unity of all in each place'. This is, however, impossible. The basic problem of 'catholicity among places' is that, in today's world, churches are no longer territorially divided but coexist in the same place.

The second unity statement of the WCC was launched in Nairobi in 1975. Interestingly, the notion of place has disappeared and catholicity is defined as follows: 'The one Church is to be envisioned as a conciliar fellowship of local churches which are themselves truly united. In this conciliar fellowship, each local church possesses, in communion with the others, the fullness of catholicity ...'[2]

The Nairobi statement is more straightforward but also more vague than New Delhi. It does not spell out what it means to be 'truly united'. Common decision-making structures are probably presupposed in the notion of conciliarity. But the local churches, spoken of in the plural, continue as autonomous bodies which may coexist in the same territory. This is not an obvious conclusion, since one can read 'truly united' to mean the same kind of local merger as in New Delhi. But it is also possible, and more probable, to read Nairobi so that the conciliar fellowship is already the true unity, within which 'each local church' continues its existence.

Since each local church possesses full catholicity, no universality needs to be presupposed. Let us label this idea as 'catholicity of each local church'. In practice, the concept of place is in Nairobi replaced with the phrase 'local church'. The problem of different local churches in the same territory is simply avoided through employing the view that each local church in communion with others already possesses the fullness of catholicity.

The third unity statement issued at Canberra in 1991 enriches the previous statements by introducing the language of *koinonia*/communion more strongly than its predecessors. The statement speaks in classical terms of 'one, holy, apostolic and catholic Church'. It holds that a full communion 'will be expressed on the local and the universal levels through conciliar forms of life and action'. The unity statement further says that churches are bound together at all levels of their life.[3] The Canberra statement no longer holds that each local church would be per se catholic, but it leans toward a concept of catholicity which emphasizes the universal level more strongly than Nairobi. The concept of catholicity in Canberra thus lies somewhere between New Delhi and Nairobi.

The fourth and most recent unity statement of Porto Alegre 2006, titled *Called to Be the One Church*, is by far the longest text. The concept of unity is in many ways similar to Canberra 1991, but particular topics are formulated more extensively. The paragraph on catholicity reads as follows:

> The catholicity of the Church expresses the fullness, integrity and totality of its life in Christ through the Holy Spirit in all times and places. This mystery is expressed in each community of baptized believers in which the apostolic faith is confessed and lived, the gospel is proclaimed and the sacraments are celebrated. Each church is the Church catholic and not simply part of it. Each church is the Church catholic, but not the whole of it. Each church fulfills its catholicity when it is in communion with the other churches. We affirm that the catholicity of the Church is expressed most visibly in sharing holy communion and in a mutually recognized and reconciled ministry.[4]

The new unity statement is not only the longest, but also in many ways the most balanced formulation of catholicity in the history of the unity statements of the WCC. As the Canberra statement, the Porto Alegre text finds that the dilemma of local and universal catholicity needs to be solved so that both aspects are adequately respected. Each church can call itself 'catholic', but at the same time the reality of catholicity is fulfilled in the universal communion. Let us label this view 'we-and-others catholicity'.

In the four unity statement we can see an elegant, though somewhat accidental, tendency leading to the gradual disappearance of the view of spatial catholicity. In New Delhi, catholicity is ensured through the concept of place. In Nairobi and Canberra, the concepts of 'local', or 'local and universal', still define the spatial component. But in Porto Alegre, the spatial component has disappeared (it only occurs in the phrase 'all times and places'). Churches are no more in 'each place' nor are they called 'local churches'. They and their catholicity are defined without spatial concepts. Each church may be everywhere, as is proper in the age of internet and globalization.

At the Porto Alegre assembly, a new ecclesiological document, NMC, was launched. This statement contains an important passage on catholicity. It is formulated with the help of two earlier Faith and Order texts, namely *Confessing the One Faith* and *The Nature and Purpose of the Church*.[5] At the same time, NMC broadens and deepens the Porto Alegre unity statement. The relevant passage reads as follows:

> The Church is catholic because God is the fullness of life 'who desires everyone to be saved and to come to the knowledge of the truth' (1 Tim. 2:4), and who, through Word and Spirit, makes his people the place and instrument of his saving and life-giving presence, the community 'in which, in all ages, the Holy Spirit makes the

believers participants in Christ's life and salvation, regardless of their sex, race or social position' (no. 12).

In NMC, as well as in its predecessors, the emphasis is more clearly placed on God as giver and guarantor of catholicity. An attempt to spell out the trinitarian dimension of catholicity is also undertaken. No reference to concrete place or locality is made, but universality is highlighted. The concept of place appears as a non-local attribute of the Church: God makes God's people, i.e. the Church, 'the place' of salvation. The Church is not a concrete place, but it is nevertheless a concrete gathering of God's people and a 'place' in this sense. In addition, the issue of equality among all humanity is mentioned. Through its emphasis on universality and equality rather than on the catholicity of local churches, NMC in its way exemplifies 'we-and-others catholicity'.

Can Protestant theologians recognize their own tradition in these documents? The Reformation movement in Germany adopted the Nicene faith and taught the catholicity of the Church. The Reformers criticized the Roman Church for being too external. As a consequence of this criticism, Lutheran confessional writings sometimes translate catholic as *allgemeine, christliche* ('common' or 'Christian'). This is done in order to spell out that catholicity cannot be an external or formal sign and criterion of true Church, but it remains an article of faith, a hidden reality. If the Church is made an 'external government' (*politia externa*), it will easily become a particularistic organ and thus lose its universal character. A catholic church consists of human beings who are scattered around the whole earth but who hold to the same faith, same Christ, same Holy Spirit, and same sacraments. It should be noted that although Protestants criticize the externalist view of catholicity, they do not move to a consistent internalism or spiritualism. Sacraments and other external signs remain necessary.[6]

In principle and in theological terms, the theocentric and non-spatial way of expressing catholicity in the most recent WCC statements should be compatible with these basic features of Protestant ecclesiology. The statements presuppose that the true, catholic church is scattered around the globe. 'We-and-others catholicity' may therefore be a more fruitful model for Protestants than 'catholicity among places' or 'catholicity of each local church'.

In reality, however, things are more complex. Protestants may be theologically global, but in church practice we remain bound to our local and national circumstances. Protestant churches are very autonomous bodies within their national and 'spatial' boundaries. The criticism of external forms is not only used to downgrade superficial formalism, but also in order to withdraw from binding international and interchurch agreements and structures which are interpreted in terms of problematic external government. In reality, Protestants therefore often tend to favour the model of 'catholicity of each local church' because it is a complacent solution to the problem of Christian universality.

Unity

For a deeper understanding of unity and catholicity, let us turn briefly to the models and realizations of unity found in the ecumenical movement. I will not, however, go through the ecumenical history for a second time. Instead, I will raise the issue of various inherent tensions found in the models of unity. These tensions are probably familiar to most of us and they can be expressed in different ways. My intention is to present them in such a guise that they may shed light on the issue of catholicity.

In the work of the WCC, three different but related ecclesiological tensions influence the drafting of texts and the ongoing renewal processes of the ecumenical movement. The so-called unity statements can be described as attempts to cope with these basic tensions. *The first tension is found between two principles, 'no models of unity' and 'unity statements'.* The famous *Toronto Declaration*, a text which until today states the requirements of membership in the WCC, holds: 'Membership in the WCC does not imply the acceptance of a specific doctrine concerning the nature of Church unity.'[7] A member church need not adopt any models concerning the nature of unity. In reality, however, member churches have approved the above-mentioned unity statements which clearly contain visions of church unity.

Thus New Delhi 1961 says that unity 'is being made visible as all in each place ... are brought ... into one fully committed fellowship'. Nairobi 1975 speaks of 'conciliar fellowship' and Canberra 1991 of 'the unity of the Church as *koinonia*'. Porto Alegre 2006 repeats this language and affirms the Nicene Creed, but says also that the Church 'is called to manifest its oneness in rich diversity'. Until Canberra 1991, the development of unity statements may be regarded as attempt to overcome Toronto 1950.

In Porto Alegre, however, the sheer length of the statement and the use of expressions like 'rich diversity' may prompt the question whether the churches again retreat to the non-affirmation of any specific view of unity, as it was stated in Toronto 1950. This doubt is strengthened by a closer reading of the commentary document, NMC. In NMC, the biblical insights spelled out in nos. 14–17 offer a platform in which no specific model of church unity is preferred but a plurality is affirmed. It is said that the 'canon of the New Testament testifies to the compatibility of unity and diversity' (no. 16). Moreover, 'to honour the varied biblical insights into the nature and mission of the church, various approaches are required' (no. 17). The biblical part of NMC tends to exclude any preferred models and to affirm a variant of ecclesiological pluralism. This feature corresponds to the 'no models' minimalism of Toronto 1950 rather than to the unity statements mentioned above.

The second tension exists between the identity of the WCC as a 'fellowship of churches' and the nature of unity as communio/koinonia. If the WCC is, again according to Toronto 1950, regarded as a mere instrument of ecumenism, we should make a clear distinction, on the one hand, between instrumental fellowship (i-fellowship) and, on the other hand, the 'real' *koinonia* or communion of churches (k-fellowship). Again, the unity statements attempt to bridge the difference between i-fellowship and k-fellowship. Many Christian World Communions, e.g., the Lutheran World Federation and the Leuenberg Church Fellowship, define themselves as communions in the sense of k-fellowship. The WCC cannot do this, but it nevertheless attempts to formulate the 'real' unity' which it serves as instrument. In this process, however, the theological character of the organization becomes debatable. This point has often been made by the Orthodox churches, most recently in the crisis that led to the constructive work of the so-called 'Special Commission on Orthodox Participation'.

In NMC, the second tension can be seen between nos. 24–33 and nos. 34–42. In the former part, the concept of *koinonia* is presented in strongly biblical and trinitarian terms as a participation in God. This language avoids the difficulties present in the distinction between i-fellowship and k-fellowship, since the communion among humans and institutions is not spelled out in any concrete terms. The language of participation in God, however, clearly assumes that a 'deep' communion, a k-fellowship, is meant and implied.

The latter part (nos. 34–42) continues with the topic of mission. Here, however, the tone changes significantly. The task of the Church is presented in strongly instrumental terms, as advocacy, care and proclamation. The reader now gets the impression that the communion occurs in terms of i-fellowship, as a strategic alliance for the sake of something else than the unity. Thus the tension between different meanings of fellowship/unity is not resolved.

The third tension is related to the second and concerns the tensions and differences among the terms 'church', 'communion', and 'fellowship'. Especially in European Protestantism it is common to enter a communion, *Kirchengemeinschaft*, in which each church remains an autonomous body. This is more difficult, though not totally impossible, in Catholic and Orthodox ecclesiology, given that the Church is defined as communion. Again, the unity statements attempt to formulate a careful balance between the autonomy of a participating church and the theological nature of *koinonia*.

One controversial way to express this tension is to speak of different 'ecclesial densities' pertaining to different bodies.[8] Thus, the WCC would have less ecclesial density than a confessional world communion, which in turn has less density than an individual member church. Although such quantitative terms have their obvious theological problems, various unity statements choose their terminology in order to express the shades and aspects of unity which do not conflict with the legal autonomy of a member church. Thus, the unity statements in fact do employ the idea of 'ecclesial density' in order to cope with the third tension.

In NMC nos. 57–9 the phrases 'growth in communion' and 'not yet full communion' are employed. These are clearly quantitative terms which presuppose a 'more' and 'less' of communion. But if we look at the trinitarian passages, nos. 24–33, the quantitative language disappears and Christians are in communion with God and with one another.

What do we learn from this brief identification of certain tensions within the ecumenical language of unity? Although the issue of unity is vital for all churches within the ecumenical movement, the concrete will to proceed in the search of unity is often lacking or the time is not found to be ripe. The hesitations, tensions and even contradictions present in the ecumenical language are not symptomatic of the lack of common agreement and clarity among drafters, but they reflect the hesitation of the churches. A church wants to proceed toward unity, but it also wants to preserve its identity and autonomy. This is an understandable phenomenon which can be found in many other areas of human life.

We find similar tension or oscillation in the concept of catholicity. Whereas New Delhi promotes visible unity, Nairobi is more inclined to leave local churches in peace. The communion language of Canberra was again more binding, whereas the 'rich diversity' language of Porto Alegre in turn moderates the nature of unity.

An important concept relating unity to catholicity is that of identity. Both Protestants and Orthodox have a Christian identity, and in that sense they have the 'same' identity as Christians. But the word 'same' must be left in quotation marks, since it is obvious that their confessional self-understandings differ and may often be more important for their concrete identity. Unity implies the idea of having the same identity in a rather strong sense. Catholicity, too, employs the idea of identity. The Orthodox in Finland, Russia, and Greece are in communion and in that sense participate in their 'catholic' church. Today's Lutherans may be grouped together with eighteenth-century Pietists and sixteenth-century Reformers. All of them belong to the same catholic church which stretches through the ages.

With the help of the concept of catholicity, we often distinguish between insiders and outsiders. Although ecumenically we can speak of 'we-and-others' catholicity, the historical meaning of catholicity has often been used to convey almost the opposite meaning. Catholic Christians are those who are not non-catholic and not heterodox. In this sense the concept of catholicity safeguards one's own identity and furthers unity within one's own group through time and place. For obvious reasons, this is not the meaning of catholicity promoted in the ecumenical texts. In order to discuss the issue of identity in more detail, we must turn to other theological treatises.

Identity

I will exemplify current Protestant discussion on unity and catholicity with two recent voices. In his discussion on catholicity, Hans-Peter Grosshans pays attention to the issue that the Nicean predicate of catholicity does not say much, if anything, about the content of the identity of the Church. This does not mean that catholicity is a superfluous predicate. To be catholic presupposes that the Church has an identity.[9] But the predicate of catholicity does not yet define, for instance, the relative importance of particular doctrines and rites. The Eucharist certainly belongs to a catholic church, but the mere predicate of catholicity does not yet state that this is the case. What the predicate of catholicity constitutes, however, is the requirement of sameness or integrity.

In other words, in order to be catholic, the Church has to remain the same during different ages and different places. If this requirement is fulfilled, we can say that our church is the same as the church of Luther or Calvin or Augustine, but 'different' from the church of Marcion or the Mormons. The predicate of catholicity is thus a necessary prerequisite of the possibility of doctrinal identification. But it does not yet give concrete criteria of this identification. For Grosshans, the very concept of Reformation, as re-formation, as re-receiving the identity-giving form, is a central aspect of this catholicity. Put in this way, catholicity is an indispensable feature of the Reformation churches.

Grosshans holds that the content of this identity is the being of the Church as the body of Christ. It is Jesus Christ who gives the Church the content of its identity. If we look at both the Porto Alegre and NMC texts, they are compatible with this basic tenet. According to Porto Alegre, 'the catholicity of the Church expresses the fullness, integrity and totality of its life in Christ'. In keeping with this, NMC says that, in the Catholic Church, Christians are made 'participants in Christ's life and salvation' (no. 12). The christological being of the Church is not lacking in earlier ecumenism, but it is important that the new texts explicitly bring this reality together with the issue of catholicity. Grosshans pays much attention to the spatial dimension of the Church. Too often Protestants have left this issue to the Catholics, making merely the internal aspects of catholicity explicit in their ecclesiology. For Grosshans, Church is the 'earthly space' for the truth of the gospel.[10] The concept of space thus becomes transferred to the description of the Church itself. It is not a local concept, but it nevertheless underlines the importance of having an existence in time and place. This move has an interesting parallel in NMC. In it, as we have seen, God 'makes his people the place and instrument of his saving and life-giving presence' (no. 12). The concept of place now appears as an attribute of the Church.

Calling church 'a place' may be a fruitful way of avoiding both the absolutized spatial catholicity which remains bound to the actual territories, and the implied non-spatial catholicity which can be idealized even in the age of the Internet and globalization. Church does not remain committed to a territory, but the Church in itself offers a place or an 'earthly space' for something that is not local, namely, the gospel. In such a place it becomes possible to identify the concrete church as the Church Catholic.

Another inspiring recent voice is that of Kevin Vanhoozer. He offers a more Calvinist blend of Protestantism, but one with a high respect of the doctrinal traditions of all churches. His point of departure is the authority of biblical interpretation as the criterion of the identity of the Church and thus of its catholicity. Vanhoozer aims at grounding Protestant authority structures in a manner which surpasses private interpretation but nevertheless remains true to the principle of *sola scriptura*. Like Grosshans, he sees the issue of identity as crucial for the interpretation and proclamation of the gospel message.

Following Paul Ricoeur, Vanhoozer distinguishes between two kinds of identity. Whereas the so-called idem-identity, 'hard identity' or 'what-identity', requires unchanging communal interpretation, the so-called ipse-identity, 'soft identity' or 'who-identity' can be more flexible. In ipse-identity, we can know who you are even though you sometimes adjust your views and react to new situations. Ipse-identity is not pluralism, but a non-identical repetition of central practices.

Protestant biblical interpretation can avoid both legalism and privatism with the help of conceiving its teaching and church practices in terms of ipse-identity.[11]

Remaining the same, and in that sense catholic, can be labelled as the 'ecclesial performance of Scripture'.[12] In this sense, scripture determines the range of catholicity and ipse-identity of the Church. Vanhoozer refines this basic idea with another distinction, namely that between 'cultural-linguistic' (PII) and 'canonical-linguistic' (PI) performance. Roughly, PII emphasizes that our understanding of the scripture is conditioned by ecclesial (and other cultural) traditions, whereas PI stresses the autonomy and primacy of canonical scripture. Vanhoozer prefers PI, arguing that PI and PII relate to one another as the events of 'receiving' and 'using' a text. According to PI, the believers have the possibility to become guided by the canonical text so that they sometimes can even criticize traditions on the basis of scripture. It is indeed possible to listen and to receive a text before using it.

Vanhoozer is not hostile to the concept of tradition and claims that his approach affirms the importance of historical traditions. Even *sola scriptura* presupposes an interplay between scripture and tradition. Remaining the same, in terms of ipse-identity, must leave room for some conscious and unconscious changes. The believer can, however, remain confident that the canonical scripture is capable of leading the Church through the ages. Vanhoozer affirms the christological core of scripture and holds that the Church is kept together by the content of the word of God rather than any formal or legal structure.

Looking back at the Porto Alegre and NMC texts on catholicity, we see that they both mention the Word of God and the proclamation of the gospel. In Vanhoozer's terms, scripture is not only relevant as the doctrinal content which the principle of catholicity formally safeguards. The principle of catholicity is also itself being upheld by the canonical norm of Scripture. This is, in brief, how a Protestant theologian understands canonical scripture to be the norm and guarantee of the unity and catholicity of the Church. In order to keep the Church 'the same' and in this sense catholic, scripture is the most important criterion. Canonical scripture is not merely another instance of tradition, but it has the ability to judge tradition, at least to an extent. At the same time, *sola scriptura* neither promotes private interpretation nor implies rigid literalism.

Ecclesial performance should be consonant with the canonical intentions of scripture. Ecclesial performance may vary in different times and places and it can be and should be re-formed. It would probably be an exaggeration to claim that the performance should constantly be reformed, but in any case the chain of catholicity is based on non-identical repetition. And yet, this chain builds an ipse-identity in which we can know who the Christians are. We may be to an extent uncertain of 'what' the Church finally is and even of 'what' precisely it teaches. But we do know who represents the Church and who are (and were) God's people. In this sense the Church has both unity and catholicity.

Notes

1. *Documentary History of Faith and Order 1963–1993*, ed. Günther Gassmann (Geneva: WCC, 1993), p. 3.
2. Ibid.
3. Ibid., pp. 3–4.
4. The text is available at www.wcc-assembly.info.
5. *The Nature and Purpose of the Church*. Faith and Order Paper, 181 (Geneva: WCC, 1998). See *Confessing the One Faith* (4th edn, Geneva: WCC, 1996), no. 240, and *The Nature and Purpose of the Church*, no. 12.
6. See Apology of the Augsburg Confession, in *The Book of Concord: The Confessions of the Evangelical Lutheran Church*, ed. R. Kolb and T. Wengert (Minneapolis: Fortress, 2000), pp. 175–6.
7. Toronto Declaration III, 5, in *The Ecumenical Movement: An Anthology of Key Texts and Voices*, ed. M. Kinnamon and B. E. Cope (Geneva: WCC, 1997), p. 465.
8. For this phrase, see *From Federation to Communion: The History of the Lutheran World Federation*, ed. J. H. Schjorring *et al.* (Minneapolis: Fortress, 1997), p. 236.
9. Hans-Peter Grosshans, *Die Kirche – irdischer Raum der Wahrheit des Evangeliums* (Berlin: Evangelisches Verlag, 2003), pp. 179–82.
10. Ibid., p. 298.
11. Kevin Vanhoozer, *The Drama of Doctrine* (Louisville: Westminster, 2005), p. 127.
12. Ibid., p. 167. For what follows, see pp. 167–85.

Chapter 4

COMMUNION: GOD, CREATION AND CHURCH

Paul M. Collins

My purpose in this essay is to explore the use of *koinonia*/communion in the recent Faith and Order text *The Nature and Mission of the Church* (NMC) and to offer some remarks that may assist in the processes of clarifying understanding.[1] The exploration of the use of *koinonia*/communion will be set against the background of what has become a major discourse in Christian theology during the twentieth century, which I shall refer to in terms of 'a hermeneutic of relationality'.[2] The discourse concerning a hermeneutic of relationality clearly has two strands: a strand in which relationality is applied to the Christian doctrine of God as Trinity, and by extension to *communio* ecclesiology; and another strand in which a critique is given of this application. Through an analysis of this underlying discourse I will seek to explore how these two different strands illuminate the attempt to understand the ecclesial community in relation to the divine, thus enhancing the ways in which the use of *koinonia*/communion may be received and interpreted in NMC.

In her article 'Ecclesial Koinonia in Ecumenical Dialogue',[3] Susan Wood raises the issue that ecumenical dialogues fail to address how communion 'is effected'.[4] She assumes that agreement that the divine being as Trinity 'is communion' is uncontested and at least to some extent self-evident. However, it seems to me that this is not uncontested and self-evident. Rather part of the reason that churches have found it difficult either to articulate the effecting of communion or indeed to practise it in relation at least to the advancement of the ecumenical endeavour, is precisely because what divine *koinonia* means is not clear-cut, and therefore what ecclesial *koinonia* may be is also problematic. It is in seeking at least a tentative step toward an answer to this problematic, in relation to NMC, that this essay is offered.

Is There an Iterative Usage of the Notion of Koinonia *in the Text?*

In the section 'The Church as *Koinonia*/Communion' of NMC, nos. 24–33 and 55–9, there are a number of uses of the term *koinonia*/communion. Within nos. 24–33 and 57–9 the notion of communion (*koinonia*) is used in relation to at least nine different areas of understanding or doctrine: namely, the relationship between

God the Trinity and the Church; creation and human relationships in creation; salvation and the restoration of communion; the relationship of the People of God to God, to each other and to the created order; participation as sharing and fellowship, particularly the fellowship of the Holy Spirit; baptism and eucharist; and the Church as instrument of communion in the created order.

It is reasonable to ask if this usage is in any sense an iterative process. Since communion is used to refer to different aspects of doctrine and experience, is the word used to mean different things and/or similar/overlapping things? Is this confusing or enriching? Despite possible ambiguity, I want to suggest that an inherent congruity of meaning may be found in the text, and that it is possible to interpret the use being made of the notion of *koinonia* as an iterative use. If this were made more explicit, perhaps *koinonia* would more clearly bear the weight of what is being asked of it. This could be achieved in terms of a hierarchy of doctrines, which would delineate between the application of *koinonia* to the Godhead and the divine purposes in creation and redemption, and to its application to the politics of inter- and intra-denominational relations, e.g., such usage as 'impaired communion'.

The text is careful not to espouse any one particular tradition of the conceptuality of either the Godhead or the Church. However, there is a consistency in the appeal to the notion of *koinonia*. This is traced from the Creation and Fall, through the redemption in Christ to an understanding in no. 58 of 'the communion of God the Holy One'. No. 59 reiterates the understanding of 'communion . . . first given in creation', enunciated in no. 25. Nos. 31, 34 and 59 each iterate the understanding of the divine gift of communion to all humanity as the outcome of the divine purposes in creating the world. In these understandings, there is a consistency of function in the notion of *koinonia*. While defending the interpretation of the text as an iterative usage of the notion of *koinonia*, I also perceive that the text might be interpreted in alternative ways. Thus, the text could be made to express such an iterative understanding more clearly. As in the case of the Faith and Order text, *Baptism, Eucharist and Ministry*, criticized for its implicit ecclesiology, this text might be criticized for its implicit ontology, or alternatively for its lack of an explicit understanding of the divine *ousia*. This undoubtedly reflects the extent of ecumenical agreement, which is possible at any given moment. Nonetheless, there is need for greater conceptual clarity between (a) the designation of the Trinity as communion, (b) 'communion . . . first given in creation' and (c) Church as communion. In order to pursue this quest for greater clarity, I will now trace and examine the genealogy of two strands of discourse on relationality.

Two Strands of Discourse

(a) Genealogy of a 'Hermeneutic of Relationality' in Trinitarian Theology and Ecclesiology

What is encompassed in the notion of a 'hermeneutic of relationality' undoubtedly varies among theologians. However, those who sit within this framework appeal to relationality on the basis that there is some correlation between understandings of divine being, ecclesiality, human sociality, and the relationship between God and creation. All of these are to be found in some respect in NMC, and it is on this basis that I pursue an analysis of a genealogy of a 'hermeneutic of relationality'. Leonardo Boff offers us a brief basis for this hermeneutic:

> By the name God, Christian faith expresses the Father, the Son and the Holy Spirit in eternal correlation, interpenetration and love, to the extent that they form one God. Their unity signifies the communion of the divine Persons. There, in the beginning, there is not solitude of One, but the communion of three divine Persons.[5]

Later in *Trinity and Society* he suggests how the late twentieth-century renewal in trinitarian thought is empowered particularly by an appeal to context in a broad sense: to society, community, and history, cosmic and human, as the starting point for reflection on the conceptuality of relationality.[6] 'So human society is a pointer on the road to the mystery of the Trinity, while the mystery of the Trinity, as we know it from revelation, is a pointer toward social life and its archetype.'[7] The methodological interplay between human experience and divine revelation is another feature of much of the theological reflection, which is manifested in a 'hermeneutic of relationality'.[8]

To reconstruct a comprehensive genealogy of a 'hermeneutic of relationality' as applied to Christian trinitarian thought is a task beyond the scope of this essay. What is attempted here is to identify some landmarks in the overall landscape of a 'hermeneutic of relationality', which will include some allusion to the cross-disciplinary nature of the broader interest in and landscape of 'relation'/ 'relationality'. From some perspectives, at least, the appeal to relationality in terms of a social model of the Trinity has been seen as a 'stampede'.[9] Certainly focus upon *koinonia* in ecumenical dialogue and its attendant relational implications is to be found among theologians of widely different traditions and interests. In seeking to identify the major landmark publications in this 'turn to relationality'[10] there are publications, which have sought to map this landscape. They include works edited by Christoph Schwöbel, *Persons, Divine and Human* and *Trinitarian Theology Today*, as well as his own more recent *Gott in Beziehung*.[11] Among this category of works F. LeRon Shults describes a broader philosophical landscape in *Reforming Theological Anthropology: After the Philosophical Turn to Relationality*,[12] in which he traces the appeal to relationality from Aristotle to Kant, and Hegel to Levinas. However, a comprehensive genealogy of a 'hermeneutic of relationality' is a task still to be undertaken. The lack of a clear understanding of a theological or theological/philosophical genealogy of a 'hermeneutic of relationality' puts all discussion of *koinonia* and its attendant categories and implications at a disadvantage, including the critique of this 'hermeneutic of relationality'.

Secondly there are those publications that clearly mark out the development of an appeal to a 'hermeneutic of relationality' in Christian trinitarian thinking in the second half of the twentieth century. On the whole such monographs and collections of essays began to be published in the 1980s and into the 1990s. Jürgen Moltmann is a significant contributor in this field, not only for *The Trinity and the Kingdom of God*[13] but also for the influence he exercises on others such as Leonardo Boff in *Trinity and Society*.[14] Robert Jenson, in *The Triune Identity*,[15] traced the emergence of a theological 'hermeneutic of relationality' to the patristic era, in particular to Gregory of Nyssa, marking an ongoing appeal to the 'Cappadocian Fathers'. John Zizioulas contributed to the landscape in *Being as Communion*[16] making an appeal to patristic (Cappadocian) sources as well as twentieth-century existentialist categories. The collection of essays *Trinity, Incarnation and Atonement*, edited by Feenstra and Plantinga,[17] marks a stage in the dissemination and broader examination of the conceptualities inherent in the appeal to relationality. Catherine Mowry LaCugna, in *God for Us*,[18] rooted her exposition of relationality in the human reception of the divine self-communication. Colin E. Gunton contributed a number of works to the exploration and application of a 'hermeneutic of relationality' but perhaps in *The One, the Three and the Many*[19] set out most clearly his vision of the implications of the divine relationality. Evidently there are other landmark works to which appeal could be made; what is offered here is by no means exhaustive. However, from the works selected I want to explore further a possible (re-)construction of a genealogy of a 'hermeneutic of relationality'. The appearance of landmark works in the 1980s and 1990s was preceded by a period when the components of what may now be perceived as a 'hermeneutic of relationality' were being crafted and assembled. One example of this is the development of the thought of John Zizioulas. His seminal article, *Human Capacity and Human Incapacity: A Theological Exploration of Personhood*,[20] published in 1975 and originally given as a paper in 1972, demonstrates the antecedents and components of Zizioulas' developed understanding. Zizioulas recognizes that his work stands in a continuity with such understandings of 'relationality' as those of Buber, Macmurray, Pannenberg and David Jenkins.[21] Zizioulas also appeals to the concept of *ek-stasis*, 'a movement toward communion',[22] which he argues is both a modern existentialist understanding (i.e. dependent upon Heidegger) as well as something he traces to the Greek Fathers such as Pseudo Dionysius and Maximus the Confessor. In making this identification he acknowledges the work of Christos Yannaras in bringing Heidegger's concepts into dialogue with Orthodox tradition.[23] In this brief exposition of the antecedents of Zizioulas' developed thought, a clear picture of the complexity of a genealogy of a 'hermeneutic of relationality' already emerges. It is also clear from such Orthodox writers as Nikos Nissiotis[24] that a focus on communion both ecclesial and divine was coming to be emphasized from the early 1960s. Writers such as LaCugna identify other earlier influences on development of late twentieth-century trinitarian theology, such as the work of

Théodore de Régnon,[25] while Christoph Schwöbel points to the work of Illingworth[26] in the late nineteenth century as a point of departure for reflection, thus identifying a number of Anglican theologians, who focused on the social model of the Trinity, exemplified in particular by Thornton.[27] Another stream of thought can be traced to the work of those in the *nouvelle théologie* of mid-twentieth century Roman Catholicism, which emerges in the appeal to 'communion' in *Lumen gentium* of Vatican II.[28] This stream of thought may be identified in Louis Lochet's *Charité fraternelle et vie trinitaire*,[29] published in 1956; Fraigneau-Julien's *Réflexion sur la signification religieuse du mystère de la Sainte Trinité*,[30] published in 1965; and Klaus Hemmerle's *Thesen zu einer trinitarischen Ontologie*,[31] first published in 1976. Leonardo Boff acknowledges that not only Moltmann but also M. J. Scheeben[32] and Taymans d'Eypernon,[33] explored the Trinity as 'supreme society' and thus as a model for human society. In these writings[34] can be discerned a move toward the later twentieth-century shift to relationality in the fields of trinitarian and ecclesiological exploration. Focus on a relational conceptuality of the divine and ecclesial continued into the late 1990s and the new millennium, and is witnessed in the writing of such as David Cunningham,[35] Paul Fiddes,[36] John Milbank and Catherine Pickstock,[37] Stanley Grenz,[38] and the recent collection of essays *Trinitarian Soundings*.[39]

Developments in a broader philosophical context, which influence and undergird these developments in Christian theological thought, are again too complex to come within the purview of this essay. The writings of Levinas are credited by some writers to be crucial for understanding the 'turn to relationality',[40] and in Levinas is to be found someone who clearly embraces the 'ethical relation to the other' as a central category. However, while not underestimating the contribution of Levinas to late twentieth-century understandings, it is evident that philosophical discussion of 'relation' is by no means a recent development. Sara Grant argues that 'all men, have always argued about questions of relation',[41] while Krempel argues that relation 'has in modern times replaced 'substance' or 'the absolute' as the ultimate category of reality'.[42] While not everyone would want to concur with these statements, they demonstrate that in constructing the genealogy of a 'hermeneutic of relationality' as it emerged in the latter part of the twentieth century, there are strands of thought that may be traced to early antiquity in both Europe and Asia. Thus the late twentieth-century appeal to relationality may possibly be described as a 'stampede' in terms of its renewed application to trinitarian thought and ecclesiology, but this 'turn' should also be seen in terms of a much wider and longer genealogy. In the context of both shorter and longer views of this genealogy it may be seen that both proponents of a social model of the Trinity and those who would offer a critique of this move, would benefit from a clear understanding of the evolution behind late twentieth-century conceptualities much more than is usually the case.

It should also be recognized that an element of this genealogy is also to be found within ecumenical conversation itself, and that the usage in NMC has a long lineage behind it. I have not attempted to give a detailed analysis of the emergence of the use of *koinonia* in ecumenical dialogue; however, it is useful to indicate some features of that development and also where it is recorded. A possible starting place may be found in an encyclical of the Ecumenical Patriarch from 1920, in which appeal is made to the notion of 'fellowship' among the churches.[43] At the time of the founding of the World Council of Churches, the writings of Oliver Tomkins also bear testimony to growing understanding and articulation of the relationship between the Church as community and the life of the Trinity.[44] This conceptuality is given clear expression in the report *One Lord One Baptism* (chaired by Tomkins) in 1960.[45] After that time the correlation of relationality ecclesial and divine becomes a strong theme in texts of the Faith and Order Commission and the World Council of Churches, which Mary Tanner traces in her address to the Faith and Order Conference in Santiago de Compostella in 1993.[46]

(b) Critique of the 'Hermeneutic of Relationality' in Trinitarian Theology and Ecclesiology

The resurgence of interest in the social model of the Trinity, together with an exploration of the consequences of the application of the category of *koinonia* to the Godhead and the Church, inevitably brought with it a counterpoise, a questioning of this resurgence and the potentially hegemonic use of relationality. A critique of a 'hermeneutic of relationality' has been in evidence from at least the early 1990s. John Gresham writing in 1993[47] outlined four main perspectives from which critique of the social model of the Trinity could be offered, viz.: terminological, monotheistic, christological, and feminist. These four perspectives highlight areas of concern that other less sympathetic writers have also identified. Two areas in particular emerge which offer a strong challenge to those who would espouse a 'hermeneutic of relationality'. First, there is a question about the way in which 'person' is to be understood; this in turn raises issues about the interpretation of patristic sources and terminology, particularly in relation to the 'Cappadocian Fathers'. Secondly, there is a question about the motivation for this kind of interpretation and indeed for the resurgence of interest in relationality altogether.

The questioning of the conceptuality of personhood, and the interpretation of patristic usage of terms among those who propound a relational understanding of the divine and ecclesial, was signalled by André de Halleux in the mid-1980s. Halleux rejects as simplistic the division of trinitarian conceptualities between a social Eastern model and a psychological Western model, traced to de Régnon. He argues that in the understanding of Basil of Caesarea there was perhaps never a real distinction between *hypostasis* and *ousia*.[48] From this critique Halleux suggests that Zizioulas' interpretation of the 'Cappadocian Fathers' understanding of *koinonia* as dialogical is a misunderstanding.[49] He concludes that the personalism of the Cappadocians does not have to be opposed to the language of 'essence' (*ousia*).[50] Similar concerns are raised by John Wilks in 1995,[51] especially in relation to Zizioulas' use of the Cappadocian Fathers. Fermer, writing in 1999,[52] reiterates these concerns, in particular focusing on the way in which Zizioulas extrapolates his conceptuality of the divine being as *koinonia* from the writings of the Cappadocian Fathers. In particular, Fermer argues that in the understanding of the Cappadocian Fathers the divine *ousia* was ineffable.[53] Anthony Meredith endorses this view.[54] In 2003 Norman Metzler[55] wrote arguing that despite the values in the social modelling of the Trinity, the use to which the term *persona* is put in these relational understandings cannot bear the weight being put upon it.[56] The most developed critique in this area is offered by Lucian Turcescu,[57] who argues that the conceptuality of personhood which Zizioulas argues is to be found in the writing of the Cappadocian Fathers is rather a 'newly minted concept of person (which) rests on an understanding of the Christian Trinity mainly as prototype of persons-in-relation'.[58] Such a critique of the interpretation of patristic sources leads to a second challenge, which questions where the motivation for such interpretation is to be situated. Writing in 1992 Nicholas Lash warns: 'Although the individualism which, in Western culture, infects our sense of what it is to be a human person is no help here, to exorcize [person] would not render the term more suitable for use in trinitarian theology.'[59] Implicit in his argument is a critique of those who seek to reformulate a conceptuality of personhood in order to challenge the perceived effects of the Enlightenment on understandings of human being. Sarah Coakley reiterates a critique of the argument that the appeal to the doctrine of the Trinity as 'prototype of persons-in-relation' as made in particular by Zizioulas and Gunton is designed to overcome Enlightenment 'individualism'.[60] James Mackey makes a similar point but argues more explicitly that in the social modelling of the Trinity is to be found a projection of current ideas of human relationships into the immanent Trinity,[61] resulting in what he deems to be too much certainty about the inner life of God.[62] Indeed he suggests there are 'crypto-ideologies that must always lurk in those social Trinities which have not quite abjured all knowledge of the inner being of God'.[63] Agreeing with Mackey, Fermer reinforces the attack, arguing that the relational interpretation of the divine and ecclesial to be found in the work of Zizioulas and Gunton suggests the collapse of the distinction between God and the world.[64] Metzler argues that a possible solution to the recognition that relational understandings of the divine and ecclesial are based upon contemporary understandings of persons and relationships, rather than patristic understandings, is to accept that the divine is relational in the economy, but not in the inner life of the divine.[65] Thus in this solution he rejects the foundational concept that the economic and immanent Trinity are identical, which underpins so much of the social modelling of the divine and ecclesial.[66] David Cunningham raises parallel concerns, questioning whether a 'hermeneutic of relationality' leads to an authentic expression of Christian monotheism: '... contemporary Trinitarian theology has simply presented a "kinder gentler" substantialist metaphysics. The fault lies in the assumption that the doctrine of the Trinity necessarily implies an ontology of any kind – which, in my view, it does not.'[67]

In answer to this challenge Cunningham recommends an appeal to 'partici-pation' rather than 'relationality', for he argues that participation (*perichoresis*) achieves what relationality sets out to do, but without the pitfalls. His concern to overcome ontology, which finds support in the work of Milbank and Marion,[68] is it seems to me a proper concern, whether that concern finds a solution in making a distinction between relationality and *perichoresis* is another matter particularly when so many proponents of a 'hermeneutic of relationality' set so much store by *perichoresis.*[69] Jens Zimmermann[70] also reiterates this strand of critique, but also offers a means of rehabilitating a 'hermeneutic of relationality'.

> Clearly the Trinitarian conception of the human subject is important for the recovery of theological hermeneutics. There is, however, one significant problem: most presentations of the communal model of subjectivity are not very hermeneutical. They begin in the speculative realm with the doctrine of the Trinity rather than with God's self-revelation in history. Instead of beginning in time and history, speculation begins in the eternal. The danger is that metaphysics begins to shape theology. While much of the Greek Orthodox speculation on the Trinity and personhood is attractive, its tendency to determine human subjectivity primarily through the Trinity rather than through God's self-expression in Christ is in danger of shaping God himself in our own image ...[71]

Zimmermann's solution is to appeal to Bonhoeffer's conceptuality of person-hood[72] as understood in relation to the Incarnation and the Cross. Earlier Jean Galot made similar suggestions, rooting his appeal to relationality in the 'Relational Being of Christ',[73] while also anchoring his argument in the doctrine of the Trinity. This appeal to the self-expression of the divine in Christ is echoed in the typology of trinitarian thought set out by Sarah Coakley,[74] in particular in relation to 'the Trinity construed from reflection on the death of Christ', as well as in her appeal to 'religious experience'. In using Coakley's typology to analyse and interpret the critique of the social modelling of the divine and ecclesial, two alternative approaches to 'relationality' emerge. On the one hand it would be possible to be satisfied simply with a 'hermeneutic of relationality', while on the other hand it would be possible to argue that the hermeneutic leads to an ontology of relationality. Before we turn to address this fundamental question, I want first to attend to issues surrounding person/hood.

(c) The Place of Person/hood in the Discourse

Alongside the discourse concerning a 'hermeneutic of relationality' per se there is another accompanying discourse on person/personhood, which again manifests itself in two contrary streams: one in which the 'turn to person/hood' understood in relational terms is defended and another in which person/hood is seen in primarily individualist(-ic) terms. A brief overview of these discourses will assist further in the analysis and understanding of the place of *koinonia* in NMC.

The exploration of a relational understanding of person/hood in the 1970s may be found not only in the work of Zizioulas, but also in the work of Johann Auer,[75] who raises the question of person/hood in relation to the 'person' of Jesus Christ and the Trinity and by extension to the Church. The work of Karol Wojtyla (later Pope John Paul II) also contributed to the richness of the discourse concerning a relational understanding of the human subject. Alfred Wilder,[76] reflecting on the work of Karol Wojtyla, situates his work in the post-Enlightenment context in relation to understandings of person found in Feuerbach, Marcel and Buber, over against the exposition of the Absolute Ego found in Fichte, Schelling and Hegel.

Lawerence B. Porter,[77] writing in 1980, focuses his attention in particular on the divine 'persons' arguing that the attempt to avoid the language of 'person' in trinitarian doctrine made by both Barth and Rahner does not take into account patristic innovation, found particularly in the work of Tertullian. He argues that the self-relatedness of the Godhead requires the ongoing and unresolved tension that the language of person/hood brings to the doctrine of the Trinity.[78] The mid-1980s saw a number of publications outlining the emergence of and need for a relational understanding of person/hood, of which Zizioulas' *Being as Communion* is a prime example.[79] In 1986 Hans Urs von Balthasar[80] wrote on the concept of person, setting out something of a genealogy of the term itself as well as of those who have defended a relational understanding of it. In counterpoint to this development among theologians, an alternative discourse is manifest in other disciplines, especially among philosophers, who have argued either that the self or the person is a construct, or have continued to defend the Enlightenment individualist understanding of person/hood,[81] over against which a 'hermeneutic of relationality' has in general been developed.

Emerging from the discourse on the relationality of person/hood two themes may be discerned: firstly an understanding of person in terms of act, and secondly that 'act' is to be understood in terms of (self-)donation. An underlying strand to these themes may be traced to the influence of Husserl.[82] The human person is to be understood as a living subject, thus human subjectivity is defined in terms of consciousness, self-knowledge and self-possession, which are to be recognized in human freedom.[83] Another influence is traced to Whitehead, mediated in the Christian reception of his thought by Hartshorne and Cobb.[84] In this conceptuality, 'God is not to be understood as a unique non-temporal actual entity but rather as a personally ordered society of actual occasions'.[85] The divine act of being is understood as an activity rather than as a state; and that activity is understood as the 'interrelating' of the divine 'persons'. Bracken argues that 'this activity of interrelating is never exactly the same in two successive moments. The three divine persons, in other words, experience change in their ongoing relationality to one another.'[86] Such an understanding of person/hood and relationality has particular resonances with the discourse on 'différence' and repetition to which I will return below.

Writing on the understanding of person/hood to be found in the work of Karol Wojtyla, Robert A. Connor argues that the philosophical/theological tradition has failed to provide 'a satisfactory ontological model to explain the ever-emerging awareness of person as an intrinsically relational being'.[87] However, he suggests that in the thought of Karol Wojtyla such a model may be emerging, through his use of a phenomenology of the acting subject. Wojtyla's conceptuality of person/hood understood in terms of the double effect of intrinsic will allows for (a) the transcending action itself and (b) immanent and lasting determination within the agent, which Connor interprets as 'a model for growth by relating'.[88] Here the suggestion that the person is 'ever-emerging'[89] resonates with the conceptuality of difference and repetition. An interesting extension of this understanding of person/hood in terms of act is to be found in the writing of Joseph Ratzinger (now Pope Benedict XVI). Writing in relation to the doctrine of the Trinity he discusses the personhood of the Father: 'the first person does not generate in the sense that to the complete person the act of generating a son is added, but the person *is* the act of generating, of offering oneself and flowing out ... the pure actuality'.[90] He reiterates this understanding in a later work arguing that 'The person is identical with this act of self-donation'.[91] The richness of discourse on person/hood adds further to the sense of the complexity of the genealogy of relationality. However, the appeal to 'act conceptualities' may assist in seeking to address the question of an ontological expression of relationality.

(d) Relationality: Hermeneutic or Ontology of Koinonia?

The need for a decision emerges as to the possibility or indeed desirability when speaking of a 'hermeneutic relationality' of whether this should lead to a metaphysical/ontological understanding of the relationality of the divine and ecclesial. As I noted above when using Sarah Coakley's typology to analyse and interpret the critique of the social modelling of the divine and ecclesial, there are two possible alternative approaches to 'relationality': on the one hand a 'hermeneutic of relationality', which assumes no particular ontological claims, and on the other hand an explicit ontology of relationality. It is to this fundamental decision/question that we must turn.

In pursuit of this question concerning relationality, Rowan Williams' essay on 'Trinity and Ontology' is instructive. In his appropriation of Donald MacKinnon's appeal to the tragic in the life of Christ, Rowan Williams points to the need to begin reflection on relationality from the 'world of particulars', rather than from an *a priori* understanding of the Godhead: '... what we first know is the reality we subsequently come to know as derivative, transposed from what is prior'.[92] Sustaining this position is evidently problematic, for as both Williams and Coakley point out, despite the appeal to the 'particularity' of the Cross in the trinitarian thought of Moltmann, the interpretation of the world of particulars is construed against a background of 'more than a whiff of Hegelian dialectics'.[93] A parallel critique might be offered of others who defend a 'hermeneutic of relationality'. Thus, in seeking to clarify the usage of *koinonia* in NMC, the question must be posed as to whether a relational understanding of the divine and ecclesial is to be construed upon *a priori* understandings, be they scriptural, patristic or contemporary; or upon 'the world of particulars' as evidenced in the scriptural witness and experienced in the lived Tradition of praxis and worship. If it is to be argued that the latter is preferable, being less open to charges of importing extraneous ideologies, then the decision relating to metaphysical/ontological understandings of relationality still remains to be addressed. Alan Torrance suggests a possible way forward in terms of understanding the connections to be made between the interpretation of the world of particulars and the interpretation of the God who reveals himself. Alan Torrance argues that, 'Theologically interpreted, communication presupposes the category of communion, and not the other way round'.[94] That leaves him open to the charge of appealing to an *a priori* rather than an appeal to the revelation in the Christ event.

Nonetheless his appeal to the use of *mirifica communicatio* as an interpretative tool in relation to the *mirifica communio* mediated through what he understands as the *mirifica commutatio* may still hold useful possibilities. The main issue in asking the question regarding metaphysics is the way in which the role of the mediating *mirifica commutatio* is construed. Does the encounter with the Christ event in the 'world of particulars' take us by means of the *mirifica commutatio* to the *mirifica communio*? Or is the understanding of 'communion' an *a priori* given?

In taking forward this question of ontology, the appeal to the 'world of particulars' and an awareness of how understanding of the relation between communication and communion is received and interpreted will remain crucial to formulating any 'answer'.

Toward a Proposal for Broader Conceptual Consensus

In this section I set out a way forward toward a clarification of the use of the notion of *koinonia* in NMC. The first stage in this process would be to clarify the use of *koinonia* in relation to the Holy Trinity. This would entail reaching a consensus concerning the conceptuality(-ies) holding together on the one hand the conciliar agreement of 381/2 that in the Godhead there are three hypostases and one ousia and on the other the category of *koinonia*. Those who have espoused a 'hermeneutic of relationality', among them notably John Zizioulas, have put forward such an understanding. However, as noted already, their conceptualities of personhood and *koinonia* are by no means uncontested. It is not the purpose of this essay to defend one view or another in relation to this discourse. Nonetheless Zizioulas' understanding of 'an event of communion'[95] has much to recommend it, not only in terms of its fruitfulness for ecclesial ecumenism, but also for a wider ecumenism, which as the NMC text acknowledges is the sphere of the *missio dei*. The event conceptuality for which Zizioulas argues situates discussion of *koinonia* not so much in the realm of interdenominational politics as in the realm that Caputo calls 'Radical Hermeneutics', and thus potentially also in the realm of discussion of the deconstruction of the defensive-ness of 'community' made by Derrida.

The 'event of communion' of which Zizioulas writes may be understood to embrace a conceptuality of 'communion . . . rooted in the order of creation' (NMC 25), and the 'new life of communion' (NMC 32). Each instance may be interpreted as an expression of an iterative understanding of an event conceptuality of *koinonia* which I want to suggest undergirds all existence. Church understood as 'communion' relates to this conceptuality of *koinonia* in terms of a means of enabling participation in the divine life for all humanity/the cosmos. This enabling is rooted in such practical means as the sacraments. Hence the reference in 1 Cor. 10:16 to *koinonia* remains a key first stage in building the conceptual ladder to any understanding of *koinonia* and of Church as 'communion'.

(a) Beginning from a Critique of a 'Hermeneutic of Relationality' in Trinitarian Theology and Ecclesiology

In seeking to clarify the use of *koinonia* in relation to the Holy Trinity in NMC, my first concern is to examine the understanding that is to be found among those who defend and encourage such usage, for example John Zizioulas. In an article 'The Church as Communion' (1993) Zizioulas makes it clear that, in his understanding, the appeal to a divine and ecclesial relationality is not based upon any *a priori* ideological pre-understanding. While *koinonia* might be understood in sociological terms, its adoption in trinitarian theology and ecclesiology is by no means to be rooted there.[96] Christians are not called to *koinonia* because it is good for them; rather because God is by definition relational: God is *koinonia*.[97] His non-ideological stance is rooted in the claim that, 'The Church is the body of Christ, because Christ is a pneumatological being, born, born and existing in the *koinonia* of the Spirit'.[98] Such a stance is rooted in the narrative of the Gospels, for example the Annunciation and the Baptism of Christ, thus appealing to 'the world of particulars' of divine self-revelation. It is also in relation to experience in the life of the Church that Zizioulas appeals to the idea of 'an event of communion'.[99] His understanding that the Church is bound to the very being of God emerges from his own reflection upon the life of the Church, as well as upon his interpretation of patristic sources; it is upon this basis that 'an event of communion' is an expression of a 'hermeneutic of relation(ality)', which includes the divine, ecclesial and cosmic. Zizioulas reiterates his understanding that this is rooted in experience: 'This experience revealed something very important: the being of God could be known only through personal relationships and personal love. Being means life, and life means communion'.[100] In this statement Zizioulas confirms that the conceptuality of relationality emerges from reflection upon 'the world of particulars', from a particular experience of ecclesial/eucharistic living. His conceptuality is then first and foremost a 'hermeneutic of relationality'. However, Zizioulas immediately translates this hermeneutic of relationality into an ontology of relationality: 'The substance of God, "God", God has no ontological content, no true being apart from communion'.[101] Such a leap to ontology from experience is perhaps too quick, and in the view of some too certain.

Zizioulas understands that his argument for an ontology of communion is not based upon *a priori* understandings of relationality, for he constructs his ontological understandings upon the role of the person of the Father: the 'free person'.[102] Thus a person is the cause of communion/relationality. Zizioulas' understanding of the person of the Father bears strong parallels to that of Ratzinger's understanding, which is expressed in particular in terms of self-donation.[103] However, in applying the notion of freedom to the human person, Zizioulas is careful to reject any resonance with the existentialists' quest for absolute freedom as a quest without fulfilment; thus again rejecting any *a priori* ideology. A fundamental epistemic question remains however about the construction of the role of the Father in the thought of either Zizioulas or Ratzinger: to what extent is this role rooted in the divine self-revelation and 'the world of particulars' and to what extent is this speculation; speculation which must rest upon a set of (*a priori*) preconceptions. Furthermore, to what extent is it advisable or possible to have such certainty about the inner life of God? Does commitment to the axiom that economic and immanent Trinity are identical necessarily disclose the particularity of the role of the Father? One way forward may be to take a step backwards: to resist at least for the time being the move to an ontology of relationality, and to reflect further on a 'hermeneutic of relationality'; a hermeneutic rooted in event conceptuality.

Christoph Schwöbel points to dissatisfaction with non-trinitarian thought, which gives no proper account of the person and work of Christ as well as 'disappointment with the inability of many versions of Christian theism, conceived in terms of a metaphysics of substance or a philosophy of subjectivity, to do justice to the relational "logic" of such central Christian statements as "God is Love" '.[104] Against this background a hermeneutical rather than ontological account of relationality may be more pertinent in seeking to give an account of the category of *koinonia*.

(b) Event and the 'Weakness of God'

In the quest to defend a 'hermeneutic of relationality' rather than an ontology, John Caputo, gives a timely reminder that 'This new hermeneutics would not try to make things look easy, to put the best face on existence, but rather to recapture the hardness of life before metaphysics showed us a fast way out the back door of flux'.[105] In the project to deconstruct the metaphysics of presence, *kinesis* is to be read back into *ousia*, in order to face up to time and flux, with no appeal to Greek recollection.[106] Thus, if the appeal to *koinonia* as event is to be sustained, a move toward a metaphysics of presence, enfolded in an ontology of relationality, needs to be resisted (at least initially). If the appeal to an event conceptuality of *koinonia* is an attempt to recognize *kinesis* in *ousia*, then an event of communion will be understood as a looking forwards – i.e., repetition – rather than backwards – i.e., recollection. Caputo goes on to argue for the recognition that 'Repetition ... is not repetition of the same, but a creative production which pushes ahead, which produces *as* it repeats ...'[107] However Caputo, in company with Derrida, warns against the easy achievement of the outcome of adopting an event conceptuality. Hegel, Heidegger and Gadamer are all criticized for their persistent inability to overcome recollection and presence. Caputo writes (referring initially to Gadamer):

> Even though it contains a useful critique of 'method', the question of 'truth' in *Truth and Method* remains within the metaphysics of truth. Constantin warned us about those friends of the flux who make a lot of noise about becoming, when what they have up their sleeve all along is the noiseless hush of *Aufhebung*.[108]

In his recent work *The Weakness of God*,[109] Caputo writes of 'event', in particular in terms of the name of God as an event. He sets out eight characteristics of this event, beginning with the idea that 'The event is the open-ended promise contained within a name, but a promise that the name can neither contain nor deliver'.[110] The notion of promise may be understood in that 'every event occurs against a horizon of expectation that it breaches'.[111] An event is an excess, an overflow, a surprise, an uncontainable incoming (*l'invention*), an irruption, a gift beyond economy, 'something that cannot be constricted to either the ontic or ontological order at all'.[112] If Zizioulas' phrase 'an event of communion' were to be construed in relation to Caputo's notion of event, then a new understanding of a 'hermeneutic of relationality' emerges. Communion is no longer an appeal to a metaphysics of presence but an incoming of what Derrida would understand as 'the impossible'. Such conceptualities bring new insights to the construal of communion divine and ecclesial in ecumenical dialogue in general and in relation to NMC in particular. Caputo expands upon the conceptuality of event in reference to the thought of Derrida on the impossible:

> The event begins *by* the impossible ... By that he means that the event is moved and driven by the desire for the *gift* beyond economy, for the *justice* beyond the law, for the *hospitality* beyond proprietorship, for *forgiveness* beyond getting even, for the coming of the *tout autre* beyond the presence of the same ...[113]

This event conceptuality interprets *kinesis* in terms of gift, justice, hospitality and forgiveness, which could assist the process of developing an understanding of what is to be found in NMC, in terms of the outcome of the divine gift of *koinonia*.

(c) The Weakness of God and Ecumenical Hermeneutics of Koinonia

In seeking to clarify the use of *koinonia* in NMC in seems appropriate to discuss the deconstruction of community made by Derrida. Through an interpretation of a possible etymology of community, in which he suggests that part of the word relates to the origin of 'munitions', he argues that community as a defensive and enclosed concept is in need of deconstruction.[114] A reclamation of 'community' as a less defensive and more open concept might be made on the basis of an appeal to hospitality and alterity. Such an approach raises the issue of 'communion' *vis à vis* 'the other'. Already above '*tout autre*' has emerged as a characteristic of Caputo's event conceptuality. So the question emerges: in 'an event of communion' what place is there for the 'other'? Caputo suggests that such a question is unavoidable, as he reflects that

> Lévinas's idea is to rethink the religious in terms of our obligation to the other, not in terms of becoming happy, and to rethink God, not by way of a renewed experience of the truth of Being, but by getting beyond the anonymity of Being and experiencing the God whose withdrawal from the world leaves a divine trace on the face of the stranger.[115]

In pursuing this exploration of the other in relation to *koinonia*, another question emerges: how is alterity of 'the other' to be understood? Reflecting upon internal difference Deleuze has argued that difference is to be distinguished from: *contradiction, alterity* and *negation*. Deleuze appeals to Bergson's theory and method of difference, which he distinguishes from that of Plato or Hegel's dialectic, understood in terms of internal difference,[116] Bergson rejects the internal dynamics of Plato and Hegel's thought, which he argues understands alterity in terms of contradiction. Rather alterity is to be understood in terms of difference, which is external. In the light of this it is important to examine the alterity of 'the other' in relation to the characteristics of *koinonia*. A 'hermeneutic of relationality' would need to be aware of how an approach to 'the other' might be included. Such a process raises issues concerning power. Derrida argues that in the usual reality of hospitality the host remains in control, and retains property. Thus in hospitality and hosting some hostility is always to be found.[117] However, Derrida does not suggest that this is a final outcome: rather hospitality is also 'the impossible' – pushing against 'the limit' hospitality is always to come.[118] The 'limit' suggests the dynamics of the economy of giving and receiving, including the debt of gratitude and the felt need to reciprocate. For Derrida, only the in-breaking of 'the impossible' can overcome such dynamics. For community to emerge that is unfettered by the dynamics of the economy of credit and debt of hospitality, there needs to be 'an exposure to *"tout autre"* that escapes or resists community'.[119]

The language of *tout autre* has populated trinitarian thought in such writers as Karl Barth, Jürgen Moltmann and Eberhard Jüngel. Barth, for instance, argues that God reveals himself 'in the form of something He Himself is not'.[120] The reiteration or repetition of the divine (*Wiederholung Gottes*) in this conceptuality begs many questions, which I cannot pursue in this paper. However, what is crucial for the understanding of *koinonia* is whether the divine self-revelation is simply that: the reiteration of the divine or absolute '*Ich*'? Is this, as has been mentioned above, another example of the influence of Hegel's use of *Aufhebung*? Hegel's own understanding of *Aufhebung* – annihilation, invalidation and also preservation – means that in annihilation there is also preservation: preservation of *Ich*. If such a conceptuality is extended to the Church, this could mean that the ecclesial *koinonia* is no more than an 'absolute' *Wir*. In construing a 'hermeneutic of relationality' it is crucial therefore to have a clear concept of the place of 'the other'. Is alterity to be understood as within *Ich* or *Wir*? Or is it to be understood as in terms of externality? One way in which to interpret Zizioulas' role of the Father in conceptualizing the Trinity is in terms of an external alterity as suggested by Derrida and Caputo: the Father as source of that which is other than himself. In respect of such an interpretation of Zizioulas, it might also prove beneficial to draw upon Deleuze's understanding of repetition and difference.[121] His conceptuality of repetition as other-ness and difference, rather than sameness, may prove fruitful ground for a fulsome interpretation of a relational understanding of the Godhead as *koinonia*. This in turn would inform ecclesial understandings of *koinonia* as including (radical) alterity.

In *Communion and Otherness*,[122] Zizioulas himself recognizes the need to engage with the dynamics of alterity. He draws a distinction between difference (*diastasis*) and division (*diaresis*); where difference is to be understood as part of the divine gift of creation, while division is seen as a result of the Fall.[123] Insofar as all human beings are subject to the Fall, all are involved in division, so that even within the holiness of the Church there is division. Thus he argues, 'the essence of Christian existence in the Church is *metanoia* – repentance. By being rejected, or simply feared by us, the "other" challenges or provokes us to repent.'[124] Insofar as otherness is a proper feature of the communion of the Church, Zizioulas argues that otherness is divine as well as ecclesial. The *koinonia* of the Trinity is an [absolute] expression of otherness, he claims. Thus 'Communion does not threaten otherness; it generates it'.[125] However, for *koinonia* as an expression of otherness to be shared in a cosmos riven by division, Zizioulas argues that, 'communion with the other requires the experience of the Cross'.[126] For the restoration of the divine image in the human being, it is necessary for the human person to be incorporated into Christ, including his sacrificial death and resurrection. Only thus is it possible for the Church to reflect 'in history the communion and otherness that we see in the Triune God'.[127] Thus Zizioulas roots his conceptuality of otherness and *koinonia* in the 'world of particulars' of the revelation in Christ as well as in ecclesial experience. The event of communion, which is also to be understood as an event of alterity, is an affirmation of ultimate difference. However, this difference is not divisive but uniting, grounded in ecclesial experience of *metanoia*.[128]

Conclusion

In summary this essay responds to the WCC paper NMC by seeking to clarify the coherence of the use of communion/*koinonia*, in respect of Godhead, Church and the created order. Through an analysis of the genealogy of the recent appeal to relationality and its critique the essay presents a case for pursuing a 'hermeneutic of relationality' which embraces an event conceptuality as the basis for understanding divine and ecclesial *koinonia*. This in turn suggests the need to be clearer about the Church's stance toward alterity and community, as it seeks to participate in the divine purposes of restoring and sharing *koinonia* in the created order.

Notes

1. NMC no. 8, question 4.
2. I am indebted to Professor Walter Sparn of the Theological Faculty of the University of Erlangen for this phrase.
3. Susan Wood, 'Ecclesial Koinonia in Ecumenical Dialogues', *One in Christ* 30 (1994): 124–45.
4. Ibid.: 127.
5. Leonardo Boff, *Trinity and Society*, p. 9.
6. Ibid., p. 118.
7. Ibid., p. 119.
8. See: Moltmann, LaCugna and Volf.
9. Stanley J. Grenz, *The Social God and the Relational Self* (Louisville: Westminster/John Knox Press, 2001), p. 5.
10. F. LeRon Shults, *Reforming Theological Anthropology: After the Philosophical Turn to Relationality* (Grand Rapids, MI: Eerdmans, 2003).

11. Christoph Schwöbel and Colin E. Gunton (eds), *Persons, Divine and Human: King's College Essays in Theological Anthropology* (Edinburgh: T&T Clark, 1991); Christoph Schwöbel (ed.), *Trinitarian Theology Today: Essays on Divine Being and Act* (Edinburgh: T&T Clark, 1995); Christoph Schwöbel, *Gott in Beziehung: Studien zur Dogmatik* (Tübingen: Mohr Siebeck, 2002).

12. Shults, *Reforming Theological Anthropology.*

13. Jürgen Moltmann, *The Trinity and the Kingdom of God: The Doctrine of God* (London: SCM, 1981).

14. Leonardo Boff, *Trinity and Society* (Tunbridge Wells: Burns & Oates, 1988).

15. Robert W. Jenson, *The Triune Identity: God According to the Gospel* (Philadelphia: Fortress Press, 1982).

16. John D. Zizioulas, *Being as Communion: Studies in Personhood and Church* (London: Darton, Longman and Todd, 1985).

17. Ronald J. Feenstra and Cornelius Plantinga, Jr (eds), *Trinity, Incarnation and Atonement: Philosophical and Theological Essays* (Notre Dame, IN: University of Notre Dame Press, 1989).

18. Catherine Mowry LaCugna, *God for Us: The Trinity and the Christian Life* (New York: HarperCollins, 1991).

19. Colin E. Gunton, *The One, the Three and the Many: God, Creation and the Culture of Modernity* (Cambridge: Cambridge University Press, 1993).

20. John D. Zizioulas, 'Human Capacity and Human Incapacity: A Theological Exploration of Personhood', *Scottish Journal of Theology* 28 (1975): 401–48.

21. See: Zizioulas, 'Human Capacity', 408, n. 1; Martin Buber, *I and Thou* (Edinburgh: T&T Clark, 1970); John Macmurray, *Persons in Relation*, vol. 2 of *The Form of the Personal* (London: Faber & Faber, 1961); Wolfhart Pannenberg, 'Person', in *RGG* (3rd edn) 5: 230–5; David Jenkins, *The Glory of Man* (London: SCM, 1967); *What is Man?* (London: SCM, 1970); *Living with Questions* (London: SCM, 1969).

22. Zizioulas, 'Human Capacity', p. 408.

23. See Christos Yannaras, *The Ontological Content of the Theological Notion of Person* (PhD thesis, Athens: University of Salonika, 1970 (in Greek).

24. Nikos A. Nissiotis, 'The Importance of the Doctrine of the Trinity for Church Life and Theology', in *The Orthodox Ethos*, ed. A. J. Philippou (Oxford: Holywell Press, 1964).

25. Theodore de Regnon, *Études de théologie positive sur la Sainte Trinité*, 3 vols (Paris: Retaux, 1892–98).

26. J. R. Illingworth, *Personality Human and Divine* (London: Macmillan, 1894).

27. L. S. Thornton, 'The Christian Conception of God', in *Essays Catholic and Critical*, ed. E. G. Selwyn (London: SPCK, 1926).

28. *Lumen gentium* (1964) nos. 4, 7, 8, 9, 13, 14, 15, 18, 21, 22, 24, 25, 28, 29, 41, 49, 50, 51.

29. Louis Lochet, 'Charité fraternelle et vie trinitaire', *Nouvelle Revue Théologique* 78 (2) (1956): 113–34.

30. B. Fraigneau-Julien, 'Réflexion sur la signification religieuse du mystère de la Sainte Trinité', *Nouvelle Revue Théologique* 87 (7) (1965): 673–87.

31. Klaus Hemmerle, *Thesen zu einer trinitarischen Ontologie* (Freiburg: Johannes, 1992).

32. M. J. Scheeben, *Handbuch der katholischen Dogmatik*, vol. 4 (Freiburg: 1948).

33. François Taymans d'Eypernon, *Le Mystère primordial: La Trinité dans sa vivante image* (Brussels: Desclée de Brouwer, 1946).

34. Other significant contributions to this landscape are: Leonard Hodgson, *The Doctrine of the Trinity* (New York: Charles Scribners Sons, 1944); Claude Welch, *In This Name: The Doctrine of the Trinity in Contemporary Theology* (New York: Charles Scribners Sons, 1952); E. J. Fortman, *The Triune God: A Historical Study of the Doctrine of the Trinity* (Philadelphia: Westminster, 1972); William Hill, *The Three-Personed God: The Trinity as a Mystery of Salvation* (Washington: Catholic University of America Press, 1982); Walter Kasper, *The God of Jesus Christ* (London: SCM, 1984); David Brown, *The Divine Trinity* (LaSalle, IL: Open Court, 1985); Joseph Bracken, *The Triune Symbol: Persons, Process and Community*

(Lanham, MD: University Press of America, 1985); John J. O'Donnell, *The Mystery of the Triune God* (London: Sheed and Ward, 1988); Elizabeth Johnson, *She Who Is: The Mystery of God in a Feminist Theological Discourse* (New York: Crossroad, 1992).

35. David S. Cunningham, *These Three Are One: The Practice of Trinitarian Theology* (Oxford: Blackwell, 1998).

36. Paul S. Fiddes, *Participating in God: A Pastoral Doctrine of the Trinity* (London: Darton, Longman and Todd, 2000).

37. John Milbank and Catherine Pickstock, *Truth in Aquinas* (London: Routledge, 2001).

38. Stanley J. Grenz, *The Social God and the Relational Self* (Louisville: Westminster/John Knox Press, 2001).

39. Paul Louis Metzer (ed.), *Trinitarian Soundings in Systematic Theology* (London and New York: Continuum, 2005).

40. Shults, *Reforming Theological Anthropology*, p. 32.

41. Sara Grant, *Sankaracarya's Concept of Relation* (Delhi: Motilal Banarsidass Publishers, 1999), p. 1. See also: John Locke, *An Essay Concerning Human Understanding*, vol. 1. (London: Dent; New York: Dutton, 1972); and Immanuel Kant, *Critique of Pure Reason* (London: MacMillan, 1933), pp. 111–15.

42. L. Krempel, *La Doctrine de la relation chez saint Thomas* (Paris: Librairie Philosophique J. Vrin, 1952), ch. 1.

43. *Unto the Churches of Christ Everywhere*, Encyclical of the Ecumenical Patriarchate, 1920.

44. Oliver Tomkins, *The Wholeness of the Church* (London: SCM, 1949), p. 71.

45. *One Lord, One Baptism*. Faith and Order Paper, 29 (London: SCM, 1960), pp. 13–14.

46. Mary Tanner, 'Opening Remarks', in *On the Way to Fuller Koinonia*. Faith and Order Paper, 166, ed. Thomas F. Best and Günther Gassmann (Geneva: WCC, 1994).

47. John L. Gresham, 'The Social Model of the Trinity and Its Critics', *Scottish Journal of Theology* 46 (3) (1993): 325–43.

48. André de Halleux, '"Hypostase" et "Personne" dans la formation de dogme trinitaire (ca. 375–381)', *Revue d'Histoire Ecclésiastique* 79 (1984): 663.

49. André de Halleux, 'Personnalisme ou essentialisme trinitaire chez les Pères cappadociens?' *Revue théologique de Louvain* 17 (1986): 143–4.

50. André de Halleux, 'Personnalisme': 265.

51. John G. F. Wilks, 'The Trinitarian Ontology of John Zizioulas', *Vox Evangelica* 25 (1995): 63–88.

52. Richard M. Femer, 'The Limits of Trinitarian Theology as a Methodological Paradigm', *Neue Zeitschrift für systematische Theologie und Religionsphilosophie* 41 (2) (1999): 158–86.

53. Ibid.: 174.

54. Anthony Meredith, *The Cappadocians* (Crestwood, NY: St Vladimir's Seminary Press, 2000).

55. Norman Metzler, 'The Trinity in Contemporary Theology: Questioning the Social Trinity', *Concordia Theological Quarterly* 67 (3) (2003): 270–87.

56. Ibid.: 284.

57. Lucian Turcescu, 'Prosopon and Hypostasis in Basil of Caesarea's Against Eunomius and the Epistles', *Vigiliae Christianae* 51 (4) (1997): 374–95. See also his: '"Person" versus "Individual", and Other Modern Misreadings of Gregory of Nyssa', in *Re-Thinking Gregory of Nyssa*, ed. Sarah Coakley (Malden, MA: Oxford: Blackwell, 2003); and his *Gregory of Nyssa and the Concept of Divine Persons* (New York: Oxford University Press, 2005).

58. Turcescu, in *Re-Thinking*, p. 98.

59. Nicholas Lash, *Believing Three Ways in One God: A Reading of the Apostles' Creed* (London: SCM, 2002), p. 32.

60. Sarah Coakley, 'Why Three? Some Further Reflections on the Origins of the Doctrine of the Trinity', in *The Making and Remaking of Christian Doctrine: Essays in Honour of Maurice Wiles*, ed. Sarah Coakley and David A. Pailin (Oxford: Clarendon Press, 1993), p. 35.

61. James Mackey, 'Are There Christian Alternatives to Trinitarian Thinking', in *The Christian Understanding of God Today*, ed. James M. Byrne (Dublin: The Columba Press, 1993), p. 67.

62. Ibid., p. 68.

63. Ibid., p. 74.

64. Fermer, 'The Limits of Trinitarian Theology': 173.

65. Metzler, 'The Trinity in Contemporary Theology': 284.

66. Karl Barth, *Church Dogmatics* I.1, pp. 333, 382; Karl Rahner, *The Trinity* (London: Burns and Oates, 1970), p. 22.

67. Cunningham, *These Three Are One*, p. 9.

68. John Milbank, 'Theology without Substance: Christianity, Signs, Origins', *Literature and Theology*, 2 (1) (1988): 1–17; and 2 (2) (1988): 131–52; Jean-Luc Marion, *God without Being: Hors-Texte* (Chicago: Chicago University Press, 1991).

69. E.g., Moltmann, *Kingdom*, pp. 174–6; Boff, *Holy Trinity*, pp. 14–16; Gunton, *The One*, pp. 163–6; LaCugna, *God for Us*, pp. 270–8; Paul Fiddes, *Participating in God*, passim.

70. Jens Zimmermann, *Recovering Theological Hermeneutics: An Incarnational-Trinitarian Theory of Interpretation* (Grand Rapids, MI: Baker Academic, 2004). p. 71. Ibid., p. 283.

72. Dietrich Bonhoeffer, *Sanctorum Communio* (London: Collins, 1963), p. 40.

73. Jean Galot, *Who Is Christ? A Theology of the Incarnation* (Rome: Gregorian University Press; Chicago: Franciscan Herald Press, 1980), pp. 305–13.

74. Coakley, *Why Three?*, pp. 31–9.

75. Johann Auer, *Person: Ein Schlüssel zum christlichen Mysterium* (Regensburg: Verlag Friedrich Pustet, 1979).

76. Alfred Wilder, 'Community of Persons in the Thought of Karol Wojtyla', *Angelicum* 56 (1979): 211–44.

77. Lawerence B. Porter, 'On Keeping "Persons" in the Trinity: A Linguistic Approach to Trinitarian Thought', *Theological Studies* 41 (3) (1980): 530–48.

78. Ibid.: 548.

79. E.g., Catherine Mowry LaCugna, 'The Relational God: Aquinas and Beyond', *Theological Studies* 46 (4) (1985): 647–63; Joseph Ratzinger, 'Concerning the Notion of Person in Theology', *Communio: International Catholic Review* 17 (1990): 439–54; Kenneth L. Schmitz, 'The Geography of the Human Person', *Communio: International Catholic Review* 13 (1986): 27–48.

80. Hans Urs von Balthasar, 'On the Concept of Person', *Communio: International Catholic Review* 13 (1986): 18–26.

81. See: Derek Parfit, *Reasons and Persons* (Oxford: Oxford University Press, 1984); Michael Carrithers, Steven Collins, and Steven Lukes (eds), *The Category of the Person: Anthropology, Philosophy, History* (Cambridge: Cambridge University Press, 1985); Charles Taylor, *Sources of the Self: The Making of Modern Identity* (Cambridge, MA, Harvard University Press, 1989); John Foster, *The Immaterial Self: A Defence of the Cartesian Dualist Conception of the Mind* (London and New York: Routledge, 1991).

82. See Wilder, 'Community of Persons in the Thought of Karol Wojtyla': 221.

83. Ibid.: 222, 223.

84. E.g., Alfred North Whitehead, *The Adventure of Ideas* (New York: Free Press, 1967), p. 169; see also his *Process and Reality: An Essay in Cosmology* (Cambridge: Cambridge University Press, 1929); Charles Hartshorne, *The Divine Relativity: A Social Conception of God* (New Haven and London: Yale University Press, 1964); John Cobb, *A Christian Natural Theology* (Philadelphia: Westminster, 1965), pp. 188–92.

85. Joseph A. Bracken, 'Subsistent Relation: Mediating Concept for a New Synthesis?' *The Journal of Religion* 64 (2) (1984): 193.

86. Ibid.: 194.

87. Robert A. Connor, 'The Person as Resonating Existential', *American Catholic Philosophical Quarterly* 66 (1) (1992): 56.

88. Ibid.: 56.

89. See also, John S. Grabowski, 'Person: Substance and Relation', *Communio: International Catholic Review* 22 (1995): 139–63.
90. Joseph Ratzinger, 'Zum Personverständnis in der Theologie', in *Dogma und Verkündigung* (Munich: Wewel, 1973), pp. 205–23, at 211.
91. Joseph Ratzinger, 'Concerning the Notion of Person in Theology', *Communio: International Catholic Review* 17 (1990): 444.
92. Rowan Williams, *On Christian Theology* (Oxford : Blackwell, 2000), p. 161.
93. Ibid., p. 160; Coakley, 'Why Three?', p. 34.
94. Alan J. Torrance, *Persons in Communion: Trinitarian Description and Human Participation* (Edinburgh: T&T Clark, 1996), p. 4.
95. Zizioulas, *Being as Communion*, p. 15.
96. John D. Zizioulas, 'The Church as Communion', *St. Vladimir's Theological Quarterly* 38 (1994): 5.
97. Ibid.: 6. For existential structure or Buber's structure of existence, see *Being as Communion*, p. 17.
98. Ibid.
99. Ibid., p. 15.
100. Ibid., p. 16.
101. Ibid., p. 17.
102. Ibid., pp. 17–18.
103. Ratzinger, 'Concerning the Notion of Person in Theology': 444.
104. Christoph Schwöbel and Colin E. Gunton (eds), *Persons, Divine and Human, King's College Essays in Theological Anthropology* (Edinburgh: T&T Clark, 1991), p. 10.
105. John D. Caputo, *Radical Hermeneutics: Repetition, Deconstruction and the Hermeneutic Project* (Bloomington: Indiana University Press, 1987), p. 1.
106. Ibid., p. 2. See also: Kierkegaard, *Repetition* (1843): *Kierkegaard's Writings*, vol. VI: *'Fear and Trembling' and 'Repetition'*, ed. Howard Hong and Edna Hong (Princeton: Princeton University Press, 1983).
107. Caputo, *Radical Hermeneutics*, p. 3.
108. Ibid., p. 6.
109. Caputo, John D., *The Weakness of God: A Theology of the Event* (Bloomington: Indiana University Press, 2006).
110. Ibid., p. 3.
111. Ibid., p. 4.
112. Ibid., p. 5.
113. Ibid., p. 111.
114. Jacques Derrida, *On the Name* (Stanford: Stanford University Press, 1995), p. 46; *The Politics of Friendship* (London and New York: Verso, 1997), pp. 296–9.
115. John D. Caputo (ed.), *The Religious* (Malden, MA and Oxford: Blackwell Publishers, 2002), p. 5.
116. Gilles Deleuze, 'Bergson's Conception of Difference', in *The New Bergson*, ed. John Mullarkey (Manchester: Manchester University Press, 1999), p. 49.
117. John D. Caputo (ed.), *Deconstruction in a Nutshell: A Conversation with Jacques Derrida* (New York: Fordham University, 1997), p. 110; see also, Jacques Derrida, *Spectres of Marx* (New York and London: Routledge, 1994), p. 172.
118. Caputo, *Deconstruction in a Nutshell*, p. 112.
119. Ibid., p. 124; see also, John D. Caputo and Michael J. Scanlon (eds), *God, the Gift, and Postmodernism* (Bloomington: Indiana University Press, 1999), p. 77; see also Jacques Derrida, *Points … Interviews 1974–1994* (Stanford: Stanford University Press, 1995), p. 355.
120. Karl Barth, *Church Dogmatics* 1.1 (Edinburgh: T&T Clark, 1975), p. 316.
121. Gilles Deleuze, *Repetition and Difference* (London and New York: Continuum, 2004).

122. John D. Zizioulas, *Communion and Otherness*. Orthodox Peace Fellowship, Occasional Paper, 191 (1994); also *Communion and Otherness* (London and New York: T&T Clark, 2006), especially ch. 1.
123. Zizioulas draws upon the work of Maximus the Confessor in making this distinction.
124. Zizioulas, *Communion and Otherness*, 1994.
125. Ibid.
126. Ibid.
127. Ibid.
128. Also see: Christoph Schwöbel, 'Human Being as Relational Being: Twelve Theses for a Christian Anthropology', in *Persons Divine and Human*, Thesis 9, 160–2. Also Dietrich Bonhoeffer, 'A Wedding Sermon from a Prison Cell, May 1943', in *Letters and Papers from Prison* (London: SCM, 1971), p. 46.

Chapter 5

The Church as 'Creation of the Word and of the Holy Spirit' in Ecumenical Documents on the Church: A Roman Catholic Exercise in Receptive Ecumenism

Peter De Mey

In this chapter I will discuss, in chronological order, three accounts on the nature of the Church which are the result of recent ecumenical dialogues on a global level. The first one is the 1990 document *Towards a Common Understanding of the Church*, which completed the second phase of the Reformed–Roman Catholic international dialogue. The second one, issued from another bilateral dialogue between Lutherans and Roman Catholics, is the 1993 document on *Church and Justification*. Last but not least, I will pay attention to the ongoing dialogue process on *The Nature and Mission of the Church* (NMC) which is taking place within Faith and Order. In view of the sometimes quite negative official reactions by some churches to *Baptism, Eucharist and Ministry* (BEM) it became clear that a renewed reflection on the common understanding of the Church was necessary. In 1998 a first document on *The Nature and Purpose of the Church* (NPC) was proposed for discussion among the participating churches as 'a stage on the way to a common statement'. Eight years later, the Ninth General Assembly of the World Council of Churches in Porto Alegre, Brazil, announced the publication of 'a new study document' on *The Nature and Mission of the Church* which in fact is not substantially different from its predecessor. The assembly did adopt a short document on ecclesiology, *Called to Be the One Church*, as 'an invitation to the churches to renew their commitment to the search for unity and to deepen their dialogue', as it is mentioned in the subtitle. The second edition of the study document is intended to assist the churches in this process.[1]

I will not focus on these documents as a whole, but on one particular way of describing the nature of the Church which one discovers in all three documents, namely a reflection on the Church as 'Creation of the Word and of the Holy Spirit'.[2] This is definitely not a way of reflecting on the nature of the Church that is very familiar to Roman Catholics. In fact it originates in the theology of Martin Luther, as will become clear in my next section. This notion, however, is also not completely foreign to Roman Catholic ecclesiology. The reflection on 'The Mystery of the Church', in the first chapter of *Lumen gentium*, starts with the well-known and carefully formulated statement that 'the church is in Christ as a sacrament or instrumental sign of intimate union with God and of the unity of all humanity'.[3] The words 'in Christ' indicate that the Roman Catholic Church is aware that its sacramental mission is completely dependent upon Christ. The Council also pays attention to the relationship between Church and Incarnation in the title and opening line of *Lumen gentium*, stating that 'Christ is the light of the nations', and comes back to this relationship in the final paragraph of Chapter 1 (LG 8). There, the relationship between the Church as Christ's mystical body and the Church as a 'visible structure', 'equipped with hierarchical structures', is explained by referring to the relationship between the assumed nature and the divine Word in 'the mystery of the incarnate Word'. The Council Fathers remain aware of the difference between Church and Incarnation in stating that it is 'no mean analogy'.

Another way to describe the mystery of the Church in *Lumen gentium* is by explaining that the Church is the work of the Triune God. It is the 'eternal Father', who 'decided to call together all those who believe in Christ within holy church' (LG 2). The faithful 'make up one body in Christ through the sacrament of the Eucharistic bread' (LG 3). The Spirit 'dwells in the church and in the hearts of the faithful as in a temple' (LG 4). The final paragraph of Chapter 2, thereby indicating that the first and second chapters of *Lumen gentium* have been conceived as a unity, presents the three originally Pauline metaphors together: 'So the church prays and works at the same time so that the fullness of the whole world may move into the people of God, the body of the Lord and the temple of the holy Spirit, and that all honour and glory be rendered in Christ, the head of all, to the creator and Father of all' (LG 17).

The final text of *Lumen gentium* contains beautiful examples of how the Roman Catholic Church has been trying to formulate its reflection on the Church in an ecumenically open way. There are, therefore, a few statements which seem to contain an implicit reference to the notion of the Church as creation of the Word and of the Spirit – e.g., the statement that the Spirit 'rejuvenates the church through the power of the gospel' (LG 4) and the idea that the gospel which Jesus asked the apostles to proclaim everywhere 'is for all time the principle of all life for the church' (LG 20).

In the three mentioned dialogues, representatives of the Roman Catholic Church have been able to cooperate and subscribe to a rich ecumenical reflection on the Church as creation of the Word and of the Spirit. One of the major problems in the ecumenical dialogue, however, is that by now we have received of a great number of ecumenical documents expressing different stages of convergence between the Christian churches. However, clear signs of reception of the results of the ecumenical dialogue, in the life of the believers as well as in declarations and decisions taken by the highest authority structures of the churches participating in these dialogues, are lacking. We are, for example, still waiting for a papal encyclical or a document on the Church by the Congregation for the Doctrine of the Faith in which the image of the Church as creation of the Word and of the Spirit would be used in a positive way, as is the case in the documents which we will now study.[4] At the same time, of course, a more positive account of the Church as sacrament of God's grace (*sacramentum gratiae*) in theological statements issued by the Lutheran or Reformed Church at national or world level, would contribute to a better reception of the achievements of the ecumenical dialogues as well. Nevertheless, it remains important that theologians contribute to the process of reception as well, by indicating which ideas in the dialogue texts need to be integrated in the self-understanding of their own Church.[5]

The Church as Creatura Verbi in Lutheran Ecclesiology

Stat fixa sententia, ecclesiam non nasci nec subsistere in natura sua, nisi verbo Dei. 'Genuit', inquit, 'nos verbo veritatis' (Jak 1,18).[6]
Ecclesia enim creatura est Euangelii, incomparabiliter minor ipso, sicut ait Jacobus: voluntarie genuit nos verbo veritatis suae, et Paulus: per Euangelium ego vos genui.[7]
Ecclesia enim nascitur verbo promissionis per fidem ... Verbum dei enim supra Ecclesiam est incomparabiliter, in quo nihil statuere, ordinare, facere, sed tantum statui ordinari, fieri habet, tanquam creatura.[8]
... cum per solum Euangelium concipiatur, formetur, alatur, generetur, educetur, pascatur, vestiatur, ornetur, roboretur, armetur, servetur, breviter, tota vita et substantia Ecclesiae est in verbo dei, sicut Christus dicit 'In omni verbo quod procedit de ore dei vivit homo'.[9]
Die Kirche macht nicht das Wort, sondern sie wird von dem Wort.[10]
Nam cum Ecclesia verbo dei nascatur, alatur, servetur et roboretur, palam est eam sine verbo esse non posse, aut si sine verbo sit, Ecclesiam esse desinere.[11]

A brief summary of the background of this notion in Lutheran ecclesiology[12] will help us better to understand why recent ecumenical dialogues have been able to appreciate its ecumenical potentiality.

First of all, it needs to be emphasized that Luther is only able to make statements like the above because for him the Word of God is a multifaceted reality. It may refer to God's creative and revelatory word, to Jesus Christ, the Word become flesh, to the biblical text, and finally to God's word as preached or administered in the sacraments. The latter distinction helps Roman Catholics to understand that the sacraments are not disconnected from the Word of God. The preaching of the word is sometimes described by Luther as 'verbum invisibile' and the administration of the sacraments as 'verbum visibile'. Luther also distinguishes between the internal and external dimensions of the Word of God.

Furthermore, the creation of the Church through the Word is always mediated by the Spirit.[13] The Church does never receive the Word through its own efforts. It is the Spirit who makes it possible that human beings receive the Word of God by reading the Holy Scripture or by listening to the proclamation of the Word in the community – the external dimensions of the Word – and as a result the same Spirit speaks to them internally, within their hearts, and elicits their response of faith. Against the enthusiasts, however, Luther insists that the Spirit does not act apart from the Word, and, against the medieval Church, which derived its interest in hierarchical structures from its christocentrism; he insists that they do not have access to the Word apart from the Spirit. Therefore, the Church is, in the first instance, a spiritual reality. The dependence of the community on the Word is also a continuous process, a *creatio continua*, so that the Church simply ceases to exist if it is disconnected from the Word (and the Spirit).

Lutheran ecclesiologists, however, seem to have a different view on the question whether Luther had only the invisible Church in mind when he spoke about the Church as *creatura Verbi*. Christoph Schwöbel insists that the notion of Church as *creatura Verbi* applies only to the one, holy, catholic and apostolic Church, and not to any of the Christian churches. He warns against the 'heresy of orthodoxy' and the 'heresy of orthopraxis', by which human doctrines or ecclesial practices are to be identified as God's work. The churches, however, receive the mission to testify to God's revelation in Christ by proclaiming the gospel of Jesus Christ in word and sacraments.[14] Gudrun Neebe for her part believes that the notion is applicable to the visible Church as well, since Luther distinguishes between the internal and external operations of the Holy Spirit.[15]

Finally, Christoph Schwöbel is also able to treat the ecclesiology of Calvin as part of the same chapter on the Church as creation of the Word of God, even if he is aware that, especially in the 1559 edition of the *Institutio*, Calvin pays much more attention to the organization of the visible Church than Luther would allow.[16]

Reformed–Roman Catholic Dialogue: The Images of Church as Creatura Verbi and Sacramentum Gratiae Are Complementary

The bilateral dialogue between representatives of the World Alliance of Reformed Churches and the Secretariat for Promoting Christian Unity of the Roman Catholic Church usually takes its time in publishing documents expressing a convergence between both churches. The first phase of the dialogue, which started in 1968, was concluded in 1977 with a final report on *The Presence of Christ in Church and World*.[17] Reflections on the relationship between Church and Incarnation are found in the first three sections of the document entitled, 'Christ's Relationship to the Church' (13–23), 'The Teaching Authority of the Church' (24–42) and 'The Presence of Christ in the World' (43–66), whereas the latter sections deal with 'The Eucharist' (67–92) and 'On Ministry' (93–111). Both churches recognize that the Church is in fact the human response to what is called in a subtitle 'Christ's Unifying Action'. Therefore, as no. 16 states: 'There was complete agreement in presenting ecclesiology from a clear christological and pneumatological perspective in which the Church is the object of declared faith and cannot be completely embraced by a historical and sociological description.'

Before dealing with confessions of faith and the infallibility of the Church, the second section of this document first discussed the teaching authority of the Holy Scripture. The important insight that Scripture and Tradition are no longer seen by both denominations as 'two different sources' is clarified in no. 26 with an appeal by both traditions to the image of Church as *creatura Verbi*. 'We are agreed that as *creatura Verbi* the Church together with its Tradition stands under the living Word of God.'

The third section reflects in a Trinitarian way on the presence of Christ in the world. The section culminates in a common understanding of 'the Church as the effective sign of Christ's presence in the World' (60–6).

The 1990 document *Towards a Common Understanding of the Church* culminates the second phase of the Reformed–Catholic dialogue on ecclesiology.[18] The document consists of four chapters. In the *first chapter*, 'Towards a Reconciliation of Memories' (12–62), the Reformed churches and the Roman Catholic Church each narrate 'the path taken by each communion' since the time of the Reformation. Thanks to this self-critical rereading of histories it has been possible to rediscover the common ground which exists between both churches, also in ecclesiological matters. The 'Common Confession of Faith' which is offered in *Chapter 2*, focuses on two christological claims and also reflects on the ecclesiological implication thereof: our Lord Jesus Christ is the only mediator between God and humankind (64–76) and we are justified by grace, through faith (77–9). Through his Incarnation and salvific work Christ Jesus is the foundation of the Church (80–8). When it comes to a systematic reflection on the Church, in *Chapter 3* (89–144), the common discourse has become a complementary one, at least in the first part of the chapter, which focuses on the 'more Reformed' concept of the Church as *creatura Verbi* (95–101) and the 'more Catholic' concept of the Church as 'sacrament of grace' (102–10). Areas of divergence continue to be the views of both churches on 'continuity and discontinuity in church history' (114–24), and on 'the church's visibility and ministerial order' (125–37). Finally, in *Chapter 4* of the document, 'The way forward' (145–64) is being articulated.

For our purposes chapters 2 and 3 deserve close attention. The Dutch Roman Catholic theologian Henk Witte rightly wonders: if Chapter 3 maintains that each of the churches has its favourite church model, then could not some implicit ruptures in the apparently harmonious christological foundation of Chapter 2 be discovered as well?[19] Let us first look at the two church models in Chapter 3. In comparison with the previous document, in which 'the dialogue partners used the term together in order to characterize the subordination of the Church to the living Word of God', it is obvious that in Chapter 3 '*creatura Verbi* has become *the* expression of the typical Reformed concept of the Church'. The document makes reference to the 'threefold form' of the Word – 'the word incarnate, the word written, the word preached' (96) – and holds that the Church is dependent upon this word in at least three ways: 'the church is founded upon the word of God; the church is kept in being as the church by the word of God; the church continually depends upon the word of God for its inspiration, strength and renewal' (97). Within this model, however, no separation is made between the word and Spirit of God, 'for it is the power of the Spirit that enables the hearing of the word and the response of faith' (98). The 'more Catholic' concept is defended with an appeal to a large number of scriptural texts and to almost all texts of Vatican II in which the model occurs. The Church can be called a visible sign and instrument of the unique mediation of God's salvation which Christ brought about 'in the mystery of his incarnation, life, death and resurrection' (108). The document insists, however, that 'the application of the category "sacrament" to the church is doubly analogical' (104). One is aware that Christ is 'the primordial sacrament of God'

(104) and that 'the church is called a sacrament by analogy to the liturgies of baptism and the eucharist' (106). It must be repeated once again, however, that these clarifications occur in a section of the paragraph which belongs to the converging part of the document, and that 'more Reformed' and 'more Catholic' is not the same as 'exclusively Reformed' or 'exclusively Catholic'. Therefore, after introducing the two different concepts of the Church, the document stresses the potential complementarity of the two images:

> The two conceptions, 'the creation of the word' and 'sacrament of grace', can in fact be seen as expressing the same instrumental reality under different aspects, as complementary to each other or as two sides of the same coin. They can also become the poles of a creative tension between our churches (113).

Henk Witte discovered that there is a hesitation in Chapter 2 to provide an unambiguous answer to the question as to what constitutes the centre of Christology.

> Wherever thinking is based on the importance of the content, the gift and the elaboration of salvation, the mystery of Jesus' death and resurrection constitutes the centre. Wherever thinking is based on the importance of God's presence in history and in the Church, the mystery of incarnation constitutes the centre.[20]

These are some examples of both approaches:

> In that mystery of death and resurrection we confess the event which saves humanity [68]. This is why we believe that the people of God gathered together by the death and resurrection of Christ does not live solely by the promise [83]. When the church faithfully preaches the word of salvation and celebrates the sacraments ... it carries out in its ministry the action of Christ himself [86].
>
> Fundamental for us all is the presence of Christ in the church [80]. The novelty introduced by the incarnation of the Word does not call into question the continuity of the history of salvation [81]. Nevertheless we believe that the coming of Christ, the Word incarnate, brings with it a radical change in the situation of the world in the sight of God. Henceforth the divine gift which God has made in Jesus Christ is irreversible and definitive [82]. The inauguration of the church takes place in time and in stages related to the unfolding of the Christ-event [84].

According to Witte it would be incorrect to assume that the Protestant side was responsible for the paschal-soteriological Christology and the Roman Catholic side for the incarnational-presence one. In the past it was typical for Western theology as a whole to focus on the Incarnation, i.e., 'the downward movement from God to man', and this almost in a juridical way. The emphasis on the resurrection was rather to be found in orthodox thinking, which also was particularly interested in the ascending movement of human deification or *theosis*. In contemporary theology different answers can be given on the issue of the centre of Christology by both Catholic and Protestant theologians.

This twofold christological approach in Chapter 2 is not reflected in the two models of Church in Chapter 3. Both the 'more Reformed' model of the Church as *creatura Verbi* and the 'more Catholic' model of the Church as *sacramentum gratiae* are focused on the Incarnation. A reflection on the nature of the Church of this kind may involve the danger of forgetting the difference between Christ and the Church. A better integration of paschal Christology – one of the two lines of thought of Chapter 2 – would not only have made the document more coherent, but might have led to a greater attention for the mystery of Christ's presence and absence in the Church.

The third phase of the Reformed–Catholic dialogue on ecclesiology, which focused on the Church as community of common witness to the Kingdom of God, has resulted in a new report which will be published very soon. It is highly significant that the new document contains some kind of auto-criticism with regard to the reflections on the Church as creation of the Word and sacrament of Grace in *Towards a Common Understanding of the Church* (1990). Section 5.1 of the new document is now entitled: 'The Church as Creation of the Word and Sacrament of Grace in light of the Kingdom'. The discovery that patristic authors 'do emphatically relate the church to the Word and to the grace of God' (192) leads the commission to conclude:

> We can now affirm, in light of our investigation both of the kingdom and of the patristic literature, not only that these visions are mutually informative and complementary but also that neither is fully adequate without the other. A 'sacramental' church that does not give proper place to the Word of God would be essentially incomplete; a church that is truly a creation of the Word will celebrate that Word liturgically and sacramentally. If our churches differ according to these two visions, perhaps it is less because either church is convinced that the church is only *creatura verbi* or only *sacramentum gratiae* and more because each tradition has emphasized one aspect to the point of deemphasizing or neglecting the other.

Lutheran–Roman Catholic Dialogue: Both Churches Hold onto the Images of the Church as 'Creature of the Gospel' and 'God's Pilgrim People, Body of Christ and Temple of the Holy Spirit'

In the Lutheran–Catholic dialogue we had to wait until its third phase before a systematic dialogue on the Church was undertaken. This process of reflection took nine years and concluded in 1993 with the publication of an extensive document on *Church and Justification* (1993).[21] The first three chapters of this document articulate the basic ecclesiological convictions which both churches hold in common. The first chapter serves only as an introduction. It clarifies the relation between Church and justification by saying that both have their foundation in the mystery of Christ and the Holy Trinity and are a gift of God (1–9). The second chapter reflects on 'The abiding origin of the Church' (10–47). With an appeal to 1 Cor 3.11 it is made clear that Jesus Christ is the only foundation of the Church. Of course, attention is also given to the relationship between the Church and

Israel. It is been emphasised that it is the whole of the Christ-event, consisting in Christ's proclamation, cross and resurrection and the Pentecost event, which is the foundation of the Church. In the last section of the chapter, both dialogue partners consider the image of the Church as 'creature of the gospel' as a valid way to reflect together on the foundation of the Church. Earlier on, the Lutheran–Catholic dialogue had already used this model in 1972 in the so-called Malta Report on *The Gospel and the Church*: 'As *creatura et ministra verbi*, the church stands under the gospel and has the gospel as its superordinate criterion'. In *Church and Justification* the Lutheran roots of this concept are clearly recognized. The image of the Church as *creatura evangelii* highlights the Church's complete dependence on the gospel. The Church received the mission to proclaim the gospel in word and sacrament. This proclamation takes place in the power of the Holy Spirit and on the foundation of the apostles. Still, the document is also able to refer to two passages of the Second Vatican Council which highlight the link between gospel and Church.

> The conviction that the church lives out of the gospel also determines the Roman Catholic understanding of the church. In Vatican II's Dogmatic Constitution on the Church we read, '... the gospel ... is for all time the source of all life for the church' (LG 20) and the Decree on the Church's Missionary Activity says that the 'chief means of the implantation of the church is the preaching of the gospel of Jesus Christ' (AG 6).

One would not do justice to the biblical testimony on the Church, however, if the common reflection on the Church would focus exclusively on the christological foundation of the Church and if the trinitarian dimension of the Church would be omitted.[22] Therefore, the third chapter (48–106) focuses on 'The Church of the Triune God'. Attention is paid to the Pauline models of the Church as 'God's pilgrim people, body of Christ and temple of the Holy Spirit'. More particularly, 'the communion of the three divine persons is constitutive for the being and life of the church' (63). In the last section of this chapter the document explains that the concept of '*koinonia*/communion' has become important for both churches. In fact the Church is understood by Lutherans and Catholics as 'the *communio ecclesiarum* as local, regional and universal communion' (79). Near the end of the chapter, a first difference between Catholics and Lutherans is mentioned which pertains to the Lutheran and Catholic understanding of the local church.

The dialogue process, however, also revealed further areas of divergence on ecclesiology. These are reported in Chapter 4 (107–242). For our purpose the following one is worth mentioning:

> A comparison of Lutheran and Catholic views of the church cannot disregard the fact that there are two fundamentally inseparable aspects of being church: on the one hand, the church is the place of God's saving activity (the church as an assembly, as the recipient of salvation) and on the other it is God's instrument (the church as ambassador, as mediator of salvation). But it is one and the same church which we speak of as the recipient and mediator of salvation. In the course of the history of theology, the emphases have been variously placed. While Lutherans see the Church

mainly as the recipient of salvation, as the 'congregation of the faithful', *congregatio fidelium*, contemporary Catholic theology emphasizes more the Church as the mediator of salvation, as 'sacrament' of salvation (108).

The idea that the Church is the *congregatio fidelium*, the place where the believers receive the gift of salvation, is typically Lutheran, but it belongs to the common medieval heritage and it has been reaffirmed by Vatican II, as the document states. The exposition on the Church as *sacrament of salvation* leads to the conclusion 'that the church is instrument and sign of salvation and, in this sense, "sacrament" of salvation'. The Catholic dialogue partners take seriously the remaining reservations which the Lutherans have with regard to the latter notion.

Faith and Order: A Consensus in Describing the Church as 'Creation of the Word and of the Holy Spirit' and as 'People of God', 'Body of Christ' and 'Temple of the Holy Spirit'

The latest edition of *The Nature and Mission of the Church*[23] is divided into three chapters, the first of which deals with 'The Church of the Triune God'. According to its three subtitles it focuses subsequently on 'The Nature of the Church' (9–33), 'The Mission of the Church' (34–42), and 'The Church as Sign and Instrument of God's Intention and Plan for the World' (43–7). In a somehow strange way, when describing the nature of the Church, the document first discusses 'The Church as a Gift of God: Creation of the Word and of the Holy Spirit' (9–13) and thereafter four 'Biblical Insights': (a) 'The Church as People of God'; (b) 'The Church as the Body of Christ'; (c) 'The Church as Temple of the Holy Spirit'; and (d) 'The Church as *Koinonia*/Communion'.

It is most likely that the representatives of the Protestant churches insisted that the first image used to describe the nature of the Church would be the Church as 'Creation of the Word and of the Holy Spirit (*creatura Verbi et creatura Spiritus*)'. This subsection starts and ends with insisting that the Church has its origin not in human efforts but in God's initiative.

> The Church is called into being by the Father 'who so loved the world that he gave his only begotten Son, that whoever believes in him shall not perish, but have eternal life' (Jn 3: 16) and who sent the Holy Spirit to lead these believers into all truth, reminding them of all that Jesus taught (cf. Jn 14: 26). The Church is thus the creature of God's Word and of the Holy Spirit. It belongs to God, is God's gift and cannot exist by and for itself (9).

The Church is not merely the sum of individual believers in communion with God, nor primarily the mutual communion of individual believers among themselves. It is their common partaking in the life of God (2 Pet. 1.4), who as Trinity, is the source and focus of all communion. Thus the Church is both a divine and human reality (13).

In no. 10 it is emphasized that 'the Church is centred and grounded in the Word of God' and the threefold nature of the Word is made clear.[24] Immediately following, the second part of the title is explained: 'Faith called forth by the Word of God is brought about by the action of the Holy Spirit (cf. 1 Cor. 12.3). According to the Scripture, the Word and the Spirit are inseparable' (11). In a solemn way no. 12 states that the *notae ecclesiae* are ascribed to this Church. 'Being the creature of God's own Word and Spirit, the Church of God is one, holy, catholic and apostolic.'

In *The Nature and Mission of the Church* issues that do not form part of the consensus have been given a different layout. At the end of this first subsection a first area of divergence is being dealt with: 'The institutional dimension of the Church and the Work of the Holy Spirit'. Francis Sullivan, who commented on the remaining divergences in an article in *Ecumenical Trends*, wonders whether this is the appropriate place to treat this difficulty, since the reflections on the Church as creation of the Word and of the Holy Spirit in the body of the text deliberately omitted any reference to the institutional dimension of the Church.[25]

Three problems are mentioned. The first one relates to the question 'whether the preaching and the Sacraments are the means of, or simply witnesses to, the activity of the Spirit through the divine Word, which comes about in an immediate internal action upon the hearts of the believers'. Sullivan believes that the preceding reflections on the notions of the Church indicate the existence of a convergence. When speaking about the oneness of the Church the document states that God made the Church 'a foretaste and instrument for the redemption of all created reality' (12). When speaking about the catholicity of the Church it is emphasized that God, 'through Word and Spirit, makes his people the place and instrument of his saving, life-giving, fulfilling presence'.

A second area of divergence pertains to the relationship between the ordained ministry, especially the episcopacy, and the Word and Spirit of God. The document is aware that for some churches the ordained ministry almost is 'a guarantee of the presence of truth and power of the Word and Spirit of God in the Church'. For other churches, however, the Word and Spirit of God remain the norm of all church structures.

A final point of divergence pertains to the apostolicity of the Church. Some churches believe that apostolic faith requires 'institutional continuity' whereas other churches hold that it was necessary to leave this continuity in order to safeguard the apostolic faith.

As I mentioned earlier, the first chapter of the document also explains the nature of the Church by referring to the plurality of images of the Church in scripture. In the new edition the presentation of the different biblical images is preceded by an appraisal of diversity, which is inspired by the Report of the Fifth World Conference on Faith and Order in Santiago de Compostela.

It is essential to acknowledge the wide diversity of insights into the nature and mission of the Church which can be found in the various books of the New Testament and in their interpretation in later history. Diversity appears not as accidental to the life of the Christian community, but as an aspect of its catholicity, a quality that reflects the fact that it is part of the Father's design that the story of salvation in Christ be incarnational. Thus, diversity is a gift of God to the Church (16).

Conclusion

Is it possible to indicate, by way of conclusion, some convergent lines throughout the three texts that we have studied? The most striking conclusion is, in my opinion, that the Catholic theologians involved in these dialogues were willing to consider the image of the Church as creature of the Word as part of their common ecumenical reflections on the nature of the Church. In view of the fact that all texts describing this image pay attention to the role of the Spirit as well we don't have to worry about the differences in the titles: '*creatura Verbi*', 'creature of the Gospel', and 'creation of the Word and of the Holy Spirit'. And even if this image is presented in the Reformed–Catholic dialogue as a 'more Reformed' concept of the Church, the Catholic dialogue partners agreed to its relevance for reflecting on the nature of the Church.

We also observed a willingness among the Reformed theologians to consider the 'more Catholic' image of the Church as sacrament of God's grace as complementary to the one of Church as creature of the Word. However, in the other documents it has become clear that there is not yet a convergence concerning this image. Nevertheless, all churches were able to affirm that the Church is an instrument and sign of salvation.

Unfortunately, as I noted in my introduction, we will still have to wait for a document from Rome in which the image of the Church as *creatura Verbi* forms part of the Catholic teaching on the nature of the Church.

Notes

1. 'Text on Ecclesiology: Called to Be the One Church. An Invitation to the Churches to Renew their Commitment to the Search for Unity and to Deepen their Dialogue', *The Ecumenical Review* 58 (2006): 112–17, at 112 n. 2.
2. This insight, however, seems to have been discovered first in ecumenical dialogues at national level. A good example is the 1984 document *Kirchengemeinschaft in Wort und Sakrament* of the Bilaterale Arbeitsgruppe der Deutschen Bischofskonferenz und der Kirchenleitung der Vereinigten Evangelisch-Lutherische Kirche Deutschlands, which states in paragraph 13, the first paragraph on a section on 'Wort Gottes und Kirche':

   Der Ursprung der Kirche in ihrer Stiftung wie die Tatsache, dass ihr neue Glieder durch Glaube und Taufe zugeführt werden, ihre Bewahrung und Erneuerung, wird in der Heiligen Schrift auf das Wort Gottes zurückgeführt. Insofern bleibt die Kirche Geschöpf des Wortes ('creatura verbi') und zugleich Dienerin des Wortes ('ministra verbi'), das ihr übertragen ist (Mt 28,19–20) Als Grund wie als Auftrag steht das Wort Gottes über der Kirche.
3. *Lumen gentium* no. 1. I use the Vatican II translation of Norman P. Tanner, SJ, *Decrees of the Ecumenical Councils* (Washington, DC: Georgetown University Press, 1990).
4. Even if much more can be said about this text, it can be deplored that the recent *Responses to Some Questions Regarding Certain Aspects of the Doctrine of the Church* (29 June 2007) by the Congregation for the Doctrine of the Faith refers only to Roman Catholic doctrinal sources

and make no reference to texts resulting from the ecumenical dialogues in which the Roman Catholic Church has been involved for more than four decades.

5. A detailed study of the process of reception of the results of the Lutheran–Catholic dialogue and a similar plea for a more profound reception can be read in Harald Goertz, *Dialog und Rezeption: Die Rezeption evangelisch-lutherisch/römisch-katholischer Dialogdokumente in der VELKD und der römisch-katholischen Kirche. Eine Studie im Auftrag der VELKD* (Hannover: Lutherisches Verlagshaus, 2002). In another paper I have analysed the way in which episcopal collegiality has been treated in a number of dialogue texts in which the Roman Catholic Church was involved. If the Catholic Church were to take seriously what their representatives have been able to say in common with representatives of other churches, then the distinction between 'affective' and 'effective' collegiality would become highly problematic. See, Peter De Mey, 'Is "Affective" Collegiality Sufficient? A Plea for a More "Effective" Collegiality of Bishops in the Roman Catholic Church and its Ecumenical Implications', in *Friendship as an Ecumenical Value: Proceedings of the International Conference Held on the Inauguration of the Institute of Ecumenical Studies (Lviv, 11–15 June 2005)* (Lviv: Ukrainian Catholic University Press, 2006), pp. 132–53.

6. Martin Luther, *Sermo praescriptus praepositio in Litzka* (1512): WA 1,13,38–40.

7. Martin Luther, *Resolutiones Lutherianqe super propositionibus suis Lipsiae disputatis* (1519): WA 2,430,6–8.

8. Martin Luther, *De captivitate Babylonica ecclesiae praeludium* (1520): WA 6,560,33–561,1.

9. Martin Luther, *Ad librum eximii Magistri Nostri Ambrosii Catharini ... responsio (1521):* WA 7,721,10–14. This is partially a citation from Augustine who had stated that 'Ecclesia verbo Dei generatur, alitur, nutritur, roboratur'.

10. Martin Luther, *Vom Missbrauch der Messenhh* (1521): WA 8,491.

11. Martin Luther, *De instituendis ministris Ecclesiae* (1523): WA 12,191.

12. The following sources have been helpful in this regard: Gerhard Sauter's chapter on 'Der Ursprung der Kirche aus Gottes Wort und Gottes Geist' in Walter Kern, Hermann Joseph Pottmeyer and Max Seckler (eds), *Handbuch der Fundamentaltheologie. 3. Traktat Kirche* (Freiburg: Herder, 1986), pp. 198–211; Brunero Gherardini, *Creatura Verbi: La Chiesa nella teologia di Martin Lutero* (Rome: Vivere In, 1994); Gudrun Neebe, *Apostolische Kirche: Grundentscheidungen an Luthers Kirchenbegriff unter besonderer Berücksichtigung seiner Lehre von den notae ecclesiae*, Theologische Bibliothek Töpelmann, 82 (Berlin: de Gruyter, 1997); the chapter on 'Das Geschöpf des Wortes Gottes: Grundeinsichten der reformatorischen Ekklesiologie', in Christoph Schwöbel, *Gott in Beziehung. Studien zur Dogmatik* (Tübingen: Mohr Siebeck, 2002), pp. 345–77; and Gottfried Wilhelm Locher, *Sign of the Advent: A Study in Protestant Ecclesiology* (Fribourg: Academic Press, 2004).

13. This is well reflected in the title of the essay by Gerhard Sauter, referred to in the previous footnote, *Der Ursprung der Kirche aus Gottes Wort und Gottes Geist*, and in a subsection of the book by Locher entitled 'The Spirit Creates the Church through the Word'.

14. Compare the sections on 'Was die Kirche nicht tun kann' and 'Was die Kirche tun kann und muss', in *Gott in Beziehung*, pp. 372–7.

15. Gudrun Neebe, *Apostolische Kirche*, p. 191:

> Diese Rede Luthers vom äusserlichen und innerlichen Wirken des Heiligen Geistes und die Wendung 'die Kirche' scheinen mir ein Hinweis darauf zu sein, dass Luther die Kirche als Gesamtzusammenhang meint, wenn er sie als Geschöpf des Wortes Gottes bezeichnet. Gottes (inneres) Wort schafft den Glauben und verbindet damit die Glaubenden mit Gott und miteinander zur Kirche als geistlicher Gemeinschaft, während Gottes (äusseres) Wort gleichzeitig die Glaubenden als leibliche Gemeinschaft um Wort und Sakrament versammelt. In diesem Sinne beschreibt Luther die Kirche als geistliche und leibliche Gemeinschaft als Geschöpf des Wortes Gottes.

16. See the sections 'Auf den Fundamenten aufbauen: Calvin' and 'Regeln für die Amtsführung', in *Gott in Beziehung*, pp. 363–72 and the section on 'Johannes Calvin', in Ulrich Kühn, *Kirche*. Handbuch Systematischer Theologie, 10 (Gütersloh: Gerd Mohn, 1980), pp. 58–75.

17. 'The Presence of Christ in Church and World: Final Report of the Dialogue between the World Alliance of Reformed Churches and the Secretariat for Promoting Christian Unity, 1977', in Harding Meyer and Lukas Vischer (eds), *Growth in Agreement. Reports and Agreed Statements of Ecumenical Conversations on a World Level*. Faith and Order Paper, 108 (Geneva: WCC, 1984), pp. 434–63.
18. 'Toward a Common Understanding of the Church. Second Phase, 1984–1990', in Jeffrey Gros, Harding Meyer and William G. Rusch (eds), *Growth in Agreement II. Reports and Agreed Statements of Ecumenical Conversations on a World Level, 1982–1998*. Faith and Order Paper, 187 (Geneva: WCC, 2000), pp. 780–818.
19. Henk Witte, 'On Christological Ground', in Martien E. Brinkman and Henk Witte (eds), *From Roots to Fruits: Protestants and Catholics towards a Common Understanding of the Church* (Geneva: World Alliance of Reformed Churches, 1998), pp. 33–59. For this entire section I am indebted to the research of this ecclesiologist.
20. Ibid., p. 45.
21. 'Church and Justification', in Jeffrey Gros, Harding Meyer and William G. Rusch (eds), *Growth in Agreement II. Reports and Agreed Statements of Ecumenical Conversations on a World Level, 1982–1998*. Faith and Order Paper, 187 (Geneva: WCC, 2000), pp. 485–565.
22. This is also the view of Harding Meyer in his article on 'Kirche und Rechtfertigung. Die dritte Phase des internationalen Dialogs 1986–1994', reprinted in Meyer, *Versöhnte Verschiedenheit: Aufsätze zur ökumenischen Theologie II. Der katholisch/lutherische Dialog* (Paderborn: Bonifatius, 2000), pp. 104–28, at p. 113: 'Diese christologische Begründung von Kirche muss jedoch in ihrer "trinitarischen Dimension" gesehen werden, wenn sie dem biblischen Zeugnis entsprechen und Missverständnisse vermeiden will.'
23. *The Nature and Mission of the Church*. Faith and Order Paper, 198 (Geneva: WCC, 2005).
24. This is done by means of a citation of no. 96 of the Agreed Statement *Towards a Common Understanding of the Church* of the Reformed–Roman Catholic Dialogue: '... it is the Word of God made flesh: Jesus Christ, incarnate, crucified and risen. Then it is the word as spoken in God's history with God's people and recorded in the scriptures of the Old and New Testaments as a testimony to Jesus Christ. Third, it is the word as heard and proclaimed in the preaching, witness and action of the Church.'
25. Francis Sullivan, 'The Nature and Purpose of the Church. Comments on the Material inside the Boxes', *Ecumenical Trends* 32 (2003): 145–53.

Chapter 6

PENTECOSTAL PERSPECTIVES ON *THE NATURE AND MISSION OF THE CHURCH*: CHALLENGES AND OPPORTUNITIES FOR ECUMENICAL TRANSFORMATION

Wolfgang Vondey

The Faith and Order document *The Nature and Mission of the Church* (NMC) is the first major ecumenical consensus statement with the promise of containing significant contributions from the Pentecostal community. The text has solicited a wide response from a variety of Christian traditions since its inception in 1998, then entitled *The Nature and Purpose of the Church*.[1] Pentecostals, who generally have not been involved in large measure in any ecumenical endeavour, are beginning to consider the implications of this ecumenical consensus statement for the development of their own ecclesiological identity.

The process of study on NMC among Pentecostals has taken place in the ecumenical studies group of the Society for Pentecostal Studies. The interest group was formed in 2001 and currently represents the only formally organized, ecumenical think-tank among Pentecostal scholars, theologians, pastors and laypersons. Although no formal response to the Faith and Order document exists from Pentecostal churches, the ecumenical studies group has engaged a number of scholars in discussion of the consensus statement and produced a series of statements on the ecumenical text.[2] These attempts not only reveal the increasing ecumenical commitment among Pentecostals; they also reflect a maturing ecclesiology among the ethnically, culturally and theologically diverse Pentecostal community.

In the twenty-first century, the growing Pentecostal community struggles to formulate its ecclesiological perspective. This essay is based on the assumption that this struggle is symptomatic of the larger ecumenical endeavour to form a global ecumenical ecclesiology. I begin by outlining Pentecostal perspectives on the Faith and Order document. The second part focuses on the fact that the title of the consensus statement was changed from 'The Nature and Purpose of the Church' to 'The Nature and Mission of the Church' and examines the implications of this change for an ecumenical ecclesiology. Rather than offering a selective view of Pentecostal engagement with the key themes of the document, I present a summary of Pentecostal perspectives on the Church's mission and its relationship to the Church's nature and purpose.[3] This allows me to draw some systematic conclusions in the final part of the chapter on the implications of Pentecostal thought for the development of an ecumenical ecclesiology. While a form of typological (attribute-oriented) ecumenism was symptomatic for much of the ecumenical agenda in the twentieth century, I suggest that an archaeological (origin-oriented) ecumenism would better serve the ecumenical agenda.

Pentecostal Perceptions of The Nature and Mission of the Church

A desire to establish the unity of the churches is recorded among Pentecostals ever since the emergence of so-called Classical Pentecostalism in North America at the beginning of the twentieth century, even though Pentecostals did not engage in official ecumenical dialogue until the 1970s.[4] At the beginning of the twenty-first century, Pentecostals have taken the first steps away from remaining anonymous ecumenists toward full, albeit solicited, participation in the ecumenical movement.[5] Interaction with NMC at this stage reveals that the heart of the ecumenical endeavour among Pentecostals is formed largely by a concern for a genuine Pentecostal identity in the global ecclesial landscape. Ecumenical concerns are driven by the Pentecostal self-perception as elements of the work of God's Spirit in the world as well as by recent scholarly efforts to develop a global theology informed to a large extent by a Pentecostal worldview.[6] Four approaches to the ecumenical consensus statement can be identified at this stage:

First, *Pentecostal perspectives on the nature of the text and its function as an ecumenical document*: Pentecostal scholars situate NMC in the context of larger ecumenical efforts in the second half of the twentieth century to produce broad consensus statements on individual issues of doctrine and praxis. Particular references can be established to the publication of the convergence document *Baptism, Eucharist and Ministry* (BEM) of 1982.[7] Critique of that text, particularly from the Roman Catholic and Orthodox perspectives, clearly went beyond the agreements reported in BEM and pointed to issues of visible separation that require further and deeper attention to the questions of ecclesiology.[8] The Orthodox evaluation of BEM anticipates much of the Pentecostal attitude toward the nature of NMC: 'Differences stated in the document show the reality of the divisions among churches rather than the weakness of the text'.[9] Nevertheless, similar to the Catholic perspectives, Pentecostals point to 'a somewhat underdeveloped ecclesiology'[10] and the further need to resolve some of the remaining problematic differences in contemporary theologies of the Church. Much 'depends on the churches and their desire and ability to structure their life and to fulfill their ministry in such a way as to implement creatively the principles'[11] upheld by the consensus statement. The lessons learned from BEM could serve well in the refining of NMC as a global ecumenical text.

Second, *Pentecostal perspectives on the structure and central themes of the document*: Pentecostals generally situate NMC within the formative influence of the official Pentecostal–Roman Catholic dialogue and its documents *Perspectives on Koinonia* (1989) and *Evangelization, Proselytism and Common Witness* (1997). Agreement is found largely on the basis of an ecclesiology that portrays the Church as *koinonia* or trinitarian communion, although the basis for this theology is perceived less as an abstract and speculative concept than an experiential, doxological reality.[12] Frank Macchia points out: 'Since koinonia can be said to occur "in the Spirit" as the bond of love (both within God, between God and humanity, and within creation), the accent of … [NMC] is not necessarily in tension with Pentecostal worship'.[13]

In general, Pentecostals would likely reconsider the formal structure of the document before offering any critique of its central themes. Concerns among Pentecostals about the content of the text focus on the historical reality of the Church, the relationship of Church and Trinity, the (minimal) conditions of ecclesiality, as well as the ministry of the Church and its relationship to spiritual gifts, healing, and worship.[14] Pentecostals always like to ask: 'What is God doing in our midst?'[15]

Third, *Pentecostal perspectives on the potential ecumenical ramifications of the document*: Pentecostals view the document, at the least, as a summary of ecumenical discussions on the Church and a work in progress. From an ecclesiological perspective, the text challenges Pentecostals to consider more carefully the role of baptism, the Eucharist, and social justice as part of Christian initiation, vocation, and ministry. The notion of *koinonia* challenges the sometimes triumphalistic attitude of Pentecostals toward the life of faith.[16] On the other hand, Pentecostals lament that the text does not address the unity of the Church more explicitly and extensively as part of a global ecumenical ecclesiology.[17] The prominent place the document gives to Jesus' prayer for unity in John 17 reflects the ecumenical convictions of early twentieth-century North American Pentecostalism, which saw itself as a movement of the Holy Spirit at the beginning of the global fulfilment of Jesus' prayer.[18] NMC, on the other hand, is based almost exclusively on ecclesiologies of traditional churches in the West and ignores, for example, the changes in faith and praxis in the southern hemisphere, not only among Pentecostals. As a result, the charismatic, doxological and evangelistic elements of the Christian life are not integrated in a vision of worldwide Christian unity. Pentecostals see potential ramifications of NMC as strongest in the area of ecclesiology proper (e.g., faith, baptism, Eucharist, ministry, church government) and as weakest in the actualization of Christian unity in the culturally, ethnically and linguistically diverse churches of global Christianity.

Fourth, *Pentecostal perspectives on the development of an ecumenical ecclesiology*: the search for a genuine Pentecostal ecclesiology reveals the analytical-critical position of Pentecostals to NMC and the Pentecostal evaluation of the promises and opportunities that the document entails with regard to the future development of an ecumenical ecclesiology in general. Pentecostals are apprehensive of the ecclesiological task as it relates to a global ecumenical perspective of faith and praxis as long as this task seems to be carried out within the confines of the hypothesis that there exists a singular, universal ecclesiology. In its place, many Pentecostals suggest that there exists a plurality of ecclesial self-understandings and nuances that are theologically complementary and desirable since they are often born from and determined by a community's experience and praxis of faith rather than a division of doctrine.[19] As a result, the immediate task of ecclesiology is seen as much in the formal 'declaration' of convergence as it is found in the 'actualization' and 'application' of an ecumenical praxis in the Christian ecclesial communities. In Pentecostal terms, this is frequently explained in the form of a person's 'story'.

The Pentecostal use of 'story-telling' is essentially a criterion for spiritual discernment that narrates and reflects on the human encounter with and experience of the Holy Spirit. The story is a linguistic-communicative expression of the human experience of the Spirit of God. At the same time, a person's story also makes that encounter with the Holy Spirit present in the moment of telling the story and thereby continues to transform both the speaker and the audience.[20] NMC's implicit choice to offer a systematic presentation of the content of ecclesiology without giving voice to individual stories from the various traditions suggests that its authors envision the existence of one universal story of the Church that allows the particular traditions of thought to be expressed in global unison. On the other hand, the hermeneutic of the Pentecostal community leaves room for the possibility that there exists more than one story and, as a consequence, more than one thematic locus that stands at the beginning of an ecumenical ecclesiology and that shapes its expression.

The Relationship between the Purpose and the Mission of the Church

The recent initiative to rename the Faith and Order document and to replace the term 'purpose' with the term 'mission' bears immediate consequences in light of the four Pentecostal approaches outlined above: the nature of the text and its function as an ecumenical document, the structure and central themes of the document, the potential ecumenical ramifications of the text, and the development of an ecumenical ecclesiology. I suggest that the change in terms from 'purpose' to 'mission' is a fortuitous one. It reflects the ecumenical insight that the God-given intention for the Church is realized in history and actualized in the world only when the Church pursues its purpose with a sense of unity, integrity, urgency and mission. The divine 'purpose' of the Church is an essential part of the Church as mystery and cannot be fully explained in any document, while the focus on 'mission' speaks of the divine purpose primarily as it is revealed to the Church in history. To this end, NMC speaks with particular frequency about the Church's mission in terms of 'proclamation' and 'concrete actions' in the world.

The new title of the document implies that the mission of the Church is intrinsically connected with its nature as the Church. Indeed, NMC acknowledges that 'mission ... belongs to the very being of the Church ... which is inseparable from the other three attributes of the Church – unity, holiness and catholicity' (no. 35). In this regard, the text speaks of the Church's nature essentially in terms of worship, service and proclamation (no. 36) in relation 'both to the nature of God's being and the practical demands of authentic mission' (no. 35). 'The mission of the Church is to serve the purpose of God' and hence 'the Church cannot be true to itself without ... preaching the Word, bearing witness to the great deeds of God and inviting everyone to repentance ... , baptism ... and the fuller life' of

Christian discipleship (no. 37). This task is cast primarily in the image of the proclamation of the gospel 'in word and deed' (nos. 35, 110) which entails advocacy and care for the poor and marginalized, the exposure and transformation of unjust structures, works of compassion and mercy, and the healing and reconciliation of relationships between creation and humanity (no. 40). The heart and integrity of the Church's mission is formed by 'witness through proclamation, and concrete actions in union with all people of goodwill' (no. 47). Illustration 1 offers a broad synthesis of NMC's ecclesiology of mission.

Illustration 1: NMC Ecclesiology

Church = nature + mission (proclamation + concrete action)

A focus on the Church's mission has also been an important part of the Pentecostal dialogue with the Roman Catholic Church and a major theme during its fourth phase, 1990–97. Significantly, Pentecostals in this dialogue bound the meaning of mission not to 'proclamation' and 'concrete actions' but more intimately to 'evangelization' – a task that is understood explicitly as a response to Christ's commission in the Scriptures and a witness to the same Christ as Lord and Saviour in the world today in light of the expectation of Christ's imminent return in judgement and the hope of a new creation.[21] Simply put, for Pentecostals mission is evangelization. However, this emphasis should not be perceived as a reduction of the missionary task of the Church to the articulation of the gospel but rather as a preference in theological focus and positioning of the ecclesial self-understanding of Pentecostals in the ecumenical landscape. NMC highlights that 'evangelization is ... the foremost task of the church' (no. 110), but the lack of any further definition of this task reveals the underlying assumption that evangelization is largely synonymous with the ministry of service and proclamation advocated throughout NMC.[22] Put differently, no distinction is made between evangelization and service, on a missiological level, and between evangelization and mission, on the ecclesiological level. This neglect is particularly surprising in light of the recent emphasis on 'new evangelization' in many Christian traditions.[23] In the context of the four Pentecostal perspectives that I have outlined, this aspect points to a number of critical issues and questions:

1. *The nature of the text and its function as an ecumenical document.* Despite Pentecostal participation in the drafting process of NMC, the document reflects very little Pentecostal language. As a consensus statement that combines the views of various ecclesial traditions, this cannot be expected. Even so, from a global ecumenical perspective, the language of the document should reflect and invite the participation of all churches in casting a common vision of the nature and mission of the Church. The question is, therefore, can Pentecostal observers find their theological position reflected in the document? The ethnic, economic, and sociocultural diversity among Pentecostals accentuates this question and shifts the attention geographically and ecclesiologically away from the West and toward the southern hemisphere to include greater theological emphasis on liberation, exorcism, healing, the transformation of cultures, dialogue among religions, and

the reconciliation of nations. In order to function as an ecumenical consensus text in the twenty-first century, Pentecostals call for a more consistent integration of non-Western Christians who experience the nature and mission of the Church in ways often radically different from the established European and North American mindset.[24] The successful functioning of NMC as a global consensus statement will depend largely on the preservation and accentuation of the languages and stories of the various ecclesial traditions in the final document.

2. *The structure and central themes of the document.* A successful revision of the nature and function of the document will depend largely on the structure of the text and its themes. At this time, many Pentecostals would be hard pressed to find their emphasis on mission as evangelization reflected in the text of the ecumenical document. Pentecostal concerns focus essentially on the document's definition of the Church's mission in terms of proclamation and concrete actions and may be summarized as follows:

First, mission *as* evangelization places emphasis on 'proclamation' only insofar as the act of proclamation encompasses not only the content of the message of salvation but also the whole life of the Christian and the community. Proclamation is therefore always a witness to the gospel in worship and holiness, a task that Pentecostals find accomplished primarily through the work of the Holy Spirit.[25] NMC speaks of proclamation primarily as a verbal process and situates it in the communication of the gospel through words and a fleeting comment on 'the love of its members for one another, the quality of its service to those in need, a just and disciplined life and a fair exercise of power and authority' (no. 88).[26]

Second, mission *as* evangelization places emphasis on 'concrete actions' only insofar as these actualize the substance and manner of what is proclaimed in a person's witness to the world. NMC neglects to point out not only what kind of concrete actions belong to the nature and mission of the Church and thus form 'the practical demands of authentic mission' but also how these actions are made possible and how these demands can be met in the Church. The Pentecostal community views the 'baptism in the Holy Spirit' as essential for every believer to receive empowerment for Christian witness. NMC acknowledges the gifts of the Holy Spirit as necessary for the fulfilment of the Church's mission (no. 83) yet speaks of them primarily in terms of obligations, responsibility and accountability without first referring to the Spirit's empowerment for evangelization through words of wisdom, knowledge, prophecy, spiritual discernment, sanctification, healing, or the working of miracles.

The notion of 'mission *as* evangelization' reflects the emphasis Pentecostals place on the doxological, eschatological and charismatic aspects of the life of the Church that form the heart of the Church's mission.[27] NMC says surprisingly little about the role of praise, worship or spiritual warfare in mission. Absent from the Church's proclamation and concrete actions is any sense of urgency. The Church is 'open to the free activity of the Holy Spirit' while being exposed to change, individual, cultural and historical conditioning, and the power of sin (no. 50), yet nothing is said about the concrete individual, cultural and historical forms this work of God's Spirit takes in the Church and in the world. In other words, NMC runs the risk of disconnecting eschatology and pneumatology from ecclesiology. The result portrays the Church as a heavenly city in a constant stage of missionary pilgrimage without any social, political, cultural or moral impact on the world here and now as it presents the possibility of opening to the full realization of the Kingdom of God at any time and any place. This concern reflects not only the centrality of eschatology in Pentecostal ecclesiology but also a different way of telling the story of the Church to a global audience.

3. *The potential ecumenical ramifications of the ecumenical text.* The Faith and Order document holds a number of promises for the Pentecostal community as an ecumenical consensus on the nature and mission of the Church begins to emerge. The chief benefit is the mere exposure to the ecumenical consensus already achieved; a reality still unknown to many Pentecostals. The value Pentecostals place on pneumatology, eschatology, and doxology for an understanding of the Church could be complemented by the emphasis NMC places on trinitarian theology, history, and service in the world. Pentecostals could learn about the unity and agreement already existing among the visibly divided churches and the significance of preserving and nourishing that unity for the fulfilment of the Church's eschatological mission. In praxis, this means that Pentecostals, among others, are called to consider the implications of an emerging theological convergence on the nature and mission of the Church and the concrete steps that can be taken toward mutual recognition in the faith and praxis of the churches. NMC proposes to be a work in progress.[28] The success of this endeavour depends not only on what is being said in the document but also on how it is being said and whether it ever reaches those who should listen.

In the second half of the twentieth century, the ecumenical movement produced a number of significant consensus statements. From a Pentecostal perspective, the ecumenical ramifications of the global consensus process depend only secondarily on the challenge to accept the implications of these common affirmations into the life of the churches. The primary challenge remains to this day to introduce the agreed statements first of all to the various communities that participated in its production.[29] This is a particular challenge among the numerous Pentecostal communities, which still lack the structures, institutional support, public recognition, and promotion of the ecumenical agenda. The task of incorporating an ecumenical sensitivity in the life of its communities rests only partly on the shoulders of Pentecostals. It is fundamentally a task that has to be supported by the whole ecumenical community.

4. *The development of an ecumenical ecclesiology.* The successful circulation and implementation of the final document among Pentecostal churches and communities could speak to the importance of the ecclesial life in communion and could call Pentecostals to consider the significance of the sacramental and liturgical life, ministry, and social justice in a way that has not been achieved by previous ecumenical documents. Notwithstanding well-known concerns about the predominance of sacramental categories in the ecclesiology of NMC, the development of an ecumenical ecclesiology is not likely to be hindered by distinctions of ecclesial praxis but challenged more immediately by ecumenical prejudices, assumptions and generalizations.[30] The most important among those is the presumed antithesis of Pentecostalism and ecumenism.

Pentecostals today see no fundamental contradistinction between a Pentecostal and an ecumenical ecclesiology. On the contrary, Pentecostal theology must be considered ecumenical in its essence by virtue of the origin in and emergence of Pentecostals from virtually all forms and branches of the visibly divided churches. Rather than perceiving Pentecostal communities as distinct from the established theological and religious traditions from which they emerged, the ecclesiality of worldwide Pentecostalism can be perceived only in continuing awareness of other confessions not as an alternative to but as a root and source of Pentecostal life and praxis. This insight has far-reaching consequences not only for the ecumenical perception of Pentecostalism but for the identity of the ecumenical enterprise itself. The search for a global consensus on the nature and mission of the Church that includes the ecclesiological struggle of Pentecostals effects a dynamic redefinition of the ecumenical agenda.

Pentecostalism and the Search for an Ecumenical Ecclesiology

In recent years, ecumenical scholars have begun to take more seriously the concern that Pentecostals might develop their theology in ecumenical anonymity and apart from a formative experience with the larger Christian world. While North American Pentecostals at the beginning of the twentieth century spoke of their own movement in largely ecumenical terms that emphasized the holiness and unity of the churches, subsequent decades turned attention away from the ecumenical agenda and toward the preservation of a distinctive Pentecostal form of thought.[31] Ecumenical concerns re-emerged with the formation of the Roman Catholic–Pentecostal dialogue in the 1970s, the Reformed–Pentecostal dialogue and the Orthodox–Pentecostal dialogue in the 1990s, the formation of the WCC–Pentecostal Joint Consultative Group in 2000, recent attempts to initiate a dialogue between Pentecostals and Lutherans, and the formation of the ecumenical studies group of the Society for Pentecostal Studies. Nonetheless, the endeavour to define Pentecostalism from an ecumenical perspective frequently gives the impression that Pentecostals are defined by a reintegration of an independently developed theological agenda into the existing ecclesial traditions instead of a retrieving from, reconstructing with and reappropriating of the theological heritage evident in Pentecostal thought.

At the end of the twentieth century, the ecumenical image of Pentecostalism was typically constructed on the basis of already existing Pentecostal communities and denominations, distinct from other traditions, and with little reference to the ecclesial origins and ecumenical development of these communities. Pentecostalism has been presented as existing in contradistinction to other traditions and not as originating from or developing out of a historical struggle with existing Christian confessions. For example, the perception of Pentecostalism as an alternative to Roman Catholicism neglects to show that this choice can only be perceived as an alternative if Catholicism remains inherently connected with the emerging Pentecostal tradition. Similarly, one cannot speak of Pentecostalism as an alternative to the Reformed tradition, Lutherans, Baptists, or Methodists, without acknowledging the (theological, liturgical, pastoral, cultural, or ethical) roots of many Pentecostals in those traditions. In his seminal work, *Pentecostal Spirituality*, Steven J. Land remarks on this aspect.

> Pentecostalism flows in paradoxical continuity and discontinuity with other streams of Christianity. Insofar as it retains similarity to the first ten years of the movement, it is more Arminian than Calvinist in its approach to issues of human agency and perseverance. It is more Calvinist than Lutheran in its appreciation of the so-called 'third use of Law' to guide Christian growth and conduct. It is more Eastern than Western in its understanding of spirituality as perfection and participation in the divine life (*theosis*) ... Pentecostalism is more Catholic than Protestant in emphasizing sanctification-transformation more than forensic justification, but more Protestant than Catholic in the conviction that the Word is the authority over the church and tradition for matters of faith, practice, government and discipline ... Pentecostalism therefore exists in continuity but differentiating discontinuity with other Christian spiritualities.[32]

Overall, Pentecostal theology, worship, and liturgy can no longer be presented over against but rather within the religious and ecumenical landscape. While a form of phenomenological (typological-descriptive) ecumenism is symptomatic for much of the ecumenical perception of Pentecostals in the twentieth century, I suggest that an archaeological (origin-oriented) ecumenism would better serve the ecumenical agenda. A Pentecostal perspective on the nature and mission of the Church considers not only the present state of visible separation among the churches but also the origin of currently divided thought and experience in those churches as well as the continuity and discontinuity of influence among those communities.

It is a prominent exercise among Pentecostals to locate the origins of the Pentecostal heritage in the movements and revivals that preceded and accompanied the emergence of the movement and from which Pentecostals gained their theological emphases, such as Methodism and the nineteenth-century holiness revivals.[33] Walter Hollenweger, pioneer of academic research on Pentecostalism, ventured the thesis that Classical Pentecostalism 'started as an ecumenical revival movement *within* the traditional churches'.[34] However, the subsequent establishment of Pentecostal churches and denominations is often perceived *as distinct from* the established theological and religious traditions from which they emerged: Pentecostalism is not Methodism. This distinction is drawn even more radically when it comes to the established mainline churches that reject the Pentecostal experience under the presupposition that 'they' (Pentecostals) are not 'we' (Catholics, Lutherans, etc.). At the beginning of the twenty-first century, ecumenical scholars in the Pentecostal tradition recognize that this distinction can only be perceived if those participating in Pentecostal theology continue to be aware of Pentecostalism as an alternative to other confessions.[35] In other words, one can only say that Pentecostalism is not Catholicism if one is aware of Catholic teaching and how Pentecostal thought has distinguished itself from it. Put differently, a more ecumenical way of expressing the theological diversity would be to say that Pentecostals are no longer Catholic (or Methodist or Baptist or

Buddhist or Hindu). From an ecumenical perspective of history, this expression would indicate that the Holy Spirit was not poured out on (already-existing) Pentecostals but on Catholics or Methodists or Calvinists who then became Pentecostals because they are able to uphold the Pentecostal worldview as an alternative to their own origins in the ecumenical context.

As a consequence, if we no longer examine Pentecostalism in a typological-descriptive manner as already established in the global ecumenical context but begin to see it as a continuing movement in and out of the various confessions and religions, we may retrieve an ecumenical theology of Pentecostalism from the teachings of the various Christian traditions instead of trying to reintegrate Pentecostalism into the existing ecumenical landscape. An observation of the continuing mutual influence of the Christian traditions will undoubtedly prove to be of great benefit to the reconciliation of Christian traditions with one another.

The success of formulating an ecumenical ecclesiology from a global perspective will largely depend on the choices the churches make with regard to those whose worldview is different.[36] An ecumenical perspective that integrates Pentecostalism will have to state not only that Pentecostal ecclesiology is different from others but also to what extent Pentecostal ecclesiology is no longer the same. For example, according to John Calvin, the Protestant Reformation emerged from a protest against Roman Catholic doctrine, praxis and government.[37] This protest can only be perceived as long as Catholic doctrine remains part of the self-definition of the Reformation. At the point when Protestantism has completely isolated itself from Catholic thought, Protestantism will cease to exist. Yet as long as it exists, it also establishes itself as an alternative to its own origins in the Catholic tradition in order to 'show that the particular remedies which the Reformers employed were apt and salutary'.[38] Similarly, Evangelicalism emerged as a consequence of pietism and the Great Awakening in North America and as a reaction to the Enlightenment. The reaction to the Enlightenment continues to be the initiatory and transformative force of Evangelical theology and must be taken into consideration when we define Evangelical thought in the present.

This principle of continuing ecumenical influence is illustrated vividly in Paul's Letter to the Romans when the apostle addresses the question of justification. Although he can say that the righteousness of God is revealed apart from the Law, the Law still remains a part of God's righteousness and witnesses to God's righteousness (see Rom. 3.21). A person is justified by faith apart from the Law but this does not nullify the Law (v. 28). On the contrary, the newfound justification by faith upholds the Law (v. 31). Likewise, we can say that Pentecostalism is revealed apart from other confessions and yet these confessions still remain as part of the Pentecostal tradition. In fact, it is Pentecostalism that upholds and establishes these confessions as other. The same is true for all of the visible divided churches that exist in continuing mutual influence with each other. We may refer to this as the principle of ecumenical transformation.

In light of this perspective, Pentecostals begin to engage in ecumenical reflection on what makes them unique in the global ecclesial context. At the same time, they also ask the question to what extent Pentecostals remain indebted to and are transformed by Catholic, Lutheran, Methodist, Calvinist, Evangelical or other forms of thought and praxis. Ecumenically, Pentecostals not only find their theology reflected in other confessions but also acknowledge the influence of other confessions on their own worldview. Practically, Pentecostals have begun to ask difficult ecumenical questions: Can Pentecostals who were once Catholic ever leave behind their Catholic roots without jeopardizing the kind of Pentecostalism they chose? Can third-generation Classical Pentecostals in North America say that they have purged their theology completely from any Methodist thought? Is the form of traditioning that Pentecostals call for possible without any reference to the continuing influence of other Christian traditions on the emerging Pentecostal worldview?[39] When the ecumenical community begins to ask similar questions, it will likely discover that finding a consensus on the nature and mission of the Church means also to acknowledge one's inheritance in other traditions that formed and continue to inform one's own identity.

As a result, an ecumenical way of expressing the Pentecostal contribution to an ecumenical ecclesiology would be to say that Pentecostals are no longer pursuing the ecclesial life from which they emerged although they remain ecclesiologically bound to their experience of that life. There exists a variety of 'experiences' among Pentecostals depending on the negative or positive influence of particular forms and elements of ecclesial faith and praxis on a person's life. For example, some may have found the celebration of the Eucharist life-transforming while others have lost all sense about its significance in the daily ritual of the ecclesial life in which they were raised. Some Pentecostals experience a strict ritual format of worship as a limitation of the public demonstration of their faith, while others are longing for more liturgical and ritual manifestations of faith in their churches.

Pentecostals would reserve room for such experiences and migrations within and among ecclesial communities as part of the nature and mission of the Church which, not only for Pentecostals, is always being renewed. In many ways, therefore, the ecclesial experience of Pentecostals finds the mission of the Church starting not outside of its boundaries but within.[40] From there the Church's mission extends into the world only to return again to itself. Worship, service and proclamation are acts of the churches that originate within the churches and are directed toward the churches in order to affirm the unity, holiness, catholicity and apostolicity of the one Church beyond the churches and into the world. This continuous dynamism is what moves the whole Church along the way and confronts it with the Kingdom of God. In essence we have here a sketch of an ecumenical ecclesiology from a Pentecostal perspective (see Illustration 2).

Illustration 2: Pentecostal Ecclesiology

Church = mission = evangelization $\left\{ \begin{array}{l} \text{transformation} \\ \text{confrontation} \\ \text{urgency} \end{array} \right\}$ inside toward toward
the > the > kingdom
Church world of God

This ecclesiological concept stands in sharp contrast to the theology of NMC, which speaks of the Church as a combination of its nature and mission and defines the latter in terms of proclamation and concrete action (see Illustration 1). For

Pentecostals, Church is a reflective, discerning reality that finds consensus about its nature and mission not only in formal statements but in an often painful process of repentance, forgiveness, conversion and renewal in and among the churches while the Church proclaims the gospel to the world. Ecumenical transformation is an essential part of preserving and establishing the ecclesial identity not only of the Pentecostal tradition. I suggest that this form of evangelistic, contextual, critical, non-triumphant and pragmatic Pentecostal ecclesiology has much to say to what often appears as an idealistic, romantic and authoritarian ecclesiology in the text of NMC. In light of these insights, the next stages in the development of an ecumenical consensus on the nature and mission of the Church will likely prove to become a catalyst in the development of a genuine ecclesiology in the Pentecostal traditions which, surprisingly, still have not produced a comprehensive theology of mission.

Notes

1. See World Council of Churches, *The Nature and Mission of the Church: A Stage on the Way to a Common Statement*. Faith and Order Paper, 198 (Geneva: WCC, 2005) and its predecessor *The Nature and Purpose of the Church: A Stage on the Way to a Common Statement*. Faith and Order Paper, 181 (Geneva: WCC, 1998).
2. See Veli-Matti Kärkkäinen, '*The Nature and Purpose of the Church*: Theological and Ecumenical Reflections from Pentecostal/Free Church Perspectives', *Ecumenical Trends* 33 (7) (2004): 1–7; Jeff Gros, 'Pentecostal Response to *The Nature and Purpose of the Church*', *Ecumenical Trends* 33 (7) (2004): 1; Thomas P. Rausch, 'A Response to Veli-Matti Kärkkäinen on *The Nature and Purpose of the Church*', *Ecumenical Trends* 33 (7) (2004): 8–11; Frank D. Macchia, '*The Nature and Purpose of the Church*: A Pentecostal Response', *Ecumenical Trends* 34 (7) (2005): 1–6; Edmund Rybarczyk, 'A Response to Dr. Frank Macchia', *Ecumenical Trends* 34 (7) (2005): 7–10; Caleb Oladipo, 'A Response to Dr. Frank Macchia', *Ecumenical Trends* 34 (7) (2005): 10–12.
3. A synopsis of these perspectives was published in Wolfgang Vondey, 'Pentecostal Perspectives on *The Nature and Mission of the Church*', *Ecumenical Trends* 35 (8) (2006): 1–5, and is used here with kind permission of the editorial board.
4. Cf. Walter J. Hollenweger, 'The Pentecostal Movement and the World Council of Churches', *The Ecumenical Review* 18 (July 1966): 310–20; Cecil M. Robeck, Jr, 'Pentecostals and the Apostolic Faith: Implications for Ecumenism', *Pneuma: Journal of the Society for Pentecostal Studies* 9 (Spring 1987): 61–84; Jeffrey Gros, 'Pentecostal Engagement in the Wider Christian Community', *Mid-Stream* 38 (4) (1999): 26–47.
5. Cf. Veli–Matti Kärkkäinen, '"Anonymous Ecumenists"? Pentecostals and the Struggle for Christian Identity', *Journal of Ecumenical Studies* 37 (1) (Winter 2000): 13–27.
6. Cf. Jackie David Johns, 'Pentecostalism and the Postmodern Worldview', *Journal of Pentecostal Theology* 7 (October 1995): 73–96. See the recent endeavours of Amos Yong, *The Spirit Poured Out on All Flesh: Pentecostalism and the Possibility of Global Theology* (Grand Rapids: Baker Academic, 2005); Frank D. Macchia, *Baptized in the Spirit: A Global Pentecostal Theology* (Grand Rapids: Zondervan, 2006).
7. See Kärkkäinen, 'The Nature and Purpose of the Church': 1–2.
8. See Michael A. Fahey (ed.), *Catholic Perspectives on Baptism, Eucharist, and Ministry. A Study Commissioned by the Catholic Theological Society of America* (Lanham, MD: University Press of America, 1986), pp. 9–24; Gennadios Limouris and Nomikos Michael Vaporis (eds), *Orthodox Perspectives on Baptism, Eucharist, and Ministry* (Brookline, MA: Holy Cross Orthodox Press, 1985).

9. Limouris and Vaporis, *Orthodox Perspectives*, p. 95.
10. See this observation of the Catholic response to BEM in Fahey, *Catholic Perspectives*, p. 24.
11. Limouris and Vaporis, *Orthodox Perspectives*, p. 95.
12. See Macchia, 'The Nature and Purpose of the Church': 3–4.
13. Ibid.: 4.
14. See Kärkkäinen, 'The Nature and Purpose of the Church': 6.
15. Macchia, 'The Nature and Purpose of the Church': 4.
16. Ibid.: 4.
17. See Macchia, 'The Nature and Purpose of the Church': 1–2.
18. Cf. Cecil M. Robeck, Jr, 'Taking Stock of Pentecostalism: The Personal Reflections of a Retiring Editor', *Pneuma: The Journal of the Society for Pentecostal Studies* 15 (3) (Spring 1993): 37. See Charles F. Parham, *A Voice Crying in the Wilderness* (Baxter Springs, KS: Apostolic Faith Bible College, 1902, 1910; 3rd edn, n.d.), pp. 61–7; W. F. Carothers, *The Baptism with the Holy Ghost and Speaking in Tongues* (Houston: W. F. Carothers, 1906–07), p. 25; W. J. Seymour, 'Christ's Messages to the Church', *The Apostolic Faith* 1 (11) (October 1907–January 1908): 3; idem, 'The Baptism of the Holy Ghost', *The Apostolic Faith* 2 (13) (May 1908): 3.
19. See Yong, *The Spirit Poured Out on All Flesh*, pp. 121–202; Simon Chan, 'Mother Church: Toward a Pentecostal Ecclesiology', *Pneuma: The Journal of the Society for Pentecostal Studies* 22 (2) (Fall 2000): 177–208; Miroslav Volf, 'The Nature of the Church', *Evangelical Review of Theology* 1 (26) (2002): 68–75; Veli-Matti Kärkkäinen, *An Introduction to Ecclesiology: Ecumenical, Historical & Global Perspectives* (Downers Grove, IL: Intervarsity, 2002), pp. 167–233.
20. See, for example, Kenneth J. Archer, *A Pentecostal Hermeneutic for the Twenty-first Century: Spirit, Scripture and Community* (London: T&T Clark, 2004); idem, 'Pentecostal Story: The Hermeneutical Filter for the Making of Meaning', *Pneuma: The Journal of the Society for Pentecostal Studies* 26 (1) (Spring 2004): 36–59; Simon Chan, *Pentecostal Theology and the Christian Spiritual Tradition* (Sheffield: Sheffield Academic Press, 2000), pp. 17–39; Scott A. Ellington, 'History, Story, and Testimony: Locating Truth in a Pentecostal Hermeneutic', *Pneuma: The Journal of the Society for Pentecostal Studies* 23 (2) (Fall 2001): 245–63; Roger Stronstad, 'Pentecostal Experience and Hermeneutics', *Paraclete* 26 (Winter 1992): 14–30; Amos Yong, *Spirit-Word-Community: Theological Hermeneutics in Trinitarian Perspective* (Burlington, VT: Ashgate, 2002), pp. 221–74.
21. See 'Evangelization, Proselytism and Common Witness: The Report from the Fourth Phase of the International Dialogue (1990–1997) between the Roman Catholic Church and Some Classical Pentecostal Churches and Leaders', *Pneuma. Journal of the Society for Pentecostal Studies* 21 (1) (Spring 1999): 11–51; see also Veli-Matti Kärkkäinen, 'Evangelization, Proselytism, and Common Witness: Roman Catholic–Pentecostal Dialogue on Mission, 1990–1997', *International Bulletin of Missionary Research* 25 (1) (January 2001): 16–18, 20–22; idem, *Ad Ultimum Terrae: Evangelization, Proselytism and Common Witness in the Roman Catholic Pentecostal Dialogue, 1990–1997*. Studies in the Intercultural History of Christianity, 117 (Frankfurt: Peter Lang, 1999).
22. See also Neville Callam, 'The Mission of the Church in the World Council of Churches' Text on the Nature and Purpose of the Church', *International Review of Mission* 90 (358) (2001): 239.
23. See, for example, Wolfgang Vondey, 'New Evangelization and Liturgical Praxis in the Roman Catholic Church', *Studia Liturgica: An International Ecumenical Review for Liturgical Research and Renewal* 36 (2) (2006): 231–52.
24. See Amos Yong, *The Spirit Poured Out on All Flesh*, pp. 167–202; Allan Anderson, *An Introduction to Pentecostalism: Global Charismatic Christianity* (Cambridge: Cambridge University Press, 2004), pp. 187–286; David Martin, *Pentecostalism: The World Their Parish* (Oxford: Blackwell, 2002); Manuel Quintero, *Jubileo: La Fiesta del Espíritu: Identidad y Misión del Pentecostalismo Latinamericano* (Maracaibo, Venezuela: Comisión Evangélica Pentecostal Latinamericana, 1999).

25. Cf. Carmelo E. Alvarez, 'Mission as Liberating Spirit: Disciples and Pentecostals in Venezuela', *Discipliana* 62 (4) (2002): 116–28; J. A. B. Jongeneel, 'Ecumenical, Evangelical and Pentecostal/Charismatic Views on Mission as a Movement of the Holy Spirit', in *Pentecost, Mission and Ecumenism: Essays on Intellectual Theology: Festschrift in Honour of Professor Walter J. Hollenweger*, ed. J. A. B. Jongeneel (Frankfurt: Peter Lang, 1992), pp. 231–46; Veli-Matti Kärkkäinen, 'Mission, Spirit and Eschatology: An Outline of a Pentecostal–Charismatic Theology of Mission', *Mission Studies* 16 (1) (1999): 73–94; Andrew M. Lord, 'Mission Eschatology: A Framework for Mission in the Spirit', *Journal of Pentecostal Theology* 11 (December 1997): 111–23; John Christopher Thomas, 'The Spirit, Healing of Mission: An Overview of the Biblical Canon', *International Review of Mission* 93 (370) (2004): 421–2.

26. Cf. Callam, 'The Mission of the Church in the World Council of Churches': 239.

27. See Vondey, 'Pentecostal Perspectives': 4; idem, 'Presuppositions for Pentecostal Engagement in Ecumenical Dialogue', *Exchange: Journal for Missiological and Ecumenical Research* 30 (4) (2001): 351–2.

28. The subtitle of NMC calls it 'a stage on the way to a common statement'. On the process see also Alan D. Falconer, 'The Church: God's Gift to the World – on the Nature and Purpose of the Church', *International Review of Mission* 90 (359) (2001): 396–7.

29. Cf. Vondey, 'Presuppositions for Pentecostal Engagement': 356–58; idem, 'Appeal for a Pentecostal Council for Ecumenical Dialogue', *Mid–Stream* 40 (3) (July 2001): 45–56.

30. Cf. Rybarczyk, 'A Response to Dr. Frank Macchia's Paper': 9.

31. See Vondey, 'The Symbolic Turn': 226–44; Kärkkäinen, 'Anonymous Ecumenists': 13–27.

32. Steven J. Land, *Pentecostal Spirituality: A Passion for the Kingdom* (Journal of Pentecostal Theology Supplement 1; Sheffield: Sheffield Academic Press, 1993), pp. 29–30.

33. See Donald W. Dayton, *Theological Roots of Pentecostalism* (Peabody, MA: Hendrickson, 1986).

34. Walter J. Hollenweger, 'The Pentecostal Movement and the World Council of Churches', *The Ecumenical Review* 18 (July 1966): 313; idem, *Pentecostalism: Origins and Developments Worldwide* (Peabody, MA: Hendrickson, 1997), pp. 334–66.

35. See Wolfgang Vondey, 'Pentecostalism and the Possibility of Global Theology: Implications of the Theology of Amos Yong', *Pneuma: Journal of the Society for Pentecostal Studies* 28 (2) (2006): 289–312.

36. On the Pentecostal worldview, see Johns, 'Pentecostalism and the Postmodern Worldview': 73–96.

37. John Calvin, 'The Necessity of Reforming the Church', in *Calvin: Theological Treatises*, ed. J. K. S. Reid (Philadelphia: Westminster Press, 1954), pp. 185–6.

38. Ibid., p. 186.

39. Cf. Vondey, 'Pentecostalism and the Possibility of Global Theology': 299–303.

40. See the emphasis on change and conversion within the Church in Groupe des Dombes, *Pour la conversion des églises: Identité et changement dans la dynamique de la communion* (Paris: Centurion, 1991).

Chapter 7

ARE COUNCILS AND SYNODS DECISION-MAKING? A ROMAN CATHOLIC CONUNDRUM IN ECUMENICAL PERSPECTIVE

Bradford E. Hinze

One of the most valuable formulas developed by the Faith and Order Commission of the World Council of Churches (WCC) states that 'at every level of the Church's life, the ministry of oversight must be exercised in personal, collegial and communal ways'. This principle was introduced in *Baptism, Eucharist and Ministry* (BEM) and elaborated upon in *The Nature and Mission of the Church* (NMC).[1] It is valuable because it provides an instrument and template for evaluating ecclesiological doctrines and pastoral practices. Specifically, this triadic formula introduces a *comprehensive relational framework* that enables members of individual churches along with their ecumenical partners to identify and witness to the *assets* of their own tradition and to recognize their *deficiencies*, and so to exchange their distinctive *gifts* and to acknowledge their distinctive *wounds* as they search for healing, communion, and catholic fullness together.[2] This can contribute to the processes of mutual accountability and mutual learning associated with receptive ecumenism as it invites ongoing conversion and reformation.[3]

In this ongoing journey of churches as gifted and wounded, as *semper purificandae* and *semper reformandae*, each church faces its own challenges, what can be identified in some instances as conundrums. One example is provided by Roman Catholics, who since the Second Vatican Council have had their own struggles, and had to face conundrums, with implementing a more relational vision of the communal and collegial approach to the exercise of the personal authority of the pope, bishops and priests.

A Catholic Conundrum: Shared Responsibility without Shared Decision-Making

Following the teachings of the Second Vatican Council (1962–65), Catholics were encouraged to implement conciliar and synodal structures of governance at various levels of the church – parish pastoral councils, diocesan pastoral councils and synods, presbyteral councils, and the international synod of bishops.[4] The Code of Canon Law issued in 1983 established these various structures with wider involvement and participation of representative members of the Church, but with the proviso that these bodies are to be consultative only and not decision-making. Councillors and synod delegates – lay people, religious, and clergy – were approved to offer advice to the leader – pastor, bishop or pope – who has the authority of decision-making.[5] These bodies were neither required, nor permitted, to make decisions collectively with the ordained leader. Ecumenical councils are the exception, not the rule.

The consultative-only clauses in the 1983 Code of Canon Law symbolize the compromise reached at Vatican II between a hierarchical ecclesiology that had reached its zenith in the second half of the nineteenth and early twentieth centuries and the new affirmation of shared responsibility in the Church based on the recovery of the sacramental foundation of episcopal authority and collegiality, and the baptismal mandate of all members of the Church to participate fully and actively in the Spirit-anointed offices of Christ and the realization of the identity and the pastoral mission of the Church. The Council attained widespread consensus on the theological foundations for shared responsibility in the Church, but was unable in the time allotted to work out their implications in relation to the long-standing practices of a hierarchical ecclesiology. One often finds in the Vatican II documents the two ecclesiological trajectories juxtaposed, but not fully integrated. The consultative-only formula in Canon Law established what can be described as an asymmetrical implementation of these two ecclesiological orientations in favour of previously established patterns of the exercise of hierarchical authority over the wider involvement of the laity, religious, and clergy in shared responsibility by means of shared decision-making.

After forty years of experimentation with conciliar and synodal forms of governance in the Church, the conundrum is whether there can be shared responsibility in the Church without shared decision-making. This issue has not gone unnoticed by ecumenists.[6] Some Catholics believe that it would be sufficient and certainly much better than it is right now, if we could simply implement genuine consultative procedures as specified by the Code, even though they are not mandated by the Code. My own position is that, in order to fulfil the vision and promise of Vatican II, councils and synods at parochial, diocesan, regional, national and international levels should be mandated and granted the authority doctrinally and canonically to engage in collective discernment and decision-making in order to actualize shared responsibility and mutual accountability in the Church, while further developing the relational and interdependent model of personal authority of pope, bishop and clergy.

What Perspective Is Offered by the Faith and Order Documents?

What follows is an analysis of the treatment of personal, collegial and communal aspects of ministerial oversight in *Baptism, Eucharist and Ministry* and in *The Nature and Mission of the Church* to determine what these documents assert about the decision-making character of synods and councils.

Historical Antecedents of the Triadic Principle

Before examining these two Faith and Order documents, I think it is helpful to acknowledge that they stand in relation to contributions from earlier works of the Faith and Order Commission and bilateral discussions. Four sources merit special attention.

The first source, the First World Conference on Faith and Order at Lausanne in 1927 (no. 26, commentary), is identified in BEM, which reads:

> In view of (i) the place which the episcopate, the council of presbyters, and the congregation of the faithful, respectively, had in the constitution of the early Church, and (ii) the fact that episcopal, presbyteral, and congregational systems of government are each today, and have been for centuries, accepted by great communions in Christendom, and (iii) the fact that episcopal, presbyteral and congregational systems are each believed by many to be essential to the good order of the Church, we therefore recognize that these several elements must all, under conditions which require further study, have an appropriate place in the order of life of a reunited Church ... [To complete the sentence from the original document:] and that each separate communion, recalling the abundant blessing of God vouchsafed to its ministry in the past, should gladly bring to the common life of the united Church its own spiritual treasures.[7]

Episcopal forms of church governance are utilized by Catholics, the Orthodox, Anglicans, Methodists, and sometimes by Lutherans. Presbyteral forms are employed by the Reformed tradition of governance by a group of elders either through a presbytery that governs at a certain regional level, and session or consistory at the congregational level. The congregational system is governed by a local association of believers and is best represented by the Free Church tradition that includes the United Church of Christ, Baptists, and Disciples of Christ.[8] The terms personal, collegial and communal were subsequently developed as correlative terms for episcopal, presbyteral and congregational. However, each category in BEM functioned beyond the original context of origin for the designations episcopal, presbyteral and congregational by representing different forms of governance within a given church tradition, for example, personal can imply papal or episcopal or some other ordained form of personal ministry; the same argument could be made about collegial modes of exercising authority.[9]

A second source emerged as a result of the growing attention given to ordained ministry and laity by the Faith and Order Commission. The Lausanne triad – episcopal, presbyteral and congregational – did not receive much attention until the Fourth World Conference on Faith and Order held in Montreal in 1963, which 'called for a study on the relation and distinction between special ministry, as one gift among the many gifts, and the ministry of the whole people of God'. This resulted a decade later in the Accra Report, *One Baptism, One Eucharist and a Mutually Recognised Ministry*, the precursor of BEM.[10] The Accra Report did not use the triadic principle and said little about the ministry of oversight (*episkopé*) and the personal minister associated with this ministry (*episkopos*). To address this deficiency, a small consultation was convened in Geneva in 1979 to reflect upon episcopacy. A paper delivered by Orthodox theologian John Zizioulas on the early Church proved to be pivotal in the development of the three dimensions of oversight. Zizioulas gave special attention to the *episkopé* in relation to the local eucharistic community.

> The early Church refused to recognize any [episcopal] ministry or [collegial or conciliar] structure which would by-pass or ignore the local church ... The synods never became in the early Church a superstructure over and above the local communities, and for this reason they never acquired authority in themselves: they always had to be *received* by the communities in order to be fully valid. The conclusion from all this may sound strange but it seems inevitable: episcopacy, as it developed in the first three centuries, also with regard to councils, meant anything but the subjection of the laymen to the higher authority; it meant, on the contrary, that a ministry existed through which the Church remained in the final analysis a *concrete community*.[11]

The Geneva Memorandum issued by those gathered for the consultation responded to the question: 'How is *episkopé* to be exercised in the Church?' with the answer '*episkopé*' has three dimensions: 'personal, collegial, and communal' – changing Lausanne's triad, personal, presbyteral and congregational. They concluded, 'personal *episkopé* can only be carried out in a collegial way. The authority of the one to provide the focus of the community needs to be tested by a group ... *Episkopé* has a communal dimension. It is exercised not over the community but with the collaboration and participation of the community.'[12]

Two additional sources issued in 1976 may have influenced the participants at the 1979 Geneva consultation and the 1982 that published BEM. The third source is the Anglican–Roman Catholic International Commission document called the Venice Statement on *Authority in the Church*.[13] Three levels of church authority can be identified in the document: the first is designated in terms of Christian authority operative in the community (nos. 3–6), the second is the authority of the individual ordained bishop, and the third level is the collective authority of the bishops called conciliarity. First, the community and each of its members are responsible to humankind and to each other as bearers of authoritative witness. 'This is Christian authority: when Christians so act and speak, men perceive the authoritative word of Christ' (no. 3). Second, the bishop has special authority in the community, but not in isolation. 'All those who have ministerial authority must recognize their mutual responsibility and interdependence' (no. 5). This personal and collegial authority of bishops is related to the first communal level: 'the perception of God's will for his Church does not belong only to the ordained ministry but is shared by all its members' (no. 6). The community is to discern, assess and respond to the teachings of the ordained ministers (no. 6). This culminates in a third level called conciliar authority. Councils are convened to 'discuss matters of mutual concern and to meet contemporary challenges' (no. 9). They can be local, regional, or worldwide – ecumenical. The local council is convened to take an action by making a decision assured that 'the Lord himself is present when his people assemble in his name (Mt. 18.20), and that a council may say, "it has seemed good to the Holy Spirit and to us" (Acts 15.28)' (no. 16). The role of the entire Church, individuals within the Church, and bishops in particular is further explained:

> In its mission to proclaim and safeguard the gospel the Church has the obligation and the competence to make declarations in matters of faith. This mission involves the whole people of God, among whom some may rediscover or perceive more clearly than others certain aspects of the saving truth ... But the bishops have a special responsibility for promoting the truth and discerning error, and the interaction of the bishop and the people in its exercise is a safeguard of the Christian life and fidelity (no. 18).

A document entitled *Elucidation* issued in 1981 identifies critical comments on the Venice Statement and offers an official response to them. One criticism should be noted. It is 'accused of an over-emphasis upon the ordained ministry to the neglect of the laity'. The text responds:

> In guarding and developing communion, every member has a part to play. Baptism gives to everyone in the Church the right, and consequently the ability, to carry out his particular function in the body. The recognition of this fundamental right is of great importance. In different ways, even if sometimes hesitantly, our two Churches have sought to integrate in decision-making those who are not ordained (no. 4).

The *Elucidation* text further asserts that 'there was no devaluing of the proper and active role of the laity', which is supported by the recognition of the gifts of the Spirit given to individuals for the good of the Church (no. 5), the role of the laity in discerning God's will (no. 6), and what subsequently was called the *sensus fidelium* (no. 18).

The fourth source, the French Group of Les Dombes, composed of representatives of Reformed Churches and the Roman Catholic Church, building on their 1973 statement, likewise issued a statement on the episcopal ministry in 1976.[14] This document likewise considers *episkopé* in association with the local church. It asserts that the personal authority of the *episkopos* is exercised collegially and in communion with the local community. Quoting their 1973 statement, 'The episcopal ministry is exercised "in the dependence of the community and the minister on one another"', the new document emphasizes that 'there is no *episcopos* without community' and no 'community without *episcopos*' (281). In particular, 'synods and councils are privileged moments in the exercise of episcopal vigilance over the faithfulness of the life of the churches to the apostolic witness. Their faithfulness can be guaranteed only through the mutual verification of unanimity in confessing the true faith' (282).[15]

Within the context established by these four documents, the question can now be posed: what perspective on the Catholic conundrum identified here is offered by the Faith and Order triadic principle as it has been articulated in BEM and NMC? Are councils and synods decision-making in these documents?

Baptism, Eucharist and Ministry

Five theses summarize the cumulative argument of *Baptism, Eucharist and Ministry* and are accompanied by textual evidence.

Thesis 1: The ordained and the laity are to be understood as related and interdependent. 'All members of the believing community, ordained and lay, are interrelated. On the one hand, the community needs ordained ministers ... On the other hand, the ordained ministry has no existence apart from the community' (no. 12).

Thesis 2: This relationship and interdependence is identified in terms of cooperation between the ordained and the entire community of faithful in the exercise of ministerial authority. 'The authority [of the ordained ministry] has the character of responsibility before God and is exercised with the cooperation of the whole community' (no. 15).

> Ordained ministers must not be autocrats or impersonal functionaries. Although called to exercise wise and loving leadership on the basis of the World of God, they are bound to the faith in interdependence and reciprocity. Only when they seek the response and acknowledgement of the community can their authority be protected from the distortion of isolation and domination (no. 16).[16]

Thesis 3: The triadic principle that 'the ordained ministry should be exercised in a personal, collegial, and communal way' (no. 26) further specifies the character of the relationship and interdependence of the ordained and the entire community. The personal modality refers to the action of the ordained leader. The collegial modality pertains to the collaboration of the ordained in the shared task of representing and responding to the concerns of the community. The communal modality indicates the action of the ordained ministry in relation to life and collaborative participation of the community of the faithful.

Thesis 4: The ordained and the faithful fulfil their relational and interdependent character by participating together in collective discernment and decision-making. This is the decisive step relevant to our topic. Two key passages illuminate this thesis.

> The intimate relationship between the ordained ministry and the community finds expression in a communal dimension where the exercise of ordained ministry is rooted in the life of the community and requires the community's effective participation in the discovery of God's will and the guidance of the Spirit (no. 26).
> Strong emphasis should be placed on the active participation of all members in the life and decision-making of the community (no. 27).

Thesis 5: Synodal structures of discernment and decision-making provide constitutionally – or canonically approved practices for each of the three dimensions – personal, collegial, and communal – to 'find adequate expression' (no. 27). As the document states, 'The collegial and communal dimensions will find expression in regular representative synodal gatherings' (no. 27).

The Nature and Mission of the Church

The 2005 document *The Nature and Mission of the Church* offers a more detailed analysis of the ministry of oversight and ministerial authority exercised by all the faithful and by the ordained, and more in-depth consideration of the three modalities associated with ministerial oversight. If one compares NMC with BEM on the five identified theses, the following conclusions can be reached. NMC reaffirms the first three theses in BEM: (1) the ordained and the entire community of the faithful are by nature related and interdependent; (2) as related and interdependent, the ordained and the entire community are to collaborate in the exercise of ministerial authority;[17] and (3) this collaboration is further specified in terms of the personal, collegial and communal modes of participation in ministerial authority.

Theses 4 and 5, however, merit closer scrutiny.

Concerning thesis 4, NMC differs from BEM on collective discernment and decision-making. Collective discernment and responsibility – personally, collegially, and communally – are reaffirmed in NMC, but the treatment of decision-making is both more nuanced and ambiguous. *Collegial* decision-making is reasserted, but there is no unambiguous affirmation of *communal* decision-making. Several claims lead to this conclusion.

First, NMC states more clearly than BEM that ministerial oversight (*episkope*) 'belongs to the whole Church', which implies that all the faithful participate in some way in this work of vigilance, while certain ordained persons have been given a particular responsibility in this regard (no. 94). Consequently, instead of situating, as BEM did, the triadic principle in the context of treating the exercise of ordained ministry and authority, NMC recasts the entire discussion of it in terms of the ministry of all the faithful (section D), the particular ministry of the ordained (section E), followed by the treatment of oversight: personal, communal, collegial (section F). This cumulative treatment establishes a relational understanding of all ministries and examines the ministry of oversight shared by all and specifically exercised by designated ministers within this context.

Second, there was a concern that in the aftermath of the *Geneva Memorandum* and BEM 'the triad came to be interpreted as referring almost exclusively to the structural and organizational life of the Church' rather than to the quality of the relations among members at various levels of the Church.[18] In particular, a great deal of attention was being given to the role of the laity as representatives of the community in decision-making procedures, specifically in synodal assemblies. Probably to avoid this tendency NMC offers a fuller formulation by asserting that the three modalities 'refer not only to particular structures and processes, but also describe the informal reality of the bonds of *koinonia*, the mutual belonging and accountability within the ongoing common life of the Church' (no. 94).

Third, in the paragraph devoted to the communal aspect of ministerial authority, it is stated that those ordained with ministerial oversight are to promote 'the participation of the whole community in what makes for its common life and the discernment of the mind of the faithful', which is founded on the sacrament of baptism, and that 'all the baptised share a responsibility for the apostolic faith and witness of the whole Church' (no. 96).

The conclusion drawn from these three claims is that the participation and responsibility of all the faithful is specified in terms of consultation, reception and assent. There is no explicit statement about the role of communal collective decision-making involving the lay faithful with those ordained. This is a decisive difference from BEM. *Communal* decision-making, as distinct from yet related to *collegial* decision-making, is not explicitly and unambiguously affirmed. So we read in paragraph no. 96: 'The communal dimension of the Church's life refers to the involvement of the whole body of the faithful in common consultation, sometimes through representation and constitutional structures, over the well-being of the Church and their common involvement in the service of God's mission in the world'. Does this sentence affirm a consultative-only approach to the communal dimension of the exercise of ministerial oversight, or does it imply communal decision-making by mentioning 'representative and constitutional structures?' I find the sentence ambiguous. These representative and constitutional structures may be consultative only or decision-making. The document's support of the collegial mode of decision-making is confirmed by additional statements made about synods, which will be treated below, and its ambiguity, if not total restriction, pertaining to communal decision-making is also further in evidence.

Concerning thesis 5, NMC also differs from BEM on communal synodal structures of decision-making. This topic is treated in two different contexts in NMC. In the paragraphs treating historical precedents in the early Church (no. 92) and after the Reformation (no. 93), *collegial* forms of synods are treated, but no mention is made of *communal* participation in synods. The most important statements about decision-making at synods and councils are found in the section addressing conciliarity in relation to primacy.[19] It should be noted that in the 1998 version of this document, then entitled *The Nature and Purpose of the Church*, conciliarity was identified with communality and synodality, not collegiality. In the 2005 document conciliarity is described in general terms as a characteristic of the Church, based on baptism that is operative at 'all levels of the life of the Church' (no. 99), but which operates specifically in terms of communal and collegial aspects of ministerial oversight (no. 102).

Synods – and I am assuming this pertains to councils – are convened 'to discern the apostolic truth over against particular threats and dangers to the life of the Church' (no. 100). Reception of the decrees by the entire Church affirms their importance and authority in 'fostering and maintaining universal communion'. Synods in the text appear to be *collegial* decision-making acts, not *communal*. In the following paragraph, however, a broader claim is made: 'Wherever people, communities or churches come together to take counsel and make important decisions, there is need for someone to summon and preside over the gathering for the sake of good order and to help the process of promoting, discerning and articulating consensus' (no. 101). This statement could apply to wider communal forms of discernment and decision-making, beyond collegial modalities, but this is not made explicit. Since the section is devoted to primacy, the argument is about the importance of relating primacy to conciliarity, both in terms of communal and collegial modalities. However, the role of discernment and decision-making is emphasized for collegial forms of conciliarity in synods, not communal forms. Making reference to canon 34 of the *Apostolic Canons*, the document says that 'the first among bishops would only make a decision in agreement with the other bishops and the latter would make no important decision without the agreement of the first' (102). The conclusion is that any model of primacy – universal, regional or local – as indeed any form of personal ministry 'would need to be exercised in communal and collegial ways' (no. 104), but this need not entail communal forms of conciliar decision-making.

In the end, it is clear that NMC admits that personal ministerial authority should involve a collegial dimension of oversight that includes collegial modes of discernment and decision-making with other ordained leaders. There is, however, a serious question about whether there is any room here for the role of communal modes of decision-making in synods and councils as exercised by many churches, if not in the Catholic Church. This affirmation of collegial decision is articulated in the following statements:

> Collegiality refers to the corporate, representative exercise in the areas of leadership, consultation, discernment, and decision-making. Collegiality entails the personal and relational nature of leadership and authority. Collegiality is at work wherever those entrusted with oversight gather, discern, speak and act as one on behalf of the whole Church (no. 97).

There is nothing comparable about the role of communal modes of decision-making in the Church operating in relation to personal and collegial modalities.

Amendments

Several passages in the 1998 edition that offered background doctrinal warrants for conciliar and synodal relationships in the exercise of oversight have been excised in the 2005 text. The first omission pertains to the analogy between the Trinity as a communion of persons and relations in the Church. The text reads:

> A ministry of oversight implies an ordering and differentiation within the communion of the Church. Such an ordering (*taxis*) is called to reflect the quality of ordering in the divine communion of Father, Son and Holy Spirit. The Church is a communion of co-responsible persons: no function, no gift, no charisma is exercised outside or above this communion. All are related through the one Spirit in the one Body. Such an ordering which reflects divine communion cannot imply domination or subordination (1998, no. 94).

A second text, contrasting viewpoints on the question of an order (*taxis*) and hierarchy in the divine trinitarian reality and their usefulness in determining the sacred order in ecclesial structures (see p. 49) has likewise been omitted in the 2005 text.[20]

Third, two paragraphs (nos. 99 and 100) in the 1998 version – one devoted to the ministry of discernment by the faithful based on the *sensus fidei* and *sensus fidelium*, the second on the role all baptized faithful play in 'the discernment of truth' – have been omitted in the 2005 text. This *sensus* is described in the 1998 version as 'a kind of spiritual perception, sense, discernment (flair) … by which baptised believers are enabled to recognize what is, or is not, an authentic echo of the voice of Christ in the teaching of the community; what is, or is not, in harmony with the truth of the Gospel' (no. 99). The document goes on to say: 'All must play their part in the discernment of the truth, by attentiveness to those with a special ministry of oversight and through the reception of the truth' (no. 100). Again we read: 'The communal life of the Church involves the coming together in council to seek and voice the mind of Christ for the Church in changing circumstances and in the face of the new challenges' (no. 100). It is important that this *sensus* is characterized in terms of discernment. What is noteworthy and indisputable is that this *sensus* is identified with the role played by recognition, attentiveness and reception of the truth among the faithful as conveyed by those with the special ministry of oversight (no. 100). What is puzzling is that this *sensus* is not also associated with the role of vigilance, guardianship and active participation of the faithful in discerning and decision-making in articulating the truth of the faith identity of the Church which yields consensus and also in the discernment and decisions that bear upon the Church's pastoral mission in local churches, regionally, and globally.

One final modification in the 2005 version merits comment. When the three aspects were introduced in the 1998 edition, the communal modality was treated first, followed by the personal, and then the collegial. With this ordering, the personal is thereby situated in relation to the communal, rather than vice versa. As Mary Tanner explains about the ordering in the 1998 version:

> The communal is grounded in the sacrament of baptism, which renders each person co-responsible for the faith and the mission of the Church. It emphasizes the *sensus fidei* in every member of the community. Personal oversight emerges through the discernment of the community under the guidance of the Holy Spirit and is exercised in relation to the community, both the local church and the communion of all the churches. This could turn out to be a timely correction to an over-concentration on structures and institutions, a return to the priority of the personal and the relational.[21]

In the 2005 version the personal was treated first in an order that affirms the priority of the apostolic witness and emphasizes that the ordained ministry functions as representative not merely of the Christianity community but also of the Lord to the Christian community; personal is followed by the communal, then the collegial.[22] BEM started with the personal aspect, then, treated the collegial, and finally the communal.

To conclude this section, are councils and synods decision-making in BEM and in NMC? Both documents emphasize the importance of collegial discernment and decision-making in synods. BEM also affirmed the importance of communal discernment and decision-making in synods, but the role of communal decision-making in NMC is denied or ambiguous at best. It is significant that the triadic principle has been widely, but not universally received by churches.[23] Most notably, this principle has not been utilized by the Roman Catholic Church in official documents or in ecumenical joint statements with other churches and communions. This is due to the conundrums facing the Catholic Church on the decision-making function of collegial and communal synods.

What Light Do These Documents Shed on the Catholic Conundrum?

Both BEM and NMC stand as an affirmation and encouragement of the Catholic Church's efforts in the aftermath of Vatican II to recover the doctrine and practices of episcopal collegiality at every level of the Church. Both BEM and NMC likewise assert the need to promote the active participation of the faithful in *communal discernment* of the truth of the gospel through consultation and reception, which is also important in light of Vatican II. There is a confusing message from BEM and NMC on *communal decision-making* in synods and councils. BEM affirms it, but NMC does not explicitly affirm it. NMC can be understood as subscribing to a consultative-only approach to the communal aspect of oversight, whether this was intended or not by those who crafted and approved this text. There may be some who would argue that this ambiguity or denial concerning communal decision-making shows growth in wisdom of the ecumenical community in keeping with the position and practice of Roman Catholics. If it is intended to affirm a consultative-only doctrine, I think it demonstrates the deficiency of the document.

How Can The Nature and Mission of the Church Be Improved?

The Nature and Mission of the Church has reaffirmed the importance of the relational framework provided by the triadic principle of personal, collegial and communal modalities of ministerial oversight and authority that was introduced in BEM. Moreover, it has expanded and deepened its analysis of all three aspects and their relationship to the nature and significance of synods and conciliarity. In particular, the recent version of NMC affirms the need for collegial discernment and decision-making in the Church in synodal structures. Discernment, consultation, reception and assent are the categories employed when it addresses the communal aspects of ministerial oversight. These are of utmost importance in the everyday life and practice of the Church, but the role of decision-making in communal forums like synods and councils, including the participation of representative lay members, needs to be unambiguously affirmed and situated within the larger framework of terms and relations established by the document in the following ways.

The Historical Issue: There should be some attention given in the historical section of the document to the participation of the lay faithful in collective discernment and decision-making processes, including synods and councils throughout the history of the Church in Catholic, Orthodox, Anglican, and Reformed traditions.

The Descriptive Issue: There is a need to assert descriptively that lay faithful have a decision-making role and obligation in certain communal synodal and conciliar forums in many churches at diverse levels of the church – parish/congregational, local church, regionally, nationally, and in some cases internationally.

The Prescriptive Issue: Prescriptively, the communal dimension of ministerial authority includes the importance of consultation and reception, which rests on an understanding of collective discernment. This much is prescriptively affirmed in the current version of the document. The question is whether communal decision-making needs to be included. I would propose that the decision-making can and should be affirmed at the level of principle as a constitutive ingredient in the communal modality of oversight. All of these ingredients – consultation, reception, discernment, decision-making – take on different forms at different levels of church life. Not all churches may agree that communal collective decision-making should be included at all levels of church life in all cases. However, the argument can be made prescriptively in principle, prescinding from articulating under what conditions and in what situations and with what limits such communal decision-making should take place. Within that context the document could state the areas of consensus, convergence and differences concerning what should be involved in the communal aspect of ministerial oversight.

The Theological Warrants: What are the theological warrants for the communal modality of ministerial oversight?

The first theological justification, the sacrament of baptism, is already treated in the document. The text affirms the pivotal importance of baptism in the exercise of oversight that all the faithful share in discernment and witness. 'The communal life of the Church is grounded in the sacrament of baptism. All the baptized share in a responsibility for the apostolic faith and witness of the whole Church' (no. 96). Certain questions follow. Does the authority of decision-making flows from this same baptismal charism? Does the responsibility for the faith and witness of the Church entail decision-making? Through baptism and more broadly through Rites of Christian Initiation an individual as a member of the community proceeds through a formation process so that they may learn how to discern and make decisions in one's life as an individual, but also so that as a member of a community one may participate fully in the life of the community and share in the Church's witness and mission in the world. Christian initiation into the life of faith should provide a preparation for one to learn how to discern and to make decisions as a disciple of Jesus Christ, to become a Christian agent in one's personal life and in the life of a Christian community and in the world. One is being baptized and initiated into a way of identity and mission as a Christian acting subject in the world which requires individual and collective decision-making and action in the world.

A second theological warrant is provided by the theology of *sensus fidei* and *sensus fidelium*. As I have indicated, this topic has been omitted from the 2005 version of the text. This undermines the communal modality of ministerial authority. There have been times when the doctrine of *sensus fidelium* has been used to pit the authority of the community against the authority of leaders, which simply reveals a defective formulation or application of the doctrine. There needs to be advanced a relational approach to the *sensus fidei* and the *sensus fidelium* that can establish the frame of reference for personal and collective discernment and guardianship in matters of faith. Discernment and guarding the faith of the Church is by baptism shared by all of the faithful, even though those ordained who exercise oversight personally and in collegial forms do so in particular manners, employ certain procedures, and act under certain conditions. The gift of the individual's *sensus fidei* is embedded in and reflective of the *sensus fidelium* of the entire community in the sharing of word and sacrament and in witness. Through this personal and collective form of faith one is not only able to discern the truth of the gospel, one is compelled to decide how to realize this in pastoral decisions in everyday life and in the local church. The doctrines of the *sensus fidei* and *sensus fidelium* compel all to participate and share responsibility in discerning and deciding about the pastoral mission in the local church, and these gifts from God set up the condition for the possibility of genuine consensus in decision-making and in actions.

A third and related theological warrant for communal discernment and decision-making is the anointing of the Spirit of God in baptism and the reception of the gifts of the Spirit associated with the threefold offices of Jesus Christ as priest, prophet and king. The anointing and gifts of the Spirit are bestowed so that the individual can contribute to 'the upbuilding of the Church' and participate in the mission of Jesus Christ in the world (NMC, nos. 83–4). In addition to becoming a priestly people and prophetic witness, the anointing of the Spirit provides the basis for exercising one's royal freedom in spiritual discernment and decision-making associated with the role of being vigilant, a guardian, a caretaker of the truth of the gospel in the Church and in advancing God's reign in the world.

Fourth, and finally, the doctrine of the Trinity continues to have a bearing on one's understanding of the identity of the Church – institutional and charismatic, with sacred order ('hierarchy' broadly construed) combined with non-subordinating relations, ordained and laity, unity and diversity – and on the mission of the Church. The document clearly affirms the doctrine of the Triune God as source of the Church and framework for understanding the Church, but the specific areas of convergence forged by the ongoing ecumenical discussion about the doctrine of the Trinity and its relation to the understanding of communion as they bear on ministry in general and the ministry of oversight in particular are not treated in the current version. I would propose that the ecumenical convergence about the doctrinal formulation of the Trinity as a communion of persons and the 'perichoretic' character of roles and relations provides a valuable doctrinal framework for understanding the relational and interdependent character of personal, collegial and communal aspects of oversight as it is exercised by the ordained and the laity in concert in the realization of the Church's identity and in advancing its mission. This triune relational understanding of God's identity and mission does not establish an institutional order for the Church that can be deduced, but it does provide an analogy that illuminates and should empower the members of the Church.

Notes

1. In *Baptism, Eucharist and Ministry* the text reads: 'The ordained ministry should be exercised in a personal, collegial and communal way' – Faith and Order Paper, 111 (Geneva: WCC, 1982), M no. 26. In *The Nature and the Mission of the Church*, Faith and Order Paper, 198 (Geneva: WCC, 2005), the text reads: 'Like every other aspect of ministry, episkopé both belongs to the whole church and is entrusted as a particular charge on specific persons. For this reason it is frequently stressed that, at every level of the Church's life, the ministry must be exercised in personal, communal and collegial ways' (no. 94).

2. For a recent statement on gift exchange in ecumenical relations, see the *Joint Working Group Between the Roman Catholic Church and the World Council of Churches*, Eighth Report 1999–2005 (Geneva: WCC, 2005), no. 21. On the wounded character of the churches, the recent US Lutheran–Catholic joint statement speaks of a 'mutual recognition that our ordained ministries are wounded because [of] the absence of full communion ... and that our communities are wounded by their lack of ... full catholicity' – in *The Church as Koinonia of Salvation: Its Structures & Ministries*. Lutherans and Catholics in Dialogue X, ed. Randall Lee and Jeffrey Gros (Washington: USCCB; ELCA, 2005), no. 103. The gifted and wounded character of the churches in relation to the communal, collegial and personal aspects of exercising ministerial oversight is affirmed in the BEM commentary when it states: 'In various churches, one or another [of the aspects] has been over-emphasized at the expense of others' (p. 26). This is echoed in the 1998 version of NMC (box, p. 53), with the added question: 'Each church needs to ask itself in what way its exercise of the ordained ministry has suffered in the course of history'.

3. Paul Murray (ed.), *Receptive Ecumenism: The Call to Catholic Learning* (London: Oxford University Press, 2007).

4. The issues raised by the consultative-only are treated in my book, *Practices of Dialogue in the Roman Catholic Church: Aims and Obstacles, Lessons and Laments* (London and New York: Continuum, 2006).

5. On consultative-only clauses see *Code of Canon Law: Latin–English Edition* (Washington, DC: Canon Law Society of America, 1999): The synod of bishops (canon 343); particular councils – plenary, provincial – participants who are not bishops (canons 443); diocesan synods (canon 465); presbyteral councils (canon 499, §2), diocesan pastoral council (canon 514), parish pastoral council (canon 536 §2).

6. See Lukas Vischer, 'The Reception of the Debate on Collegiality', in *The Reception of Vatican II*, ed. Giuseppe Alberigo, Jean-Pierre Jossua and Joseph A. Komonchak, trans. Matthew J. O'Connell (Washington, DC: The Catholic University of American Press, 1987), pp. 233–48, esp. p. 236.

7. Original text found in *Faith and Order Proceedings of the World Conference Lausanne, August 3–21, 1927*, ed. H. N. Bate (New York: George H. Doran Co., 1927), p. 469; cited in *Baptism, Eucharist and Ministry*, p. 26.

8. For a helpful analysis of these different forms, see Edward LeRoy Long, Jr, *Patterns of Polity: Varieties of Church Governance* (Cleveland, Ohio: The Pilgrim Press, 2001).

9. Lukas Vischer recognizes a similar expansion of the meaning of collegiality beyond episcopal relations among Catholics in the aftermath of Vatican II, see 'The Reception of the Debate on Collegiality', p. 234.

10. For what follows, on the role of the Geneva consultation in 1979 and on other matters related to the triad principle, I am deeply indebted to Mary Tanner for bringing to my attention her essay on this topic. I have drawn from an earlier manuscript entitled, 'Personal, Collegial and Communal', which has some additional material, and from the published text,

'A Case for Re-form: Personal, Collegial and Communal', which appeared in *Travelling with Resilience: Essays for Alastair Haggart*, ed. Elizabeth Templeton (Edinburgh: General Office of the Scottish Episcopal Church, 2002), pp. 103–19. For the Accra Report see *One Baptism, One Eucharist and a Mutually Recognised Ministry*. Faith and Order Paper, 73 (Geneva: WCC, 1975).

11. John Zizioulas, 'Episkopé and Episkopos in the Early Church: A Brief Survey of the Evidence', *Episkopé and Episcopate in Ecumenical Perspective*. Faith and Order Paper, 62 (Geneva: WCC, 1980), pp. 30–42, at pp. 37–8.

12. Memorandum, *Episkopé and Episcopate in Ecumenical Perspective*, pp. 6–7; the list of fourteen participants and four Faith and Order staff members is provided on p. 13.

13. International Anglican–Roman Catholic Commission, 'Authority in the Church I (Venice Statement) 1976', in *Growth in Agreement: Reports and Agreed Statements of Ecumenical Conversations on a World Level*. Faith and Order Paper, 108, ed. Harding Meyer and Lukas Vischer (New York: Paulist Press; Geneva: WCC, 1984), pp. 88–105. George Tavard offered helpful insights into the communal dimension of authority in the Venice Statement in relation to ordained and collegial modes of authority (9/9/2006).

14. Group of Les Dombes, 'The Episcopal Ministry' (1976) in *One in Christ* 14 (1978): 267–88; idem, 'For a Reconciliation of Ministries' (the actual date is 1972 although it was published in 1973) in *Modern Ecumenical Documents on the Ministry* (London: SPCK, 1975), pp. 87–107.

15. It is noteworthy that this document suggests that Roman Catholics need to be encouraged to implement collegial and synodical structures so that bishops can promote shared responsibility and decision-making with members of people of God in the local church (272, 285–6). Lutheran and Reformed theologians are admonished to overcome the kind of maneuvering associated with parliamentary procedures utilized in their presbyterian-synodical structure of decisions-making, but also by 'the restoration of the value of the ministry of episcope, including its expression in particular persons' (287).

16. The commentary on the Ministry section, no. 16, included in BEM reads:

Here two dangers must be avoided. Authority cannot be exercised without regard for the community. The apostles paid heed to the experience and the judgment of the faithful. On the other hand, the authority of ordained ministers must not be so reduced as to make them dependent on the common opinion of the community. Their authority lies in their responsibility to express the will of God in the community.

17. The affirmation of collaboration is further specified in NMC beyond the formulation in BEM in terms of the entire community's support and assent and the exercise of ministerial leadership as set apart from the community (no. 90).

18. Tanner, 'Personal, Collegial and Communal' (MS.), p. 5; cf. 'A Case for Re-Form', pp. 114–16.

19. I am not going to comment on the treatment of primacy, which is the main aim of this section, other than to say that the entire section is devoted to arguing that primacy (e.g., bishop of Rome, patriarch, archbishop, but in principle any form of ministerial oversight at any level of the Church) should exercise authority in a dynamic relation with conciliar relations, that is, explicitly understood as communal and collegial.

20. The relation of the Triune God and the Church are treated in part I of the 1998 and the 2005 editions and in a box devoted to 'The Institutional Dimension of the Church and the Work of the Spirit', but the substance of the omitted material is not reproduced in these earlier sections of the 2005 document.

21. Tanner, MS., p. 8.

22. I am indebted to John W. Hind, Anglican Bishop of Chichester, Church of England, for offering a rationale for this change of order.

23. Mary Tanner has identified the impact of the triadic principle on the work of the Anglican Communion evident in The Anglican International Theological and Doctrinal Commission, *The Virginia Report* (1997) (London: Morehouse Publishing, 1999), pp. 18–19, as well as its

reception in various bilateral statements: *The Meissen Common Statement* (1992) of the Church of England and the Evangelical Church of Germany (CCU Occasional Paper, 2, 1992); *The Porvoo Common Statement* (1993) of the Anglican churches of Britain and Ireland and the Nordic and Baltic Lutheran Churches in *Together in Mission and Ministry* (London: Church House Publishing, 1993), p. 31; *The Reuilly Common Statement* (1999) of the Anglican churches of Britain and England and the French Lutheran and Reformed churches in *Called to Witness and Service: The Reuilly Common Statement with Essays on Church, Eucharist and Ministry* (London: Church House Publishing, 1999). The triadic principle was not used in the International Anglican–Roman Catholic Commission in *The Gift of Authority: Authority in the Church III* (1998); a synodal way of life is mentioned, but it 'has very little to say about synods and nothing about a synod at the world level in which laity are present' (Tanner, MS., p. 6), which may reflect concerns raised about the role of representative laity in decision-making communal processes.

Chapter 8

IS THERE A FUTURE FOR THE CATHOLIC–PROTESTANT DIALOGUE? NON-RECEPTION AS CHALLENGE TO ECUMENICAL DIALOGUE

Korinna Zamfir

The aim of this study is to address the issue of non-reception as a phenomenon that severely jeopardizes the chances for interconfessional communion. Thus my intention is to emphasize that, notwithstanding significant results reached in Catholic–Protestant dialogue, the non-reception of these results questions the future and the rationale of such theological dialogue. My study offers a personal Catholic perspective, often pointing to parallels between the insight of the ecumenical documents and Catholic theological reflection. Despite the achieved convergence, the evolution of the ecumenical situation, and the tendency manifest in ecclesiastical declarations on all sides, points to a lack of interest by both theologians and church leadership for the reception of these common insights and in the promotion of ecclesial communion. Thus non-reception is a major issue which should be seriously analysed and addressed.

In a first section I point to some of the elements of convergence already reached, without entering into the details about the substance of this convergence or insisting on the remaining differences. The following part focuses on the levels of non-reception of the common ecclesiological insights. Afterwards, some of the causes of the non-reception are discussed. The final section comes back to the question articulated in my title and formulates some conclusions.

Existing Ecclesiological Convergence

The examination of the Catholic–Protestant (WCC and bilateral, especially Catholic–Lutheran[1]), dialogue concerning ecclesiology and related topics, such as the Eucharist and ministry reveals very diverse understandings of many previously controversial questions. As it is not the goal of this study to give a detailed presentation of the existing theological convergence, only some of the main issues will be mentioned briefly. Remaining differences notwithstanding, most of the documents express an agreement upon the trinitarian origin of the Church, as well as the Church's christological and pneumatic, spiritual, and institutional dimensions.[2]

Within ecumenical dialogue the broader entity of the Church of Christ compared with the denominations is explicitly formulated in the Toronto Declaration, and reaffirmed by *Towards a Common Understanding and Vision of the World Council of Churches*,[3] as well as by the recent *Called to Be the One Church*.[4] Although serious differences exist as to the way Catholic theology describes the relationship of the Catholic Church to the Church of Christ, in the ecclesiological texts of Vatican II and in postconciliar Catholic ecclesiology, the Church of Christ is also perceived as more inclusive than the Roman Catholic institutional body. Thus, *Lumen gentium* defines the Church as the universal sacrament of salvation that transcends the limits of the institution: the Church of Christ subsists in the Catholic Church, but several ecclesial elements, i.e., 'many elements of sanctification and of truth are found outside of its visible confines'.[5] *Lumen gentium* deliberately avoids a full identification of the two entities, dropping the unequivocal word *est* from the initial draft.[6] Subsequently, after a long tradition of denying any ecclesial realm outside the borders of the Catholic Church, conciliar theology admits that several ecclesial elements can be found outside the institutional Church, and recognizes the role of non-Catholic Christianity within the path to salvation.[7]

A fundamental paradigm defining the Church in both ecumenical documents[8] and in Catholic theology[9] is that of *communio/koinonia*. This model has become central in the main Faith and Order ecclesiological texts of the last decade,[10] which stress anew the trinitarian dimension of this communion.[11]

Consensus exists on the importance of both the universal and local church. Thus, according to *The Church: Local and Universal*, a document of the Joint Working Group of the Roman Catholic Church and the WCC (1990), the eschatological-pneumatological perspective points to the simultaneous existence and the equal importance of the universal and the local church.[12] Approaching this relationship from the angle of the divine plan of salvation, the universal Church, as a manifestation of God's saving will, is understood to have absolute priority. Nevertheless, according to its historical existence, the Church is realized in the local church, which has to preserve communion with all the other local churches.[13] This balanced description of the relationship between the universal and the local church is found in *Lumen gentium* nos. 23 and 26 as well.[14]

Agreement extends to the privileged significance of apostolic doctrine compared with the ministry carrying it. This pre-eminence of the continuity in the apostolic doctrine, alongside with the re-evaluation of the importance of the episcopacy, is stated in the ecumenical documents.[15] The Lima Document, *Baptism, Eucharist and Ministry* (BEM), emphasizes not only the witness of the whole Church, but also the importance of personal *episkope*, namely that of the bishop.[16] The importance of this kind of continuity is also expressed in Catholic–Lutheran dialogue.[17] While the Lutheran position focuses on the apostolic continuity of the whole Church,[18] it does not place the same emphasis on episcopacy as the Catholic Church does.[19] On the other hand, the Lima Document invites the churches that, because of historical reasons, have not preserved the threefold ministry, to regard episcopacy as a sign of the apostolic continuity and unity of the Church, and thereby to consider reintroducing it, although they do not lack continuity with the apostolic teaching.[20] BEM also invites the churches that have kept episcopal succession to consider that the apostolic faith, the continuity in worship and mission, could have been preserved even in those churches that have lost this type of institutional continuity.[21] Even if the Catholic Church has doubts regarding the validity of Protestant ordinations, ecumenical dialogue has made it aware of the existence of a ministry of the word and sacraments in Protestant churches, analogous to the functions of priesthood in the Roman Catholic Church. Protestant churches have also preserved the function of *episkopé*, in the original, broad sense of oversight.[22]

According to mainly postconciliar Catholic theology, episcopal succession is an important sign of apostolicity, without being identical to it, nor functioning as an automatic guarantee of it.[23] In ideal cases, there is a coincidence between the continuity of the apostolic tradition and the office serving it. However, in certain situations, apostolic tradition can be preserved in spite of an interruption of the ministerial continuity, since God can act outside the sacraments,[24] just as, in other circumstances, the apostolic teaching can be obscured notwithstanding historical continuity in ministry.[25] These facts, along with ecumenical convergence in the interpretation of ministry, allow a much more nuanced Roman Catholic approach to the apostolicity of Protestant churches. Since the apostolic character of the episcopal ministry is an integral part of the apostolicity of the Church as a whole, it is first of all the Church as a whole that ensures the continuity with the teaching and life of the apostolic Church.[26]

There is agreement about the need for a ministry ensuring *episkopé* (oversight) in a personal, collegial and communal way in both *The Nature and Purpose of the Church* and the subsequent *The Nature and Mission of the Church*. The ecumenical documents agree that the responsibility to preserve the apostolic faith is the task of the Church as a whole, but also that already in the first centuries a particular office of oversight has emerged, in order to preserve the unity of the Church in the context of a multitude of gifts and ministries.[27] Thus the more recent documents underscore the personal, communal and collegial dimension of *episkopé*.[28] In addition, documents agree upon the goal of the visible communion, through the recognition of baptism, Eucharist, ministry, and a common service and mission.[29] Significant agreement has been reached regarding the Eucharist.[30] Despite remaining divergence, considerable convergence was attained in respect to the origin and function of ordained ministry as well.[31]

The Levels of Non-Reception

Notwithstanding many ecumenical documents and the elaboration of a genuinely ecumenical ecclesiology by both Catholic and Protestant theologians, during the last decades not only have these endeavours remained without any practical consequence, but, in addition, confessional borders have been reinforced on all sides. The results of dialogue have found hardly any reception and ecumenical relations can be characterized as rather frozen. This evolution is serious, since non-reception questions the very logic of the discussions and the future of the ecumenical dialogue. The non-reception of the theological convergence is manifest at the level of the official church statements, in some theologians' position, in the self-consciousness and everyday life of the local communities, and in the tendencies marking the work of the ecumenical forums.

In what follows, my essay addresses some of these levels of non-reception, reflecting on the examples mentioned in the preceding section. Thus, this part of the article refers to statements and responses that reflect the rejection of previously formulated consensus or convergence.

(a) One of the most obvious examples of the non-reception is in the evidence found in church statements.

The aforementioned document issued by the Joint Working Group of the Roman Catholic Church and the World Council of Churches, *The Church: Local and Universal*, despite the balanced ecclesiology and its nuanced description of the relationship between the universal and the local church, has had no reception in churches. Instead the Congregation for the Doctrine of the Faith issued in 1992 a text entitled the *Communionis notio*,[32] which, besides rightly appreciating that the local church has to preserve its intimate connection with the universal Church, also formulated some problematic statements about the temporal and ontological pre-existence of the universal Church. Additionally, these statements seemed to identify the universal Church with the Catholic Church.[33]

While postconciliar Catholic theology asserts the existence of ecclesial elements outside the borders of the Catholic Church, and proposes a more comprehensive definition of the Church, deliberately avoiding an identification of the Catholic Church with the Church of Christ, the latest official statements do not admit the realization of the Church in Protestant Christianity. These communities are not seen as churches in the proper sense (*Dominus Iesus* no. 17).[34] One notices a clear shift from the inclusive ecclesiology of *Lumen gentium* no. 8 and *Unitatis redintegratio* ch. III, which emphasize the ecclesiological significance of Protestant Christianity, to the exclusive ecclesiology that stresses the full and almost sole ecclesial character of the Catholic Church, in opposition to the Protestant communities, which merely preserve elements of the Church of Christ but cannot be regarded as churches. Despite the fact that basically the words of the conciliar texts are repeated, the indisputable change in meaning reflects a clear tendency to demarcate. It has been assumed that *Dominus Iesus* merely repeats previously expressed Roman Catholic doctrine.[35] However, several Roman Catholic theologians remark that the document is an obvious manifestation of the non-reception of the conciliar and postconciliar shift in Catholic ecclesiology.[36] The same non-reception of Vatican II is noticed by some outstanding Protestant theologians such as Wolfhart Pannenberg or Eberhard Jüngel.[37] However, this position does not only characterize the statements of the Catholic Church. Thus, the 2001 ecclesiological report of the Evangelische Kirche in Deutschland entitled *Kirchengemeinschaft nach evangelischem Verständnis* (2001) clarifies that the Lutheran and Catholic position concerning the visible unity of the Church, the Petrine ministry, and the apostolic succession are incompatible.[38] This clear official statement is evidently a reaction to the Catholic *Dominus Iesus*, issued one year earlier, and this is not an unprecedented position. German Catholic–Lutheran dialogue has produced during the last thirty years many important convergence texts (one of most valuable being the study document *Lehrverurteilungen – kirchentrennend?*[39]) and has expressed a growing common understanding regarding the origin and function of ministry. This has even contributed to a convergence in the understanding of sacramentality that is acceptable to Protestant churches.[40] Yet the official reception from the Protestant side has at best been ambivalent. It is the case that, according to the Vereinigte Evangelisch-Lutherische Kirche Deutschland (VELKD), the churches of the Reformation should abstain from prejudging today's Roman Catholic understanding of the sacramental character of ordination.[41] Furthermore, both the VELKD and the Arnoldshain Conference[42] correctly argued that ordination cannot confer a higher status of grace. Yet the Arnoldshain Conference clearly rejected the idea that ordination conveys grace, as in its statement it did not distinguish between personal and office-related grace, and as such adopted a somewhat different position from that of the VELKD.[43] The Arnoldshain Conference openly stated that ordination could not be a sacrament, while the VELKD stressed that it cannot be an instrument of salvation/ of grace, being therefore different from the sacraments.[44] These positions point to the lack of reception of ecumenical convergence reached by theologians.

Convergence related to ordination and episcopacy did not lead to an official reception on either side, notwithstanding the invitation addressed by BEM to reconsider the importance of both the threefold ministry and of non-episcopal ordinations. Protestant churches did not reconsider the significance of episcopacy. The reflections regarding the possible recognition of Lutheran ordinations were not received by the Catholic Church. Thus, although the *defectus ordinis* stated by *Unitatis redintegratio* no. 22 is understood by several representative Catholic theologians as a deficiency and not a lack of valid Protestant ordained ministry[45], and in spite of the already mentioned convergence on the origin and function of ministry (BEM, M55), *Dominus Iesus* stated the invalidity of Protestant ordination. Concrete steps toward the mutual recognition of ministries suggested by *Facing Unity* in 1984 received practically no reaction, and the document was eventually forgotten.[46]

(b) The non-reception can also be noticed among theologians, albeit that more than twenty years ago Karl Rahner had thought that subsequent to ecumenical dialogue no serious theologian could perceive the teaching of another Church as fundamentally non-Christian.[47] In what follows only some examples are mentioned.

The theses elaborated by Karl Rahner and Heinrich Fries in *Einigung der Kirchen – Reale Möglichkeit* (1983) were criticized by both Catholic and Protestant theologians. Joseph Ratzinger dismissed this work as 'a forced ride to unity ... an artistic piece of theological acrobatics, which unfortunately does not exist in reality'.[48] The theses of Rahner and Fries encountered opposition from some Protestant theologians as well. Eilart Herms formulated a radical 'counter-proposal', motivated by a deep mistrust toward the Catholic Church, implying that all its involvement in the ecumenical movement was an insidious strategy meant to determine the return of the non-Catholics to Roman doctrine and papal authority. Thus, wrote Herms, the still existing fundamental opposition between the teaching of the Protestant churches and the Roman doctrine is overlooked, instead of being admitted and accepted as right and necessary.[49] Fries rightly regarded Herms' response as an expression of the '*antirömische Affekt*'.[50] The Rahner–Fries theses, though formulating a significant amount of serious theological reflection and intended to raise awareness regarding the existing theological convergence, were finally forgotten.

Another example is found in the *Common Declaration on Justification* (1999). The document is the articulation of ecumenical dialogue over many years, and clarifies many of the old controversial issues. Consequently, the signatories were able to state that in their view the remaining differences were no longer church-dividing, but were expressions of the differences in theological formulation and language. One should not neglect, of course, the remaining differences, but these should not stand in the way of the achieved convergence. Nevertheless, the document was fully rejected by a large number of Protestant theologians, as allegedly it did not provide any clarification. Rejection was partially motivated by feared ecclesiological implications.[51]

A further example concerns a position found in some Catholic circles, which questions the relevance of *Unitatis redintegratio*. This stance led the Pontifical Council for Promoting Christian Unity to issue a notification regarding the ongoing significance of this conciliar document and its consequences for Catholic involvement in the ecumenical movement.[52] Other theologians consider that ecumenical endeavours are responsible for the decrease in missionary fervour, and the rise of general religious indifference and relativism.[53] This points to a certain need to define identity in opposition to other identities.

(c) Over the last two decades, a shift has occurred in the priorities and goals of the ecumenical forums, especially in the WCC. While the issues of social justice, peace and the integrity of creation rightly enjoy major attention, theological dialogue has become a second-rank task. (It is evident from the contents of the *Ecumenical Review* or reading the WCC newsletter how seldom theological questions appear on the agenda of the WCC or are discussed in its periodicals.) A relevant example is Samuel Kobia's analysis of the new trends in the ecumenical movement.[54] While it is certain that struggles for justice and peace are extremely important, just as are attempts to open up interreligious dialogue, and while it is also true that 'Southern' Christianity has little to do with the older theological controversies of the Northern hemisphere, one cannot help wondering whether these legitimate endeavours are entitled to eclipse theological dialogue, and whether the opening toward other religions is a realistic goal, when Christianity is still unable to overcome its internal divisions.

The retreat from previously reached agreement to be seen within the forums of ecumenical dialogue is obvious if we compare the evolution of certain topics within successive documents. Within the WCC this phenomenon is rightly identified by André Birmelé, who notes some examples. Thus, while Canberra expressed a need for mutual recognition of the churches, the WCC document *Towards a Common Understanding and Vision of the World Council of Churches* (1996) returns to the position expressed by the Toronto statement, which asserts that churches do not have to recognize each other; similarly, the preamble of the

Harare Report (1998) written in the spirit of Canberra was dropped from later editions.[55]

Discussions within the WCC related to the form in which unity should be manifested: Uppsala (1968) and especially Nairobi (1975) pointed to the need for a conciliar structure. This tendency was influenced by the positive example of Vatican II that had recently taken place.[56] Church fellowship was increasingly linked to visible manifestations of unity, without promoting a theological or institutional uniformity. This idea was still preserved by Canberra,[57] although Lukas Vischer pertinently noted the vagueness of Canberra's formulation, when compared to the Nairobi statement.[58] If one considers the later ecclesiological documents, it is noticeable that the interest in a conciliar structure almost disappears, even if *The Nature and Purpose of the Church*[59] still mentions the conciliar dimension in relation to forms of exercising *episkope'* in a collegial way. In NMC nos. 97–104 the issue is also addressed, but in an explanation related to issues of conciliarity and primacy, not only primacy, but conciliarity as well is presented as a matter of disagreement between the churches. It is true that the study document issued at Porto Alegre re-emphasizes the need for full visible unity, for a *koinonia* that is expressed in the common confession of the apostolic faith, the common life including sacramental communion, the mutual recognition of members and ministries, a common mission and witness, 'through a conciliar relationship of churches in different places'.[60] But given the above-mentioned doubts expressed in NMC, one has one to wonder whether this latest invitation addressed by the Porto Alegre general assembly will find acceptance in the churches, and whether this conciliar relationship refers to regular conciliar structures.

As already noted, the Lima Document, BEM, had a very positive approach to ordained ministry and the threefold structure of ministry, even to the point of inviting those churches which have not kept this model to consider reintroducing it. This invitation was no longer mentioned in *The Nature and Purpose of the Church*, even though it relies heavily on BEM in defining apostolicity. NMC points instead to the fact that the churches remain divided about the need for a historical episcopate, and that some churches reject it.[61] The Catholic–Lutheran *Communio Sanctorum* adds no significantly new element of agreement, and, despite previous discussions, expresses the same divergence regarding sacramentality in general and in respect to ministry in particular.[62]

A decrease in agreement is also to be seen in relation to understanding the Eucharist. While BEM seemed to have reached a significant convergence (e.g., the concept of anamnesis), in *The Nature and Purpose of the Church* previously resolved issues are questioned.[63] Also in NMC in addressing the topic of the Eucharist, the issue of the presence of Christ and of the meaning of anamnesis, as well as the role of the invocation of the Holy Spirit, are indicated as matters of disagreement.[64]

Some Causes For Non-Reception

Contrary to what one would have expected, the growing convergence in so many previously church-dividing matters did not lead the churches to take steps toward mutual recognition. (I refer here in particular to the Catholic–Protestant relationship, since intra-Protestant dialogue has led to various forms of mutual recognition. On the other hand, the same can be said for Catholic–Orthodox relations.) Instead, boundaries have once again been strengthened. Due to fear of the loss of identity, independence, or prerogatives, churches have retreated from a decisive step toward fellowship. The results of ecumenical dialogue have not become part of official ecclesial doctrine, nor of broader theological reflection.

The political and sociocultural situation, as well as psychological factors, may set major obstacles in the way of church fellowship. Challenges posed to Christian identity by modern and postmodern society, including globalization and political instability, were followed by a deep fear of losing national and cultural identity, as well as political and economic independence. Increasing pressure created by a globalized world, the gradual decrease of identification-markers defining the self, and the significant pressure created by the presence of non-Christian religions have led to a growing sense of fear of losing individual and collective religious identity. Increasing fear has led to a revival of confessionalism[65] and fundamentalism.

Confessionalism and fundamentalism are expanding phenomena in all Christian traditions. In an instructive analysis of Catholic fundamentalism (an otherwise uncommon discussion, for within Christianity fundamentalism is generally associated with Evangelical movements), following the classical work of James Barr and also referring to Bruce B. Lawrence, John D'Arcy May points to the intellectual-psychological motivations lying behind this phenomenon expanding within every church. This is precisely the context out of which *Dominus Iesus* emerges. Thus, 'fundamentalism is a particular form of reaction to modernity, defensive and hostile yet in a paradoxical way rationalistic, for its basic strategy is to declare certain doctrines and principles of interpretation valid a priori and therefore immune from literary contextualization or historical criticism'.[66] This is, of course, far from being solely a Catholic phenomenon but is deeply related to a widespread fear of losing one's identity and to the need for a sense of stability and clarity.[67] In any case, it is obvious that such a mindset is incompatible with sustaining dialogue or with the reception of a convergence which might be thought to destabilize clearly defined, immutable truths.

Congar had earlier noted the intimate relationship among ecclesiology, pneumatology, and the understanding of reception. A strictly hierarchic definition of the Church diminishes the emphasis on the role of the Spirit as the source of infallibility, and reception is reduced to mere approval of the decrees issued by a higher authority.[68] Reception based on sensitivity to the action of the Spirit manifested in a dialogical theology and trust in the *sensus fidei fidelium* is dynamic communitarian reception. Conversely, it is also true that a total lack of the sense of authority can lead to non-reception as well. Evidence of this can be seen in the case of Protestant Christianity in the statements issued by the Lutheran and Reformed

World Federations, or in the documents of ecumenical forums, such as the WCC.[69] In the large, more tradition-bound and hierarchically structured churches (as the Catholic and Orthodox churches), a certain mistrust toward theologians can also be detected. Their working hypotheses and theses seem to some to be casting doubt on unquestionable and unchangeable truths. This mistrust can in certain cases reach the magnitude of an 'anti-theological affect' (Bernd Jochen Hilberath).[70] In other cases, it is not only fundamentalism, but also an unwillingness to recognize the other confession and to confer communion, that can be connected to a 'mindset that goes with holding power',[71] a factor that emphasizes the importance of church-policy factors.

Non-inclusion in the process of growing mutual understanding and spiritual fellowship experienced by the participants in the ecumenical conversation may also result in the non-reception of the theological dialogue.[72] Most theologians are not actively involved in the elaboration of the ecumenical documents, therefore they may perceive these documents as mere theoretical constructs outside their area of specialization or formulated by a narrow group without wide consultation.

An additional aspect is the shift of the focus of theological research from ecumenical dialogue to interreligious dialogue, as well as a move from classical theology to the field of religious studies. Interest in interreligious dialogue is understandable given the powerful presence of non-Christian religions in Western society. The contemporary situation is related to global political instability, and to the partly objective, and partly exaggerated fear of Islamic fundamentalism. The growing attention enjoyed by religious studies is partly due to the decrease of the interest in an 'engaged' classical theology. (It is beyond the scope of this study to make statements of value regarding this evolution.) Such tendencies in contemporary theological-religious scholarship are not illegitimate. The particular interest in interreligious and intercultural research, as well as the emergence of religious studies within many Western academic contexts, are phenomena partly motivated by the attraction of a less exhausted and thus more appealing field of investigation. This has certainly contributed to ecumenical dialogue being perceived as outdated. This tendency, of course, points to theology and theological currents as being construed in response to contemporary challenges and conflicts. But this evolution is also an expression of the continual scholarly quest for uninvestigated, perhaps 'exotic' topics, and of theology being subject to certain 'fashionable' trends.

While Western European churches are marked by the renewal of confessionalism, as a response to the fear of losing religious identity, given the expansion of the religious market that awakens insecurity, in Eastern Europe confessionalism remains a continuous presence. This phenomenon is linked to a deep traditionalism rooted in the political and cultural isolation caused by the severe oppression practised by the dictatorial regimes. Political oppression and cultural isolation have led to a deep mistrust, which continues to be handed down to the present time. Subsequently, theological dialogue is absent in some regions, and international dialogue has had a low impact on theological formation.

Korinna Zamfir

Is There Hope for a Catholic–Protestant Communion?

It is clear that in the absence of reception the most detailed and in-depth agreement is useless. Non-reception is therefore a major challenge to the future of ecclesiological dialogue and should be addressed by a clear strategy.

There are certainly factors that cannot be influenced by theologians, not even by those most committed to ecumenical dialogue. One cannot change the global political, social and cultural contexts in which theology is constructed. Nor can one change church policy, which in some churches involves control over theology and theologians, and focuses on the preservation of existing structures and boundaries. The sense of fear so manifest within certain ecclesial contexts is almost impossible to address. The struggle in some theological departments to preserve 'classical' theological disciplines appears to be doomed by the dazzling advance toward more 'modern' fields of research. In the face of such realities, church communion based on a common understanding of basic statements of faith would seem to be hopeless.

On the other hand, although it might seem to be commonplace, communication, continuous dialogue within the academic and ecclesiastic communities, and lived spiritual communion are necessary prerequisites for continuous reception. Nevertheless, one of the fundamental questions is whether theologians themselves still consider that ecclesial communion is a task deserving attention and commitment.

Despite being criticized for flaws, the recent *Princeton Proposal* (2003), elaborated by the North American Center for Catholic and Evangelical Theology, seems to be one such sign of hope. The document was born out of a desire to overcome contemporary ecumenical scepticism, even if the chances of such an initiative to produce significant changes are regarded as slim.[73] Although the *Princeton Proposal* does not formulate a radically new plan, or precisely because it builds on a previously reached agreement, namely the New Delhi vision, it marks a renewed interest in the endeavour to accomplish ecclesial communion, understood as an integral part of Christian life.[74] The specific interest of this proposal lies in the emphasis it places on visible communion,[75] which has become rather uncommon in recent years. This contrasts with the unclear view in NMC concerning ecclesial communion.[76] (This by no means diminishes the significance of the latter document.) Thus, in the *Princeton Proposal*, the confession of one Lord in one baptism, communion in the apostolic faith and in the proclamation of one gospel, eucharistic communion, the mutual recognition of ministries and of the faithful, as suggested in New Delhi, are reiterated.[77] The document emphasizes the need for a common Christian identity and criticizes illegitimate pluralism that contradicts the apostolic message. It also criticizes the maintenance of the status quo that prevents the achievement of ecclesial communion.[78] The *Princeton Proposal* even states that persisting historical divisions are not always motivated by the quest for truth.[79] The overstressed adherence to confessional identity is perceived as endangering the realization of communion, in a way that is parallel with a view expressed by the French-speaking ecumenical group of Reformed and Catholic theologians, the *Groupe des Dombes*.[80]

On the other hand, the steps articulated by the *Princeton Proposal* in the spirit of New Delhi[81] either echo earlier documents or reflect a less concrete vision compared with previous documents. Thus, the suggestion to invite members belonging to different confessions to participate in teaching forums of other churches echoes the proposal formulated in *Facing Unity* to create common forums of decision-making on the way toward a commonly recognized and practised ministry and *episkopé*. At the same time, the *Princeton Proposal* goes beyond this suggestion, since it refers not only to an executive but to a doctrinal collaboration as well.[82] Still, the vision concerning the steps to be taken toward the mutual recognition of ministries is far less concrete compared with those found in *Facing Unity*,[83] and the proposal does not really deal with eucharistic sharing.

However, the *Princeton Proposal* deserves attention precisely because it re-emphasizes the serious need for a commitment to the aim of visible communion. Despite this positive attitude, it should be noted finally that this proposal is a rather isolated initiative that does not reflect the general position of ecumenical forums. Furthermore, it is unlikely that its vision would be embraced by many European theological or ecclesial circles. Likewise, the Princeton text reflects the endeavour of a rather restricted circle, compared with the wide membership of the WCC. This again testifies to the fact that a forum having a larger and more diverse membership has greater difficulties in reaching consensus.

Conclusion

It is clear that ecclesiological dialogue makes no sense if it is not followed by reception, both theological and ecclesial. The evolution of the last two decades indicates that the answer to the question formulated in the title of my study tends to be 'no', rather than 'yes'. It is noteworthy that this overview of reception shows not only that deeper consensus and communion have not been reached, but also that previous stages of agreement have been abandoned.

Non-reception and the retreat from the move toward ecclesial communion are not due to the impossibility of reaching solutions on divisive theological matters. Nor are they the result of a failure of theological dialogue as such. Rather, the retreat from progress toward communion is related to the ineffectiveness of the second level of the dialogue, namely the implementation of its results, a level influenced primarily by non-theological factors.

However, the question regarding the future remains open. I do not claim to have an answer regarding the prospects of ecclesiological dialogue or a strategy to promote reception. My brief overview of the causes of non-reception, and the reference to a positive example (the *Princeton Proposal*) is intended to identify the barriers to reception and to emphasize the fact that those factors should be considered that can be influenced.

First, the responsibility of the theologians is enormous despite their rather limited means. The lived communion of theological and spiritual exchange among theologians should be as inviting as possible to others. It is more likely that reception will emerge from informal theological reflection and shared communion rather than from official ecclesial forums.

Secondly, a factor that can be addressed is that of the partners involved. Bilateral dialogues and agreements are an important opportunity, since it is clear that the broader the palette of confessions and theological views is, the fewer the chances for consensus, as the evolution within the WCC suggests. This by no means implies the futility of a broader dialogue. In this context, it is crucial to take very concrete steps after any reached agreement in a particular conversation.

Thirdly, one cannot deal with ecclesiological dialogue without serious reflection on the contemporary political, social, cultural and scholarly situation. It is possible that ecclesiological dialogue will eventually become completely obsolete as other more fashionable fields of research take its place. Or it is also possible that a 'common enemy', such as the challenge posed by Islamic radicalism or radically secular humanism will bring Christian denominations together in a kind of 'trench-ecumenism', a regrettable prospect indeed.

In the end, the question raised in this study is meant to invite reflection, one that aims to initiate steps toward the elaboration of a strategy promoting reception.

Notes

1. The emphasis of the Catholic–Lutheran dialogue does not imply a judgement of value regarding the importance of this particular conversation, but is simply a lens that I have chosen to examine the issue of non-reception. Obviously, the Catholic–Anglican dialogue has generated in many respects an even higher degree of convergence.
2. From New Delhi 1–2 (*Neu-Delhi. Bericht der Sektion Einheit*, in *Die Einheit der Kirche. Material der ökumenischen Bewegung*. Theologische Bücherei, 30, ed. Lukas Vischer [Munich: Mission und Ökumene, 1965]), pp. 159–81, at p. 159 to *The Nature and Purpose of the Church*. Faith and Order Paper, 181 (Geneva: WCC, 1998), no. 9, and *The Nature and Mission of the Church*, Faith and Order Paper, 198 (Geneva: WCC, 2005), nos. 9–10. Gérard Philips draws parallels between the trinitarian ecclesiological conception of *Lumen gentium* nos. 1–4 and New Delhi, in *La Chiesa e il suo mistero. Storia, testo e commento della Costituzione Lumen Gentium* (Milan: Jaca Books, 1975) originally published as *L'Église et son mystère au deuxième Concile du Vatican* (Paris: Desclée de Brouwer, 1967), p. 88. See also the document of the Joint Working Group of the Roman Catholic Church and the WCC, *The Church: Local and Universal* (1990, Study Document), nos. 1–3, 5–7, in *Information Service: The Pontifical Council for Promoting Christian Unity* 74 (III) (1990): 75–84. The importance of the visible dimension of the Church is emphasized in all those statements that address the goal of visible communion as well as the importance of ministry.
3. Toronto IV.3: 'the membership of the Church of Christ is more inclusive than the membership of their own church bodies'. 'Towards a Common Understanding and Vision of the World Council of Churches', *The Ecumenical Review* 49 (1) (1997): 13–33.
4. 'Text on Ecclesiology, *Called to Be the One Church*: An Invitation to the Churches to Renew their Commitment to the Search for Unity and to Deepen their Dialogue, 9', *The Ecumenical Review* 58 (1–2) (2006): 112–17, at 115.
5. *Lumen gentium* no. 8.
6. For the background to *Lumen gentium* no. 8, as well as its interpretation and inclusive meaning, and the open character of the 'churches and ecclesial communities' formula, used in the third chapter of *Unitatis redintegratio*, see Karl Rahner, Heribert Vorgrimler, *Kleines*

Konzilskompendium: Alle Konstitutionen, Dekrete und Erklärungen des Zweiten Vaticanums in der bischöflich genehmigten Übersetzung (Freiburg: Herder, 1967), p. 107; Medard Kehl, *Die Kirche: Eine katholische Ekklesiologie* (Würzburg: Echter Verlag, 1992), pp. 415–24; Walter Kasper, J. Drumm, 'Kirche, Theologie- u. Dogmengeschichtlich', in *LThK* 5 (Freiburg: Herder, 1996), pp. 1458–65, at p. 1469; Bernard Sesboüé, *Hors de l'Église pas de salut: Histoire d'une formule et problèmes d'interprétation* (Paris: Desclée de Brouwer, 2004), pp. 210–34; Peter Neuner, *Théologie œcuménique: La quête de l'unité des Églises chrétiennes*, trans. Joseph Hoffmann (Paris: Cerf, 2005), pp. 214–15; Peter Neuner, 'Kirchen und kirchliche Gemeinschaften', in *Dominus Iesus: Anstößige Wahrheit oder anstößige Kirche? Dokumente, Hintergründe, Standpunkte und Folgerungen*, ed. M. J. Rainer (2nd edn, Münster: LIT, 2001), pp. 196–211, at pp. 202–8; Medard Kehl, 'Die eine Kirche und die viele Kirchen', *Stimmen der Zeit* 219 (1) (2001): 3–16, at 11. For Pope Paul VI's use of 'churches' in respect to the Anglican Communion, see Philips, p. 182; Neuner, *Théologie œcuménique*, pp. 216–17. It is noteworthy that John Paul II's encyclical on ecumenism unequivocally uses the designation '*churches* and communities' in respect to Protestant Christianity, in line with *Unitatis redintegratio* and contrary to the later *Dominus Iesus* no. 17 (emphasis mine).

7. *Lumen gentium* no. 15, *Unitatis redintegratio* no. 3.

8. Already in the early texts: Lausanne III, 17–18 (Vischer, 33); Edinburgh IV, 51, *koinonia ton hagion* (Vischer, 55); New Delhi I, 2, 11, 171 (Vischer, pp. 159–61, 163, 171–2); very clearly in Canberra (*The Unity of the Church: Gift and Calling*), 2.1, 3.2; see also Roman Catholic Church, Lutheran Joint Commission, *Facing Unity: Models, Forms and Phases of a Catholic–Lutheran Church Fellowship*, 110 (1984). For a discussion of the development of communion ecclesiology in the ecumenical theology, see André Birmelé, *Kirchengemeinschaft: Ökumenische Fortschritte und methodologische Konsequenzen*; originally *La communion ecclésiale: Progrès oecuméniques et enjeux méthodologiques* (Paris: Cerf; Geneva: Labor et Fides, 2000); *Studien zur systematischen Theologie und Ethik*, 38 (Münster: LIT, 2003), pp. 289–329; cf. S.-P. Bergjan, 'Ecclesiology in Faith and Order Texts', *The Ecumenical Review* 46 (1) (1994): 45–77.

9. *Lumen gentium* 23, 26; see also Kehl, *Die Kirche*, pp. 104–5, 323–4; *Ecclesia sub Verbo Dei mysteria Christi celebrans pro salute mundi. Relatio finalis*, Engl. *The Church, Subject to the Word of God, Celebrating the Mysteries of Christ for the Salvation of the World. The Final Report of the 1985 Extraordinary Synod*, *African Ecclesial Review* 28 (1–2) (1986): 81–94; Philips, pp. 21, 490–1, 627–30; Kehl, *Die Kirche*, pp. 51–2.

10. *The Nature and Purpose of the Church* (subsequently NPC) nos. 9, 49, 51–3; *The Nature and Mission of the Church* (subsequently NMC) nos. 9–10, 24, 28–9.

11. NPC, no. 53; NMC, no. 29.

12. *The Church: Local and Universal* (esp. nos. 12–14, 19).

13. Ibid., 21–4, 35–6.

14. Philips, p. 271; Y. Congar, *Die Wesenseingenschaften der Kirche*, in J. Feiner, M. Löhrer, *Mysterium salutis. Grundriss heilsgeschichtlicher Dogmatik. Das Heilsgeschehen in der Gemeinde. Gottes Gnadehandeln* (Einsiedeln: Benzinger, 1972–73) IV/1, pp. 357–594, at p. 403; Kehl, *Die Kirche*, pp. 368–72.

15. Römisch-Katholisch/Evangelisch-Lutherische Studienkommission, *Das Evangelium und die Kirche* (Malta, 1972, in Meyer, *DWÜ* I, 248–71) para. 48, 57; *Ministry in the Church* (Römisch-Katholisch/Evangelisch-Lutherische Studienkommission, *Das geistliche Amt in der Kirche*, in Meyer, *DWÜ* I, 329–57, nos. 59–66, 77; Reformierter Weltbund – Sekretariat für die Einheit der Christen, *Die Gegenwart Christi in Kirche und Welt* in Meyer, *DWÜ* I, 487–517), nos. 100–1; World Council of Churches, Faith and Order, *Baptism, Eucharist and Ministry*. Faith and Order Paper, 111 (Geneva: WCC, 1982), M34, 37, 53; NPC, nos. 70, 88; NMC, nos. 12, 68, 71.

16. BEM, commentary to M34, *Ministry in the Church*, no. 61.

17. Ibid., nos. 62–3.

18. Ibid., no. 65.

19. Ibid., nos. 43, 66; *Facing Unity*, no. 97.

20. BEM, M25, M38, 53.
21. BEM, M37.
22. BEM, M 37, 53; *Ministry in the Church* 77; Fries, Rahner, *Einigung der Kirchen – Reale Möglichkeit* (Freiburg: Herder, 1985), p. 117.
23. Already Karl Rahner, 'Über das *ius divinum* des Episkopats', in K. Rahner, J. Ratzinger, *Episkopat und Primat* (Freiburg: Herder, 1963), pp. 70–85; cf. Kasper, 'Die apostolische Sukzession als ökumenisches Problem', in *Lehrverurteilungen – kirchentrennend?*, ed. W. Pannenberg, 4 vols (Freiburg: Herder; Göttingen: Vandenhoeck & Ruprecht, 1990), 3: 329–49, at 337; H. Fries, in Fries and Rahner, *Einigung der Kirchen – Reale Möglichkeit*, p. 116; see also B. Kötting, 'Zur Frage der successio apostolica' in frühkirchlicher Sicht', *Catholica* no. 3–4 (1973): 234–47.
24. 'Sciendum tamen quod, sicut Deus virtutem suam non alligavit sacramentis quin possit sine sacramentis effectum sacramentorum conferre, ita etiam virtutem suam non alligavit Ecclesiae ministris, quin etiam Angelis possit virtutem tribuere ministrandi in sacramentis.' Thomas Aquinas, *Summa theologica* III, q. 64, a. 7, corpus; III + Supplementum, 398.
25. W. Kasper, 'Die apostolische Sukzession als ökumenisches Problem', in ed. W. Pannenberg, *Lehrveurteilungen – kirchentrennend?* III, 337–8.
26. Congar, 'Die Wesenseingenschaften der Kirche', in MySal IV/1, 560–1.
27. BEM, M 21, 23; NPC 89–90, 91–2; NMC 83, 87, 89, 90–3.
28. NPC 98–106; NMC 90–8.
29. *New Delhi* I, 2, 11, 14; *Canberra* 2.1, 3.2, NPC 56–8; NMC 32–42; *The Church: Local and Universal* 25.
30. Römisch-Katholisch/Evangelisch-Lutherische Studienkomission, *Das Herrenmahl* (1978), in Meyer, *DWÜ* I, 271–95; *Baptism, Eucharist, Ministry* (1982); Ökumenischer Arbeitskreis evangelischer und katholischer Theologen, *Das Opfer Jesu Christi und der Kirche. Abschließender Bericht*, in K. Lehmann and E. Schlink (eds), *Das Opfer Jesu Christi und seine Gegenwart in der Kirche. Klärungen zum Opfercharakter des Herrenmahles*. Dialog der Kirchen, 3 (Freiburg: Herder; Göttingen: Vandenhoeck & Ruprecht, 2nd edn., 1983), pp. 215–38; *Lehrverurteilungen – kirchentrennend?* (1986); *Die Gegenwart Christi in Kirche und Welt* (1977); *Abendmahlsgemeinschaft ist möglich* (2003).
31. *Ministry in the Church*; BEM (M); *Die Gegenwart Christi in Kirche und Welt*; *Lehrverurteilungen – kirchentrennend?* (Amt); *NPC*; *NMC*; Bilaterale Arbeitsgruppe der Deutsche Bischofskonferenz und der Kirchenleitung der Vereinigten Evangelisch-luther-ischen Kirche Deutschlands, *Communio Sanctorum: die Kirche als Gemeinschaft der Heiligen* (Paderborn: Otto Lembeck; Frankfurt am Main: Bonifatius, 2nd edn, 2000); Lutheran World Federation–World Alliance of Reformed Churches, *Toward Church Fellowship: Report of the Lutheran–Reformed Joint Commission* (Geneva, 1989).
32. *Congregatio pro Doctrina Fidei, Schreiben an die Bischöfe der Katholischen Kirche über einige Aspekte der Kirche als Communio. Verlautbarungen des Apostolischen Stuhls, 107* (Bonn: Sekretariat der Deutschen Bischofskonferenz, 1992).
33. Esp. pp. 9, 12. For a critical discussion: Kasper, 'Zur Theologie und Praxis des bischöflichen Amtes', in W. Schreer and G. Steins (eds), *Auf neue Art Kirche sein. Wirklichkeiten - Herausforderungen - Wandlungen. Festschrift für Bischof Josef Homeyer* (Munich: Bernward bei Don Bosco, 1999), pp. 32–48; Kasper, 'Das Verhältnis von Universalkirche und Ortskirche', *Stimmen der Zeit* 218 (2000): 795–804; analysed by M. Kehl, 'Der Disput der Kardinäle: zum Verhältnis von Universalkirche und Ortskirchen', *Stimmen der Zeit* 221 (2003): 219–32; see also Kehl, *Wohin geht die Kirche? Eine Zeitdiagnose* (Freiburg: Herder, 1996), pp. 80–98. In a response to Kasper's criticism, Joseph Ratzinger rejects the assumption that *Communionis notio* would identify the universal Church with the Church of Rome (defined by Ratzinger as a local church with a universal responsibility, and not the universal Church), and formulates the alternative term of 'teleological' precedence, instead of the 'ontological' precedence. See Ratzinger, 'The Local Church and The Universal Church', *America* 185 (16) (19 November 2001): 7–11. However, the assumption is not unfounded, given the fact that no. 12, which deals with the episcopate as a source of the unity of the Church, establishes an

analogy between the visible unity of the Corpus Ecclesiarum, manifested in the Church of Rome, and the unity of the episcopal college, realized through the Bishop of Rome. This context clearly suggests an association (if not an identification) of the universal Church with the Church of Rome.

34. '... the ecclesial communities which have not preserved the valid Episcopate and the genuine and integral substance of the Eucharistic mystery, are not Churches in the proper sense; however, those who are baptized in these communities are, by Baptism, incorporated in Christ and thus are in a certain communion, albeit imperfect, with the Church.' In '*Dominus Iesus*'. For an anthology of representative theologians' reactions, see *Dominus Iesus: Anstößige Wahrheit oder anstößige Kirche? Dokumente, Hintergründe, Standpunkte und Folgerungen*, ed. M. J. Rainer (2nd edn, Münster: LIT, 2001). M. Kehl, 'Die eine Kirche und die viele Kirchen', *Stimmen der Zeit* 219 (1) (2001): 3–16 also offers a thorough analysis of the text. See also Francis A. Sullivan, 'The Impact of *Dominus Iesus* on Ecumenism', *America* 183 (28 October 2000): 13, who also assesses the reproof issued by the CDF in 1985 against Leonardo Boff's view that the Church of Christ subsists in other churches as well.

35. Thus Ratzinger states the identical ecclesiological view of LG 8 and DI 17. See interview given to Christian Geyer. 'Es scheint mir absurd, was unsere lutherischen Freunde jetzt wollen' – Die Pluralität der Bekenntnisse relativiert nicht den Anspruch des Wahren: Joseph Kardinal Ratzinger antwortet seinen Kritikern', in Rainer (ed.), pp. 29–45, at pp. 33–4.

36. B. J. Hilberath, '"Dominus Iesus"' und die Texte des Zweiten Vatikanischen Konzils', in Rainer, pp. 79–84 ('Gewiss läßt sich, auch theologisch, immer weitern forschen, – aber wäre nicht noch mehr extensivere wie intensivere Rezeption bereits vorliegender theologischer Forschungsergebnisse einzufordern? ... Sind die 35 Jahre seit Abschluß des Konzils reine Verfallsgeschichte, blauäugige Irtumsgeschichte?', p. 79). P. Neuner addresses the ecclesiological shift represented by Vatican II, speaking in this context of 'fundamentale Neubesinnung', and emphasizes the non-reception of Vatican II in DI ('Kirchen und kirchliche Gemeinschaften', in Rainer, pp. 201–11). See also P. Hünermann, 'Stellungnahme zur Erklärung der Glaubenskongregation "Dominus Jesus"', in P. Neuner (ed.), *Glaubenswissenschaft? Theologie im Spannungsfeld von Glaube, Rationalität und Öffentlichkeit*. Quaestiones Disputatae, 165 (Freiburg: Herder, 2002), pp. 167–72.

37. W. Pannenberg, 'Die Einzigkeit Jesu Christi und die Einheit der Kirche. Anmerkungen zu der Erklärung der vatikanischen Glaubenskongregation "Dominus Jesus"', *Kerygma und Dogma* 47 (2001): 203–9; E. Jüngel, 'Quo vadis Ecclesia? Kritische Bemerkungen zu zwei neuen Texten der römischen Kongregation für die Glaubenslehre', in Rainer, pp. 59–67.

38. *Kirchengemeinschaft nach evangelischem Verständnis. Ein Votum zum geordneten Miteinander Bekenntnisverschiedener Kirchen*. EKD-Texte 69, 2001, http: //www.ekd.de/EKD-Texte.

39. K. Lehmann and W. Pannenberg (eds), *Lehrverurteilungen – kirchentrennend? I, Rechtfertigung, Sakramente und Amt in Zeitalter der Reformation und heute* (Freiburg: Herder; Göttingen: Vandenhoeck & Ruprecht, 1986).

40. *Ministry in the Church* no. 33; LV/*Amt*, 161.

41. *Lehrverurteilungen in Gespräch* (subsequently LVG) 145,11–18, in W. Pannenberg and Th. Schneider (eds), *Lehrverurteilungen – kirchentrennend? IV, Antworten auf kirchliche Stellungnahmen* (Freiburg: Herder; Göttingen: Vandenhoeck & Ruprecht, 1994), p. 91.

42. VELKD: LVG 155,20; AK: LVG 47,6sk, in: *Lehrverurteilungen IV. Antworten*, p. 92.

43. LVG 146, 19–31.

44. VELKD-LV, LVG 145,20; AK-LV, LVG 42,9; 46,34skk, referred to by W. Dietz, 'Die kirchlichen Stellungsnahmen aus evangelischer Sicht. Synopse der Haupteinwände', in *Lehrverurteilungen IV. Antworten*, p. 130. However, in the response given to BEM, the Northern-Elbian Evangelical Lutheran Church does not radically reject the term of priesthood, but stresses that this can be appropriately used only for Christ (*Churches Respond to BEM, Official Responses to the 'Baptism, Eucharist and Ministry' Text*. Faith and Order Paper, 129, ed. Max Thurian, 5 vols (Geneva: WCC, 1986), 1: 50.

45. Walter Kasper, 'Zur Frage der Annerkennung der Ämter in den lutherischen Kirchen', *Theologische Quartalschrift* 151 (1971): 97–109, cited by Fries, in Fries and Rahner, *Einigung*

der Kirchen: Reale Möglichkeit, p. 112; Kasper, 'Die apostolische Sukzession als ökumenisches Problem', in *Lehrverurteilungen* III, pp. 329–49, at pp. 345–6; Fries, 'Die katholische Lehre vom kirchlichen Amt', in: *Lehrverurteilungen* III, pp. 187–215, esp. pp. 207–8; cf. Edward Schillebeeckx, 'Zur Theologie des Amtes', in *Sacramentum salutis* (Leipzig: St. Benno, 1973), pp. 392–5; Kehl, 'Die eine Kirche und die viele Kirchen', *Stimmen der Zeit* 219 (1) (2001): 14–15; Otto Hermann Pesch, who notes the contradiction between the positive conciliar statements regarding the Protestant churches and implicitly their ministry, and the intimation that these ministers are actually mere impostors, called ministers solely out of politeness ('Wer sagt, das Ökumenische gemeinsame Abendmahl "sei aus streng theologischen Gründen nicht möglich" betreibt Denkverweigerung. Gemeinschaft beim Herrenmahl. Ernste Probleme, offene Möglichkeiten', in *Imprimatur* 8 (2001), http: //www. phil.uni-sb.de/projekte/imprimatur/2001/imp010502.html).

46. *Facing Unity*, 118–39.
47. Rahner makes this statement in his explanation of the first thesis, evaluating the radically changed theological situation as a consequence of the official dialogue: Fries, Rahner, *Einigung der Kirchen: Reale Möglichkeit*, pp. 35–53, at p. 47.
48. 'Ein Par-force-Ritt zur Einheit … eine Kunstfigur theologischer Akrobatik, die leider der Realität nicht standhält', in 'Luther und die Einheit der Kirche: Fragen an Joseph Kardinal Ratzinger', *Communio* (German edn) 6 (1983): 568–82, at 573 (my translation). He accused Fries and Rahner of having suggested that confessions should march together regardless of what they were thinking, thereby misinterpreting the position of the two theologians.
49. Eilart Herms, *Einheit der Christen in der Gemeinschaft der Kirchen: Die ökumenische Bewegung der römischen Kirche im Lichte der reformatorischen Theologie. Antwort auf den Rahnerplan* (Göttingen: Vandenhoeck & Ruprecht, 1984), pp. 10–11, 14–15, 30–2, 62–5, 133–5, 199–201. What strikes one who reads Herms, besides his mistrust of the Catholic Church, is the vague and unsystematic character of his reaction. Herms does not address the theses, nor analyse them in detail, but rather puts forward a global critical assessment of intrinsically erroneous Catholic doctrine and practice. For an overview of the responses and of the critical reactions to the Rahner–Fries theses, as well as a response to Herms, see Fries, *Einigung*, pp. 157–89, esp. pp. 178–89.
50. *Einigung*, p. 179.
51. 'Professors' Statement on the "Joint Declaration"', in *Ecumenical Dialogue. Suppl. EKD Bulletin*, http: //www.ekd.de/dialogue/0498/01.html. A critical, but more open evaluation is formulated by Ch. Schwöbel, 'Konsens in Grundwahrheiten? Kritische Anfragen an die "Gemeinsame Erklärung"', in B. J. Hilberath and W. Pannenberg (eds), *Zur Zukunft der Ökumene. Die 'Gemeinsame Erklärung zur Rechtfertigungslehre'* (Regensburg: Pustet, 1999), pp. 100–28. On the other hand the Reformed criticism of the Lutheran position is also remarkable: H. Ruegger, 'Ecumenical Consideration in Connection with the "Joint Declaration"', *Ecumenical Dialogue* 33 (1990), http: //www.ekd.de/dialogue/3390.html. For a balanced evaluation see W. Pannenberg, 'Die Gemeinsame Erklärung zur Rechtfertigungslehre aus evangelischer Sicht', in Hilberath, Pannenberg, *Zur Zukunft der Ökumene*, pp. 71–8; cf. idem, 'New Consensuses, Defused Conflicts and Protestant Anxieties', *Ecumenical Dialogue* 4 (1998), http: //www.ekd.de/dialogue/0498/02.html.
52. Päpstlicher Rat zur Förderung der Einheit der Christen, *Die theologische Verbindlichkeit des Ökumenismusdekrets des II. Vatikanischen Konzils 'Unitatis redintegratio'* (2003), http: //www. vatican.va/roman_curia/pontifical_councils/chrstuni/card-kasper-docs/rc_pc_chrstuni_do-c_20031110_unitatis-redintegratio_ge.html.
53. Thus Klaus Berg, the New Testament scholar from Heidelberg, quoted by Th. Söding, 'Der lange Marsch. Ökumene – wohin?' 1, *Stimmen der Zeit* 222 (2004): 365–6, at 366.
54. S. Kobia, 'Listening to the Voice of God: New Trends in the Ecumenical Movement', *The Ecumenical Review* 57 (2) (2005): 195–204. See also N. Kosby, 'Challenges to the Ecumenical Movement: Reflections in the Context of Globalization and the War on Terror', *The Ecumenical Review* 56 (1) (2004): 40–9.

55. For the analysis of the paradigm shift within the ecumenical movement see A. Birmelé, *Kirchengemeinschaft*, pp. 298–300. This phenomenon is also criticized by the *Princeton Proposal* (2003), 17–18. See also George Lindbeck, 'The Unity We Seek', *The Christian Century* (9 August 2005): 28–31. From a different perspective, the non-operationality of the ecumenical movement despite decades of dialogue is addressed by M. Kässmann, who points to the Orthodox non-reception of ecclesiological dialogue and its consequences: 'A Voice of Dissent: Questioning the Conclusions of the Special Commission on Orthodox Participation in the WCC', *The Ecumenical Review* vol. 55 (1) (2003): 67–71.
56. Birmelé, *Kirchengemeinschaft*, pp. 294–5.
57. *The Unity of the Church: Gift and Calling*, 2.1, 3.2, http://www.wcc-coe.org/wcc/what/faith/canb.html.
58. L. Vischer, 'Is This Really "The Unity We Seek"? Comments on the Statement on "The Unity of the Church as Koinonia: Gift and Calling" Adopted by the WCC Assembly in Canberra', *The Ecumenical Review* 44 (4) (1992): 467–78, at 473–4. Vischer's criticism regarding the abandonment of the concrete 'conciliar gathering' (Nairobi) for the sake of an imprecise 'conciliar forms' is all the more telling given the even vaguer position of NMC.
59. NPC 98–100.
60. *Called to Be One Church* 2.
61. NMC 93 and its commentary.
62. *Communio Sanctorum* 83–6.
63. NPC 78–80.
64. NMC 78–81 and the related commentary.
65. The growing confessionalism as a general ecclesial phenomenon was remarked upon among others by Walter Kasper (Pontifical Council for Promoting Christian Unity, 'Introductory Report of the President Cardinal Walter Kasper', http://www.vatican.va/roman_curia/pontifical_councils/chrstuni/ecum-commit-docs/rc_pc_chrstuni_ doc_20031111_prolusio-plenary_en.html).
66. J. D'Arcy May, 'Catholic Fundamentalism? Some Implications of Dominus Iesus for Dialogue and Peacemaking', in Rainer, pp. 112–33, at p. 114.
67. Again, although it would be mistaken to regard this tendency as a specifically Catholic experience, it is noteworthy to remark the frequency of the motif of fear of dissolution and the wish for certainty in an interview of Cardinal Ratzinger: 'Heute *droht* im allgemeinen Gerede der Christusglaube zu verflachen und sich in mehr oder weniger frommes Geschwätz *aufzulösen* ... In der *Auflösung der Konturen* des Glaubens durch einen Chor widersprüchlicher exegetischer Bestrebungen (materialistische, feministische, liberationistische Exegese) zeigt sich, daß gerade der Zusammenhang mit den Glaubensbekenntnissen, also mit der gelebten Tradition der Kirche, die Wörtlichkeit der Schrift *garantiert*, sie vor Subjektivismen *schützt* und ihre Ursprünglichkeit und Maßstäblichkeit *erhält*' (J. Ratzinger, 'Interview', in Rainer, pp. 30, 44, emphasis mine).
68. See Congar's classical study on reception: 'La "réception" comme réalité ecclésiologique', in *Église et papauté. Regards historiques* (Paris: Cerf, 1994), pp. 229–66, at p. 254. He is followed by Birmelé, *Kirchengemeinschaft*, pp. 331–45, at p. 333.
69. Protestant non-reception as result of the rejection of authority was already mentioned by L. Vischer, *Überlegungen nach dem zweiten Vatikanischen Konzil* (Zürich, 1966), pp. 42–4, referred to by Birmelé, *Kirchengemeinschaft*, pp. 284–5.
70. Hilberath, 'Dominus Iesus', in Rainer, p. 80.
71. D'Arcy May, in Rainer, p. 119.
72. About the importance of the process of spiritual growth among the participants in the ecumenical dialogue: Birmelé, *Kirchengemeinschaft*, p. 337.
73. Carl E. Braaten and Robert W. Jenson (eds), *In One Body Through the Cross: The Princeton Proposal for Christian Unity – A Call to the Churches from an Ecumenical Study Group* (Grand Rapids: Eerdmans, 2003). For a critical assessment see A. K. Riggs' review in *The Ecumenical Review* 56 (2004): 522–4.
74. *Princeton Proposal* nos. 3–5.

75. Ibid. nos. 6–7.
76. While NMC continues to regard *koinonia* as a central goal to be reached (32–42), in a commentary of this issue it becomes clear that the understanding of what *koinonia* actually means continues to be controversial.
77. *Princeton Proposal* nos. 15, 46; cf. *New Delhi* I, 2.
78. *Princeton Proposal* no. 23.
79. Ibid. no. 25.
80. Ibid. nos. 30–4; see also Groupe des Dombes, *Pour la conversion des Églises. Identité et changement dans la dynamique de communion* (Paris: Centurion, 1991), p. 119.
81. *Princeton Proposal* no. 46.
82. *Princeton Proposal* no. 49; *Facing Unity*, 120–2.
83. *Princeton Proposal* no. 55.

AFTERWORD

Rt Revd John W. Hind

This 'afterword' is a contribution from the perspective of someone involved in the production of the second stage of the Faith and Order ecclesiology project.[1] It is, however, not a critique of what the authors of this collection of published lectures have said or written but rather a further comment on *The Nature and Mission of the Church* (NMC).

The ecclesiological text NMC and its earlier draft are addressed primarily to the churches, both member churches of World Council of Churches and the rather wider group of churches associated with the Faith and Order Commission. As members and as servants of their own Christian communities, students of theology have also been asked to contribute both to the internal development of responses within their own churches and to scholarly reflection in interconfessional contexts. Theology is not of course a closed shop, and both texts will rightly be scrutinized by friends and critics belonging to other churches or none. Their perspectives will also be important as the work continues to discern whether NMC is, as its subtitle claims, 'A Stage on the Way to a Common Statement'.

The origins of the study lay in the 1982 document *Baptism, Eucharist and Ministry* (BEM)[2] and in responses (and, in some cases, lack of response) to it. It was often observed that BEM contained no explicit ecclesiology. For some, this was in itself a cause for criticism. Others, however, discerned an implicit doctrine of the Church in the text and either praised or criticized the Faith and Order Commission for what they found there. Also there were a number of churches and confessional traditions who either did not respond at all or who did so with some difficulty. The six volumes of published responses[3] and the official report on the process and the responses[4] not only provide a useful tool for reviewing the BEM text itself, but also raise the question why churches responded in the way they did or did not do so.

It is not surprising that the most instant and sometimes thoroughgoing comments on BEM were frequently from those churches that are most acutely aware of the church-dividing potential of sacramental[5] disagreements. Typically these are the Western Catholic and classic Protestant churches, the so-called 'churches of the Reformation'.

The divisions that have racked Western Christendom for the last half-millennium have either not impinged on Orthodox and Ancient Oriental

Orthodox churches or have done so only indirectly or at second-hand as contact
with specifically Western schisms have forced previously unasked questions upon
them. Even more hesitation is suggested by churches in the 'developing world' on
whom historic Western divisions have been visited as part of their colonial past and
by newer churches and Christian communities, particularly of an Evangelical[6] or
Pentecostal character, for some of whom ecumenical and even ecclesiological and
sacramental categories have not been central to their preoccupations.

Although, as co-moderator of the drafting group of NMC,[7] I cannot claim to be
a disinterested observer, for me one of the most fascinating aspects of the present
collection of papers is the evidence it provides of the engagement of theologians
from the Pentecostal churches in the ecumenical movement.[8]

In this connection it is worth noting that the word 'ecumenical' itself arouses
negative as well as positive reactions.

To those who remember the etymological roots of the term in the Greek word
oikoumene, the whole inhabited world, it suggests a vision of the wholeness of the
Church, and is reflected in the constitution of the World Council of Churches:

> The primary purpose of the fellowship of churches in the World Council of Churches
> is to call one another to visible unity in one faith and in one eucharistic fellowship,
> expressed in worship and common life in Christ, through witness and service to the
> world, and to advance towards that unity in order that the world may believe.[9]

The highpoint of this vision of the unity of the Church was articulated at the 1961
New Delhi Assembly:

> The unity which is both God's will and his gift to his Church is being made visible as
> all in each place who are baptized into Jesus Christ and confess him as Lord and
> Saviour are brought by the Holy Spirit into one fully committed fellowship, holding
> the one apostolic faith preaching the one Gospel, breaking the one bread, joining in
> common prayer, and having a corporate life reaching out in witness and service to all
> and who at the same time are united with the whole Christian fellowship in all places
> and all ages in such wise that ministry and members are accepted by all, and that all
> can act and speak together as occasion requires for the tasks to which God calls his
> people.[10]

'Ecumenical' in this sense may approximate to being a synonym for 'catholic' as
expressed by St Cyril of Jerusalem in the fourth century:

> The Church, Catholic or universal, gets her name from the fact that she is scattered
> throughout the whole world from one end of the earth to the other, and because she
> teaches universally and without omission all the doctrines which are to be made
> known to mankind, whether concerned with visible or invisible things, with heavenly
> or earthly things. Then again because she teaches one way of worship to all men,
> nobles or commoners, learned or simple; finally because she universally cures and heals
> every sort of sin which is committed by soul and body. Moreover there is in her every
> kind of virtue in words and deeds and spiritual gifts of every sort.[11]

This vision of universal unity between churches one in faith, worship, witness, and service attracts some and alarms others.

To modern ears, however, the term 'ecumenical' may suggest rather a series of relationships and negotiations between divided churches which somehow have to create a unity. Some suspect in this tendencies toward indifferentism with regard to what they see as essential matters of faith and order.

This is the background against which churches are invited to respond to NMC. It would be a mistake to think this implies more interest in process than in theological content, because here, as in a number of other areas, how churches deal with issues of faith and order, life and work, and mission may be theologically significant.

The need for some common perspectives on ecclesiology is as old as Faith and Order itself and is an inevitable part of the quest for visible unity between the divided disciples of Jesus. The publication of BEM aroused wide interest, provoking not only official reactions from churches but also reflections and comments from theologians, ecumenists, and others. It also had some concrete effects in enabling changed relationships between churches, in response especially to a question about 'the consequences [each church] can draw from this text for its relations and dialogues with other churches, particularly with those churches which also recognize the text as an expression of the apostolic faith'.[12]

This led quickly to the realization that behind differences and agreements about the means of grace, the sacraments, lie differences or agreements about the nature of the Church itself. Not least of the difficulties is revealed by the very title of the World Council of Churches itself. The problem is addressed directly in the introduction to NMC: 'to participate in a council of churches ... does not imply that all members regard all other members as churches in the same way in which they regard themselves'.[13] This suspension of judgement is of course essential as separated churches and ecclesial communities[14] begin to rediscover each other and discern what authentically Christian elements they can see in each other. But, as NMC continues: 'Such courtesy is not merely pragmatic, but can contribute to a spiritual encounter between different communities in which as trust grows it becomes possible to face the theological issues together.'[15] Allowing 'each other space to use their own language to describe themselves' enables dialogue without sacrifice of principle.

In the last chapter of the 'Report on the Process and Responses' in *BEM 1982–1990*, the final section was headed 'Perspectives on Ecclesiology in the Churches' Responses'.[16] After having reviewed the general situation, the Report identified *koinonia* as a 'notion' to which many churches were giving serious attention and that might be worked on as Faith and Order continued to seek 'a convergent vision on ecclesiology'. It was recognized that this could not be the only approach although the way it was presented suggested that 'different key conceptions and images which have been especially emphasized by different Christian traditions' might 'contribute in a complementary way to an ecumenically oriented ecclesiology of *koinonia*'.

Finally, having commented on the Church as the gift of the Word of God, as mystery or sacrament of God's love for the world, as the pilgrim people of God, and as servant and prophetic sign of God's coming kingdom, the Report concluded: 'Since all these images and concepts belong to the common biblical heritage and are found in the apostolic tradition there is hope that in the future work of Faith and Order on ecumenical perspectives of ecclesiology these complementary approaches will lead to a convergent vision on the nature, unity and mission of the church.'[17]

Some commentators have suggested that *koinonia* is best understood not so much as a particular understanding of the Church and still less as a 'model' of the Church, but as an overarching approach to the mystery to which various understandings and models may contribute.

The Faith and Order Commission has continued in NMC to pursue the search for a convergent vision. Its language is fittingly modest, since if even BEM, with its high degree of agreement on issues of historic dispute between the churches, was a 'convergence text' rather than a 'consensus text' or a 'common statement', what chance would there be within a relatively short timeframe to achieve more in relation to much deeper issues of ecclesial identity and self-understanding? This is why NMC is, as its subtitle announces, 'A Stage on the Way to a Common Statement'. It is certainly important to stress the preliminary status of the document and not to limit responses by claiming too much for the present stage of the text.

The language is modest for other reasons as well. Since the early 1980s, when BEM was published, there have been a number of significant changes in the ecumenical map.

Positively, we might note the growing interest of Pentecostal churches in questions of unity and the hugely important contribution of the Special Commission on the Participation of the Orthodox in the World Council of Churches.[18] There have also been a number of church unions or changes in interchurch relations because of BEM. In many parts of the world, opportunities for collaboration and shared activity have become possible even when moves toward unity do not seem to be on the radar screen.

Negatively, the general ecumenical climate has become chillier. Some apparently promising discussions and schemes for closer relations have run into difficulties, have stopped, or even gone into reverse. Formal theological agreements have failed to yield practical results. Participation of an ever-wider range of church traditions in the ecumenical movement and the WCC also means that more and more potentially church-dividing questions have to be taken into account. In this changing situation it is by no means clear whether churches all understand even the language of full visible unity in the same way, much less the extent to which they are committed to this vision. After many years in which 'professional' ecumenists largely took this for granted as the goal, the Faith and Order Commission now considers this a subject for serious reflection as the search for ecclesiological convergence and perhaps for eventual consensus continues.

All this makes the process of responding to ecumenical texts an increasingly complex exercise. As far as ecclesiology is concerned, there are those for whom the Church is part of the gospel, and those for whom it is rather an aspect of religious sociology or of the phenomenology of religion. Between these extremes lies an infinite gradation of positions. It is therefore hardly surprising that knowing how churches react to NMC is important not only for the future work of Faith and Order but for the whole ecumenical movement.

Despite the high regard in which BEM is generally held, it does however seem to me that there was a *de haut en bas* quality about the way in which the responses were handled that only serves to feed the feeling that the WCC presumes itself to be at least in some sense a pre-, pro-, or proto-conciliar superchurch – a sign of the church of the future.

In the introduction to the first volume of responses, we read that:

> for the first time, all the Christian churches have been asked for their considered opinion concerning a doctrinal document which touches their faith at the deepest level ... The ecclesiological conviction underlying the production of the Lima document is that the churches are no less churches when they are brought together by the WCC in the person of the representatives to make a decision ... This ecclesiological conviction rests on faith in the Holy Spirit who inspires the ecumenical movement.

This is a bold statement, which may have come as a surprise to some of the churches represented on the Faith and Order Commission. As I mentioned earlier, participation in a council of churches 'does not imply that all members regard all other members as churches in the same way in which they regard themselves'. This modest limitation enables as wide as possible a range of participation at the ecumenical table. On the other hand, to assert 'that churches are no less churches when they are brought together by the WCC in the person of their representatives to make a decision' and furthermore that 'this ecclesiological conviction rests on faith in the Holy Spirit who inspires the ecumenical movement' is to make a much higher claim for the 'ecclesial density' of the institutional instruments of the ecumenical movement. Some years ago, the Congregation for the Doctrine of the Faith published a text under the title of *Dominus Iesus*, widely believed to have come from the pen of its then Prefect, Cardinal Joseph Ratzinger, now Pope Benedict XVI, in which there is reference to certain Christian churches as 'not churches in the strict sense'. Despite the careful qualifications with which this assertion was made, it is hardly surprising that many people took offence. That such a statement could be made and offence taken demonstrates however how important it is for those communities who count themselves 'churches', who participate in the ecumenical movement, and who aspire to unity in some form, to find better ways of understanding each other and, if possible, move toward some common understanding and expressing what it means to be 'the Church'. NMC seeks to contribute to this endeavour. What matters is not only (or even mainly) what different churches think about the text itself, but what the ways in which they respond reveal about what they believe about themselves in relation to the mystery of the Church. The shaded boxes in NMC suggest a number of areas that, in the mind of the Faith and Order Commission, constitute significant matters of disagreement that may be and in some cases are church-dividing.

This is why it so important to get the churches as churches to respond to the present text. We do not need to know whether it is the best theology ever. We need to know whether it conforms to what the churches believe God has revealed to them of his purposes.

I refer by way of conclusion to John Henry Newman's small but important book *On Consulting the Faithful in Matters of Doctrine*. Newman argued that the faithful have a grace-given awareness of the truth of the gospel (*sensus fidei*) to which careful attention needs to be given as interpretations of the faith are weighed. The faithful – Christ's baptized faithful – are not to be asked about their opinions, but scrutinized as to their faith. Hence the importance for Faith and Order to know what Christ's faithful believe, notwithstanding the divisions between the churches. This, rather than ecclesiastical politics, is what Faith and Order is about. The essays in this present book are a welcome contribution to the continuing reflection on the text of NMC and, more importantly, to the efforts of the churches to discern what they can say in common about the *Una Sancta*.

Notes

1. The first stage was represented by *The Nature and Purpose of the Church*. Faith and Order Paper, 181 (Geneva: WCC, 1998). This was referred to member churches and others by the 1998 WCC General Assembly at Harare. In the light of responses that it received, the Faith and Order Commission published a revised text in 2005, with a new title *The Nature and Mission of the Church*. Faith and Order Paper, 198 (Geneva: WCC, 2005).
2. *Baptism, Eucharist and Ministry* [the 'Lima text']. Faith and Order Paper, 111 (Geneva: WCC, 1982).
3. *Churches Respond to BEM*, ed. Max Thurian. Faith and Order Papers, 129, 132, 135, 137, 143, 144 (Geneva: WCC, 1986–88).
4. *Baptism, Eucharist and Ministry 1982–1990*. Faith and Order Paper, 149 (Geneva: WCC, 1990).
5. 'Sacramental' at this point is shorthand, as many of the churches of the Reformation and more newly formed churches either deny or are ambivalent about the sacramental nature of ministry and ordination. The fact that this issue was treated alongside baptism and the Eucharist might however be taken as an indication either that it may be church-dividing in the same way as the so-called dominical sacraments, or that disagreement about the place of ministry in the Church, and whether differences in this area should be church-dividing, is precisely one of the issues at stake! This is an ecclesiological question and is closely linked to the still controverted question of whether the Church as such has a sacramental character, meaning by this term that the Church not only makes use of sacramental means of grace but is constituted by them. Whether ministry and ordination (and particular forms of them) belong to the actual nature of the Church is undoubtedly church-dividing.
6. I.e., 'evangelikal' rather than 'evangelisch'.
7. The other co-moderator was Metropolitan Gennadios of Sassima from the Ecumenical Patriarchate of Constantinople.
8. See, for instance, in this volume, the essay by Wolfgang Vondey ('Pentecostal Perspectives on *The Nature and Mission of the Church*: Challenges and Opportunities for Ecumenical Transformation'). Another Pentecostal theologian, Dr Cecil (Mel) Robeck is a consultant to the Faith and Order Commission and was a member of the drafting group itself.
9. WCC Constitution III.
10. WCC Assembly New Delhi 1961. Report of the Section on Unity, para. 2, described as 'probably the greatest run-on sentence in ecumenical history'.
11. Cyril of Jerusalem, *Cat. Or.* XVIII.23.

12. BEM, preface, p. x.
13. NMC, introduction, para. 8.
14. See the Declaration *Dominus Iesus* (*On the Unicity and Salvific Universality of Jesus Christ and the Church*) issued by the Congregation for the Doctrine of the Faith in 2000.
15. NMC, introduction, para. 8.
16. *Baptism, Eucharist and Ministry 1982–1990*, V. C (1–3), pp. 147ff.
17. Ibid., p. 151.
18. The member churches of the World Council of Churches represent about one quarter (25 per cent) of the world's Christians. Its members are mainly historic or classic Protestant, Anglican and Orthodox churches. The Roman Catholic Church and many of the Pentecostal and newer Evangelical churches are not members, although some of them, especially the Roman Catholic and some Pentecostal churches, have representatives on the Faith and Order Commission, which is thus the widest forum for theological and ecumenical encounter.

Appendix

THE NATURE AND MISSION OF THE CHURCH: A STAGE ON THE WAY TO A COMMON STATEMENT

Faith and Order Paper 198
World Council of Churches, Geneva

Introduction

1. Since its beginning, and especially at the First World Conference, Lausanne, Switzerland, 1927, the Faith and Order Movement identified the unity of the Church as the very reason for its existence. Thus the By-Laws of the Faith and Order Commission state that its aim is: 'to proclaim the oneness of the Church of Jesus Christ and to call the churches to the goal of visible unity in one faith and one Eucharistic fellowship, expressed in worship and in common life in Christ, in order that the world may believe'.[1]

Since Amsterdam, 1948, this goal has been at the heart of the World Council of Churches itself. Moreover, in the Assemblies of the World Council of Churches, the particular contribution of Faith and Order has been to deepen a common understanding of this goal and of the ways to realise it. A significant contribution has been made from the Canberra Assembly (1991) in the statement 'The Church as Koinonia: Gift and Calling'.[2] This statement claims that koinonia is both the foundation and the way of living a life together in visible unity. This was echoed in the theme of the Fifth World Conference on Faith and Order, Towards Koinonia in Faith, Life and Witness. The process on 'Towards a Common Understanding and Vision of the World Council of Churches'[3] again underlines the common calling of the churches as the search for visible unity.

2. All the major documents issued by Faith and Order contribute in some way or other to the understanding of the nature and mission of the Church. Moreover, *Baptism, Eucharist and Ministry*,[4] *Confessing the One Faith: An Ecumenical Explication of the Apostolic Faith as it is Confessed in the Nicene-Constantinopolitan Creed (381)*,[5] and *Church and World: The Unity of the Church and the Renewal of Human Community*,[6] sent to the churches for response and reception, are ways of keeping alive in the churches the imperative of Christ's call to visible unity and the essential characteristics of that unity. The recent studies of Faith and Order such as on Baptism, Ethnic Identity, Anthropology and Hermeneutics have a continuing relevance to the subject. Also, the absolute centrality of ecclesiology to the ecumenical movement has been recently reaffirmed by the Special Commission on the participation of the Orthodox churches in the WCC. In the last decade work

on ecclesiology and ethics (which continued the studies, for example, on racism and the community of women and men in the Church) has contributed to the understanding of our common Christian calling in the service of humanity and creation. In its turn Faith and Order continually receives insights about the unity to which God calls us from responses of the churches to its studies, the results of the bilateral dialogues, the work in other areas of the World Council of Churches and from reflection on the experience of the United and Uniting Churches.

A. This Study

3. A study on the nature and purpose of the Church was strongly recommended by the Fifth World Conference on Faith and Order in Santiago de Compostela, Spain (1993). In endorsing this study the Standing Commission of Faith and Order identified the following reasons why this call is particularly timely:

- the time is right for Faith and Order to reflect on the different insights which its own studies offer to an understanding of the nature and mission of the Church;
- the opportunity is there for Faith and Order to draw upon the fruits of the work of other areas of the WCC and of the bilateral theological agreements;
- growth in fellowship is being experienced between Christians at local, national and world levels, not least of all in the experience of united and uniting churches;
- particular challenges in many regions call out for Christians to address together what it means to be the Church in that place;
- the situation of the world demands and deserves a credible witness to unity in diversity which is God's gift for the whole of humanity;
- the experience of the BEM process and an increasing interest in ecclesiology in many churches provide fresh insights into how many Christians understand being the Church;
- political changes and challenges in recent years are significantly altering the context in which many churches exist and therefore how they seek to understand themselves.

4. The quest for visible unity of the churches is not pursued in a vacuum but by particular Christian communities in specific and varied situations. For this reason, no single text can say everything there is to say about the Church. Faith and Order invites churches in different parts of the world to enrich this study with appropriate regional material to enable their own congregations and church members to engage directly with themes which are necessarily expressed here in quite general terms. The Commission especially encourages reflection based on actual stories of Christian life and witness in different parts of the world so that both the particular and the universal features of the Church can be more clearly understood. This is important above all from the perspective of mission, which is one of the guiding themes of this study. Mission is not an abstraction but is lived in response to the grace of God as God sends his Church in faithful witness in the

actual situations of each society. While human need is universal, the forms which that need takes vary. For some the struggle with HIV/AIDS is paramount, for others finding a language to express spiritual reality in apparently materialistic cultures. For some war, poverty and injustice are the main context for mission, for others relations with other faiths. For some the issue is spiritual and for others material want. For these reasons this text attempts to be alert to the diversity of contexts; at the same time it seeks to offer the churches some common ecclesiological perspectives which might encourage practical local reflection and so serve the quest for Christian unity in diverse environments.

B. Purpose and Method

5. The purpose of this study is finally to give expression to what the churches can now say together about the nature and mission of the Church and, within that agreement, to explore the extent to which the remaining church-dividing issues may be overcome. Thus, in the precedent *Baptism, Eucharist and Ministry* the process seems to evolve into what could be called a 'convergence' text. The present text is to enable churches to begin the first steps towards the recognition of a convergence that has emerged in a multilateral context.

6. The **main text** represents common perspectives which can be claimed, largely as a result of the work of the bilateral and multilateral discussions of the past fifty years and of the changed relationships between the churches in this period. **The material inside the boxes** explores areas where differences remain both within and between churches. Some of these differences may come to be seen by some as expressions of legitimate diversity, by others as church-dividing. While the main text invites the churches to discover, or rediscover, how much they in fact have in common in their understanding of the Church, the text in the boxes offers the opportunity for churches to reflect on the extent to which their divergences are church-dividing. In the perspective of growing convergences, the hope is that churches will be helped to recognise in one another the Church of Jesus Christ and be encouraged to take steps on the way towards visible unity.

7. The Faith and Order Commission invited churches, commissions, theological institutes, ecumenical councils and individuals to reflect on the text *The Nature and Purpose of the Church: A Stage on the Way to a Common Statement.*[7] Faith and Order is grateful to those who responded to this invitation but is conscious that the responses were not fully representative of all the churches. Nevertheless, we hope that the changes occasioned by the suggestions will be evident. One of the frequent suggestions was to strengthen the text's emphasis on mission. In making this change both in title and in content we have tried to ensure that these changes confirm the continuity with the previous work, but also to meet the new concerns.

C. The Invitation

8. In God's providence the Church exists, not for itself alone, but to serve in God's work of reconciliation and for the praise and glory of God. The self-understanding of the Church is essential for its proper response to its vocation. Despite diversities of language and theology, mutual understanding can grow when people are willing to allow each other space to use their own language to describe themselves. For example, to participate in a council of churches does not imply that all members regard all other members as churches in the same sense in which they regard themselves. Such courtesy is not merely pragmatic, but can contribute to a spiritual encounter between different communities in which as trust grows it becomes possible to face the theological issues together. Hence the crucial importance of this study on the nature and the mission of the Church.

In the light of this new revised text we request especially the churches to respond, in the manner they deem most appropriate, to the following questions:

- Does this study document correctly identify our common ecclesiological convictions, as well as the issues which continue to divide us?
- Does this study document reflect an emerging convergence on the nature and mission of the Church?
- Are there significant matters in which the concerns of your church are not adequately addressed?
- Insofar as this study document provides a helpful framework for further ecclesiological discussions among the churches:
  - How can this study document help your church, together with others, take concrete steps towards unity?
  - What suggestions would you make for the future development of this text?

I. The Church of the Triune God

A. The Nature of the Church

(I) THE CHURCH AS A GIFT OF GOD: CREATION OF THE WORD AND OF THE HOLY SPIRIT (CREATURA VERBI ET CREATURA SPIRITUS)

9. The Church is called into being by the Father 'who so loved the world that he gave his only begotten Son, that whoever believes in him shall not perish, but have eternal life' (Jn 3.16) and who sent the Holy Spirit to lead these believers into all truth, reminding them of all that Jesus taught (cf. Jn 14.26). The Church is thus the creature of God's Word and of the Holy Spirit. It belongs to God, is God's gift and cannot exist by and for itself. Of its very nature it is missionary, called and sent to serve, as an instrument of the Word and the Spirit, as a witness to the Kingdom of God.

10. The Church is centred and grounded in the Word of God. This Word has become manifest in history in various ways. '... it is the Word of God made flesh: Jesus Christ, incarnate, crucified and risen. Then it is the word as spoken in God's

history with God's people and recorded in the scriptures of the Old and New Testaments as a testimony to Jesus Christ. Third, it is the word as heard and proclaimed in the preaching, witness and action of the Church.'[8] The Church is the communion of those who, by means of their encounter with the Word, stand in a living relationship with God, who speaks to them and calls forth their trustful response; it is the communion of the faithful. This is the common vocation of every Christian and is exemplified by the faithful responsiveness of Mary to the angel of the annunciation: 'Here I am, the servant of the Lord; let it be with me according to your word' (Lk. 1.38). For this reason Mary has often been seen as a symbol of the Church and of the individual Christian, called to be Jesus' 'brother and sister and mother' in doing the will of his Father in heaven (cf. Mt. 12.50). Thus the Church is the creature of God's Word (Creatura Verbi), the Gospel, which, as a living voice, creates and nourishes the Church throughout the ages. This divine Word is witnessed to and heard through Scripture. Incarnate in Jesus Christ, the Word is testified to by the Church and proclaimed in preaching, in Sacraments, and in service (cf. Mt. 28.19–20; Lk. 1.2; Acts 1.8; 1 Cor. 15.1–11).

11. Faith called forth by the Word of God is brought about by the action of the Holy Spirit (cf. 1 Cor. 12.3). According to the Scripture, the Word and the Spirit are inseparable. As the communion of the faithful, the Church therefore is also the creature of the Holy Spirit (Creatura Spiritus). Just as in the life of Christ the Holy Spirit was active from the very conception of Jesus through the paschal mystery and remains even now the Spirit of the risen Lord, so also in the life of the Church the Spirit forms Christ in believers and in their community. The Spirit incorporates human beings into the body of Christ through faith and baptism, enlivens and strengthens them as the body of Christ nourished and sustained in the Lord's Supper, and leads them to the full accomplishment of their vocation.

12. Being the creature of God's own Word and Spirit, the Church is one, holy, catholic and apostolic. These essential attributes flow from and illustrate the Church's dependence upon God. The Church is one because God is the one creator and redeemer (cf. Jn 17.11, Eph. 4.1–6), who binds the Church to himself by Word and Spirit and makes it a foretaste and instrument for the redemption of all created reality. The Church is holy because God is the holy one (cf. Is. 6.3; Lev. 11.44–45) who sent his Son Jesus Christ to overcome all unholiness and to call human beings to become merciful like his Father (cf. Lk. 6.36), sanctifying the Church by his word of forgiveness in the Holy Spirit and making it his own, the body of Christ (Eph. 5.26–27). The Church is catholic because God is the fullness of life 'who desires everyone to be saved and to come to the knowledge of the truth' (1 Tim. 2.4), and who, through Word and Spirit, makes his people the place and instrument of his saving and life-giving presence, the community 'in which, in all ages, the Holy Spirit makes the believers participants in Christ's life and salvation, regardless of their sex, race or social position'.[9] It is apostolic because the Word of God, sent by the Father, creates and sustains the Church. This word of God is made known to us through the Gospel primarily and normatively borne witness to by the apostles (cf. Eph. 2.20; Rev. 21.14), making the communion of the faithful a community that lives in, and is responsible for, the succession of the apostolic truth expressed in faith and life throughout the ages.

13. The Church is not merely the sum of individual believers in communion with God, nor primarily the mutual communion of individual believers among themselves. It is their common partaking in the life of God (2 Pet. 1.4), who as Trinity is the source and focus of all communion. Thus the Church is both a divine and a human reality.

The Institutional Dimension of the Church and the Work of the Holy Spirit

All churches agree that God creates the Church and binds it to himself through the Holy Spirit by means of the living voice of the Gospel proclaimed in preaching and in the Sacraments. Yet they have different convictions as to:

(a) whether the preaching and the Sacraments are the means of, or simply witnesses to, the activity of the Spirit through the divine Word, which comes about in an immediate internal action upon the hearts of the believers;

(b) the institutional implications and presuppositions of the Church's being Creatura Verbi: for some the ordained ministry, particularly episcopacy, is the effective means, for some a guarantee of the presence of truth and power of the Word and Spirit of God in the Church; for others the fact that the ordained ministry, as well as the witness of all believers, are subject to error and sin excludes such a judgement, the power and reliability of God's truth being grounded in the sovereignty of his Word and Spirit which works through – but if necessary also counter to – the given institutional structures of the Church;

(c) The theological importance of institutional continuity, particularly continuity in episcopacy: whereas for some churches such institutional continuity is the necessary means and guarantee of the Church's continuity in apostolic faith, for others continuity in apostolic faith is, under certain circumstances, being kept in spite of - and even through - the break of institutional continuity.

It remains for future theological work to find out whether these differences are real disagreements or mere differences in emphasis that can be reconciled with each other.

(II) BIBLICAL INSIGHTS

14. The Almighty God, who calls the Church into being and unites it to himself through his Word and the Holy Spirit, is the Triune God, Father, Son and Holy Spirit. The Church is related to each of these divine 'Persons' in a particular way. These relations shed light upon different dimensions of the Church's life.

15. Many insights pertinent to the nature and mission of the Church are present in Scripture although it does not offer a systematic ecclesiology. The biblical understanding governing the present text is based on the common conviction that Scripture is normative and therefore provides a uniquely privileged source for understanding the nature and mission of the Church. Subsequent reflection must always engage and be consonant with the biblical teaching. The interplay of

different kinds of material – accounts of the faith of the early communities, evidence regarding their worship and practice of discipleship, indications of the various roles of service and leadership and, finally, images and metaphors used to express the nature of the community – all provide resources for the development of a biblical understanding of the Church. There also exists a rich resource to be explored in the interpretation of Scripture over the course of history. The same Holy Spirit who inspired the earliest communities guides the followers of Jesus in each time and each place as they strive to be faithful to the Gospel. This is what is understood by the living tradition of the Church.

16. It is essential to acknowledge the wide diversity of insights into the nature and mission of the Church which can be found in the various books of the New Testament and in their interpretation in later history. Diversity appears not as accidental to the life of the Christian community, but as an aspect of its catholicity, a quality that reflects the fact that it is part of the Father's design that the story of salvation in Christ be incarnational. Thus, diversity is a gift of God to the Church.[10] Not only do various passages of the New Testament use the plural 'churches' to denote that there are a variety of local churches (cf. Acts 15.41; Rom. 16.16; 1 Cor. 4.17, 7.17, 11.16, 16.1, 19; 2 Cor. 8.1; Gal. 1.2; 1 Thess. 2.14), without thereby contradicting the conviction that Christ's body is one (Eph. 4.4), but also one finds variety among the ecclesiological themes and insights addressed by individual books. The inclusion of such plurality within the one canon of the New Testament testifies to the compatibility of unity and diversity. Indeed, the discussion of the one body with many members (cf. 1 Corinthians 12–14) suggests that unity is possible only through the proper co-ordination of the diverse gifts of the Triune God.

17. To honour the varied biblical insights into the nature and mission of the church, various approaches are required. Four – 'people of God', 'Body of Christ', 'Temple of the Holy Spirit' and koinonia – have been chosen for particular comment because, taken together, they illuminate the New Testament vision of the Church in relation to the Triune God. A fully rounded approach to the mystery of the Church requires the use and interaction of all biblical images and insights (in addition to those mentioned, 'vine', 'flock', 'bride', 'household' and 'covenant community'), each of which contributes something vital to our understanding. These images counterbalance each other and compensate each others' limitations. Since every image comes out of a particular cultural context they suggest both insufficiencies and possibilities. This text seeks to relate to Scripture as a whole, not playing off one passage against another, but trying always to honour the totality of the biblical witness.

(a) The Church as People of God

18. In the call of Abraham, God was choosing for himself a holy people. The recalling of this election and vocation found frequent expression in the words of the prophets:'I will be their God and they shall be my people' (Jer. 31.33; Ez. 37.27; echoed in 2 Cor. 6.16; Heb. 8.10). Through the Word (dabhar) and the Spirit (rû'ah), God fashioned one from among the nations as servant for the salvation of all (cf. Is. 49.1–6). The election of Israel marked a decisive moment in

the unfolding realisation of the plan of salvation. The covenant between God and his people entailed many things for example, the Torah, the land and common worship, including the call to act with justice and to speak the truth. At the same time, the covenant was also clearly a relationship of communion (cf. Hosea 2; Ezekiel 16). But it is also a gracious gift, a dynamic impulse to communion which is evident throughout the history of the people of Israel, even when the community breaks the covenant. In the light of the ministry, teaching, death and resurrection of Jesus and the sending of the Holy Spirit at Pentecost, the Christian community believes that God sent his Son to bring the possibility of communion for each person with others and with God, thus manifesting the gift of God for the whole world. There is a genuine newness in the covenant initiated by Christ. Nevertheless, as 'the Israel of God' (Gal. 6.16), the Church remains related, in a mysterious way, to the Jewish people, even as a branch is grafted onto the rich root of an olive tree (cf. Rom. 11.11–36).

19. In the Old Testament, the people of Israel is a pilgrim people journeying towards the fulfilment of the promise that in Abraham all the nations of the earth shall be blessed. In Christ this promise is fulfilled when, on the cross, the dividing wall between Jew and Gentile is broken down (cf. Eph. 2.14). The Church, embracing both Jew and Gentile, is a 'chosen race, a royal priesthood, a holy nation', 'God's own people' (1 Pet. 2.9–10), a community of prophets. While acknowledging the unique priesthood of Jesus Christ, whose one sacrifice institutes the new covenant (cf. Heb. 9.15), Christians are called to express by their lives the fact that they have been named a 'royal priesthood' and 'holy nation'. In Christ who offered himself, Christians offer their whole being 'as a living sacrifice, holy and acceptable to God, which is your spiritual worship' (Rom. 12.1). Every member participates in the priesthood of the whole Church. No one exercises that priesthood apart from the unique priesthood of Christ, nor in isolation from the other members of the body. As a prophetic and royal people, Christians seek to witness to the will of God and to influence the course of events of the world. Throughout the ages, the Church of God continues the way of pilgrimage to the eternal rest prepared for it (cf. Heb. 4.9–11). It is a prophetic sign of the fulfilment God will bring about through Christ by the power of the Spirit.

(b) The Church as the Body of Christ
20. According to the design of God, those 'who once were far off have become near by the blood of Christ. For he is our peace' (Eph. 2.13–14). He overcame the enmity between Jew and Gentile, reconciling both with God in one body through the cross (cf. Eph. 2.16). This body is the body of Christ, which is the Church (cf. Eph. 1.23). Christ is the abiding head of his body and at the same time the one who, by the presence of the Spirit, gives life to it. He who cleanses and sanctifies the body (cf. Eph. 5.26) is also the one in whom 'we, though many, are one body' (Rom. 12.5; cf. 1 Cor. 12.12). The image of the body of Christ in the New Testament includes these two dimensions, one expressed in 1 Corinthians and Romans, the other developed in Ephesians.

21. It is through faith and baptism that human beings become members of Christ in the Holy Spirit (cf. 1 Cor. 12.3–13). Through the Lord's Supper their

participation in this body is renewed again and again (cf. 1 Cor. 10.16). It is the same Holy Spirit who confers the manifold gifts to the members of the body (cf. 1 Cor. 12.4; 7–11) and brings forth their unity (cf. 1 Cor. 12.12). All members of Christ are given gifts for the building up of the body (cf. Rom. 12.4–8; 1 Cor. 12.4–30). The diversity and specific nature of these gifts enrich the Church's life and enable a better response to its vocation to be servant of the Lord and effective sign used by God for furthering the Kingdom in the world. Thus the image of 'body of Christ', though explicitly and primarily referring to the Christological dimension of the Church, at the same time has deep pneumatological implications.

(c) The Church as Temple of the Holy Spirit
22. Reference to the constitutive relationship between Church and Holy Spirit runs through the whole New Testament witness. While there is no explicit image for this relationship, a vivid example is the account of the descent of tongues of fire upon the disciples gathered in the upper room on the morning of Pentecost (cf. Acts 2.1–4). The New Testament imagery that most closely approximates to this relationship is that of 'temple' and 'house'. This is so because the relationship of the Spirit to the Church is one of indwelling, of giving life from within. The Holy Spirit so enlivens the community that it becomes a herald of, and an instrument for, that general transformation of the whole cosmos for which all creation groans (cf. Rom. 8.22–23), the new heavens and new earth (cf. Rev. 21.1).
23. Built on the foundation of the apostles and prophets the Church is God's household, a holy temple in which the Holy Spirit lives and is active. By the power of the Holy Spirit believers grow into 'a holy temple in the Lord' (Eph. 2.21–22), into a 'spiritual house' (1 Pet. 2.5). Filled with the Holy Spirit, they witness (cf. Acts 1.8), pray, love, work and serve in the power of the Spirit, leading a life worthy of their calling, eager to maintain the unity of the Spirit in the bond of peace (cf. Eph. 4.1–3).

(d) The Church as Koinonia/Communion
24. The biblical notion of koinonia has become central in the quest for a common understanding of the nature of the Church and its visible unity. The term koinonia (communion, participation, fellowship, sharing) is found not only in the New Testament but also in later periods, especially in patristic and Reformation writings which describe the Church. Although in some periods the term largely fell out of use, it is being reclaimed today as a key to understanding the nature and mission of the Church. Due to its richness of meaning, it is also ecumenically useful in appreciating the various forms and extent of communion already enjoyed by the Churches.
25. The relationship between God, humanity and the whole of creation is a fundamental theme of Scripture. In the narrative of creation, man and woman are fashioned in God's image, bearing an inherent capacity and longing for communion with God, with one another and with creation as its stewards (cf. Genesis 1–2). Thus, the whole of creation has its integrity in koinonia with God. Communion is rooted in the order of creation itself and is realised, in part, in

natural relationships of family and kinship, of tribe and people. At the heart of the Old Testament is the special relationship, the covenant, established by God between God and the chosen people (cf. Ex. 19.4–6; Hos. 2.18–23).

26. God's purpose in creation is distorted by human sin, failure and disobedience to God's will and by rebellion against him (cf. Genesis 3–4; Rom. 1.18–3.20). Sin damages the relationship between God, human beings and the created order. But God persists in faithfulness despite the sin and error of the people. The dynamic history of God's restoring and increasing koinonia reaches its culmination and fulfilment in the perfect communion of a new heaven and a new earth established by Jesus Christ (cf. Revelation 21).

27. The biblical images already treated, as well as others such as 'the flock' (Jn 10.16), 'the vine' (Isaiah 5; John 15), 'the bride' of Christ (Rev. 21.2; Eph. 5.25–32), 'God's house' (Heb. 3.1–6), 'a new covenant' (Heb. 8.8–13) and 'the holy city, the new Jerusalem' (Rev. 21.2), evoke the nature and quality of the relationship of God's people to God, to one another and to the created order. The term koinonia expresses the reality to which these images refer.

28. The basic verbal form from which the noun koinonia derives means 'to have something in common', 'to share', 'to participate', 'to have part in', 'to act together' or 'to be in a contractual relationship involving obligations of mutual accountability'. The word koinonia appears in significant passages, such as the sharing in the Lord's Supper (cf. 1 Cor. 10.16), the reconciliation of Paul with Peter, James and John (cf. Gal. 2.9), the collection for the poor (cf. Rom. 15.26; 2 Cor. 8.3–4) and the experience and witness of the Church (cf. Acts 2.42–45).

29. Through the death and resurrection of Christ, by the power of the Holy Spirit, Christians enter into fellowship with God and with one another in the life and love of God:'We declare to you what we have seen and heard so that you also may have fellowship with us; and truly our fellowship is with the Father and with his Son Jesus Christ' (1 Jn 1.3).

30. The Good News is the offer to all people of the free gift of being born into the life of communion with God and thus with one another (cf. 1 Tim. 2.4, 2 Pet. 2.9). Paul speaks of the relationship of believers (cf. Gal. 2.20) to their Lord as being 'in Christ' (2 Cor. 5.17) and of Christ being in the believer, through the indwelling of the Holy Spirit.

31. It is only by virtue of God's gift of grace through Jesus Christ that deep, lasting communion is made possible; by faith and baptism, persons participate in the mystery of Christ's death, burial and resurrection (cf. Phil. 3.10–11). United to Christ, through the Holy Spirit, they are thus joined to all who are 'in Christ': they belong to the communion – the new community of the risen Lord. Because koinonia is a participation in Christ crucified and risen, it is also part of the mission of the Church to share in the sufferings and hopes of humankind.

32. Visible and tangible signs of the new life of communion are expressed in receiving and sharing the faith of the apostles; breaking and sharing the Eucharistic bread; praying with and for one another and for the needs of the world; serving one another in love; participating in each other's joys and sorrows; giving material aid; proclaiming and witnessing to the good news in mission and working together

for justice and peace. The communion of the Church consists not of independent individuals but of persons in community, all of whom contribute to its flourishing.

33. The Church exists for the glory and praise of God, to serve the reconciliation of humankind, in obedience to the command of Christ. It is the will of God that the communion in Christ, which is realised in the Church, should embrace the whole creation (cf. Eph. 1.10). The Church, as communion, is instrumental to God's ultimate purpose (cf. Rom. 8.19–21; Col. 1.18–20).

B. *The Mission of the Church*

34. It is God's design to gather all creation under the Lordship of Christ (cf. Eph. 1.10), and to bring humanity and all creation into communion. As a reflection of the communion in the Triune God, the Church is God's instrument in fulfilling this goal. The Church is called to manifest God's mercy to humanity, and to bring humanity to its purpose – to praise and glorify God together with all the heavenly hosts. The mission of the Church is to serve the purpose of God as a gift given to the world in order that all may believe (cf. Jn 17.21).

35. As persons who acknowledge Jesus Christ as Lord and Saviour, Christians are called to proclaim the Gospel in word and deed. They are to address those who have not heard, as well as those who are no longer living according to the Gospel, the Good News of the reign of God. They are called to live its values and to be a foretaste of that reign in the world. Mission thus belongs to the very being of the Church. This is a central implication of affirming the apostolicity of the Church, which is inseparable from the other three attributes of the Church – unity, holiness and catholicity. All four attributes relate both to the nature of God's own being and to the practical demands of authentic mission.[11] If in the life of the Church, any of them is impaired, the Church's mission is compromised.

36. The Church, embodying in its own life the mystery of salvation and the transfiguration of humanity, participates in the mission of Christ to reconcile all things to God and to one another through Christ (cf. 2 Cor. 5.18–21; Rom. 8.18–25). Through its worship (leitourgia); service, which includes the stewardship of creation (diakonia); and proclamation (kerygma) the Church participates in and points to the reality of the Kingdom of God. In the power of the Holy Spirit the Church testifies to the divine mission in which the Father sent the Son to be the Saviour of the world.

37. In exercising its mission, the Church cannot be true to itself without giving witness (martyria) to God's will for the salvation and transformation of the world. That is why it started at once preaching the Word, bearing witness to the great deeds of God and inviting everyone to repentance (metanoia), baptism (cf. Acts 2:37–38) and the fuller life that is enjoyed by the followers of Jesus (cf. Jn 10.10).

38. As Christ's mission encompassed the preaching of the Word of God and the commitment to care for those suffering and in need, so the apostolic Church in its mission from the beginning combined preaching of the Word, the call to repentance, faith, baptism and diakonia. This the Church understands as an

essential dimension of its identity. The Church in this way signifies, participates in, and anticipates the new humanity God wants, and also serves to proclaim God's grace in human situations and needs until Christ comes in glory (cf. Mt. 25.31).

39. Because the servanthood of Christ entails suffering it is evident (as expressed in the New Testament writings) that the witness (martyria) of the Church will entail – for both individuals and for the community – the way of the cross, even to the point of martyrdom (cf. Mt. 10.16–33, 16.24–28).

40. The Church is called and empowered to share the suffering of all by advocacy and care for the poor, the needy and the marginalised. This entails critically analysing and exposing unjust structures, and working for their transformation. The Church is called to proclaim the words of hope and comfort of the Gospel, by its works of compassion and mercy (cf. Lk. 4.18–19). This faithful witness may involve Christians themselves in suffering for the sake of the Gospel. The Church is called to heal and reconcile broken human relationships and to be God's instrument in the reconciliation of human division and hatred (cf. 2 Cor. 5.18–21). It is also called, together with all people of goodwill, to care for the integrity of creation in addressing the abuse and destruction of God's creation, and to participate in God's healing of broken relationships between creation and humanity.

41. In the power of the Holy Spirit, the Church is called to proclaim faithfully the whole teaching of Christ and to share the Good News of the Kingdom – that is, the totality of apostolic faith, life and witness – with everyone throughout the entire world. Thus the Church seeks faithfully to proclaim and live the love of God for all, and to fulfil Christ's mission for the salvation and transformation of the world, to the glory of God.

42. God restores and enriches communion with humanity, granting eternal life in God's Triune Being. Through redeemed humanity the whole world is meant to be drawn to the goal of restoration and salvation. This divine plan reaches its fulfilment in the new heaven and the new earth (cf. Rev. 21.1) in God's holy Kingdom.

C. The Church as Sign and Instrument of God's Intention and Plan for the World

43. The one, holy, catholic and apostolic Church is sign and instrument of God's intention and plan for the whole world. Already participating in the love and life of God, the Church is a prophetic sign which points beyond itself to the purpose of all creation, the fulfilment of the Kingdom of God. For this reason Jesus called his followers the 'salt of the earth', 'the light of the world' and 'a city built on a hill' (Mt. 5.13–16).

44. Aware of God's saving presence in the world, the Church already praises and glorifies the Triune God through worship and discipleship, and serves God's plan. Yet the Church does so not only for itself, but rather renders praise and thanks on behalf of all peoples for God's grace and the forgiveness of sins.

45. To acknowledge the nature of the Church as 'mysterion' (cf. Eph. 1.9–10, 5.32) indicates the transcendent character of its God-given reality as one, holy,

catholic and apostolic. The Church can never be fully and unequivocally grasped only in its visible appearance. Therefore the visible organisational structures of the Church must always be seen and judged, for good or ill, in the light of God's gifts of salvation in Christ, celebrated in the Liturgy (cf. Heb. 12.18–24).

46. As instrument of God's plan the Church is the community of people called by God and sent as Christ's disciples to proclaim the Good News in word and deed, that the world may believe (cf. Lk. 24.46–49). Thus it makes present throughout history 'the tender mercy of our God' (Lk. 1.78).

47. Sent as Christ's disciples, the people of God must witness to and participate in God's reconciliation, healing, and transformation of creation. The integrity of the Church as God's instrument is at stake in witness through proclamation, and concrete actions in union with all people of goodwill, for the sake of justice, peace, and the integrity of creation.

II. The Church in History

A. The Church in via

48. The Church is an eschatological reality, already anticipating the Kingdom. However, the Church on earth is not yet the full visible realisation of the Kingdom. Being also an historical reality, it is exposed to the ambiguities of all human history and therefore needs constant repentance and renewal in order to respond fully to its vocation.

Church as 'Sacrament'?

Although all churches agree that the church is a sign and instrument, some churches express their understanding of the reality of the church in Sacramental terms; some speak of the church as Sacrament; others do not normally use this language, or reject it outright.

The churches who use the expression 'Church as Sacrament' do so because they understand the Church as an effective sign of what God wishes for the world:namely, the communion of all together and with the Triune God, the joy for which God created the world (notwithstanding the sinfulness of Christians).

The churches who do not use the concept of Sacrament for the Church do not do so for at least two reasons, namely, (1) the need for a clear distinction between the Church and Sacraments:the Sacraments are the means of salvation through which Christ sustains the Church, and not actions by which the Church realises or actualises itself; and (2) the use of the word 'Sacrament' for the Church obscures the fact that, for them, the Church is a sign and instrument of God's intention and plan – but it is so as a communion which, while being holy, is still subject to sin.

Behind this lack of agreement lie varying views about the instrumentality of the Church with regard to salvation. Yet those who have become accustomed to call the Church 'Sacrament' would still distinguish between the ways in which baptism and the Lord's Supper on the one hand, and the Church on the other, are signs and instruments of God's plan. And those who do not use the phrase 'Church as Sacrament' would still uphold that the Church is God's holy instrument for his divine purpose (cf. next box, following §56).

49. On the one hand, the Church already participates in the communion of God, in faith, hope, love, and glorification of God's name, and lives as a communion of redeemed persons. Because of the presence of the Spirit and of the Word of God, the Church – as Creatura Verbi and Creatura Spiritus (cf. §10ff.), as the communion of all believers held in personal relationship with God by God himself (cf. §11), as the people of God (cf. §§19–20) – is already the eschatological community God wills.

50. On the other hand the Church, in its human dimension, is made up of human beings who – though they are members of the body of Christ and open to the free activity of the Holy Spirit (cf. Jn 3:8) in illuminating hearts and binding consciences – are still subject to the conditions of the world. Therefore the Church is affected by these conditions. It is exposed to:

- change, which allows for both positive development and growth as well as for the negative possibility of decline and distortion;
- individual, cultural and historical conditioning which can contribute to a richness of insights and expressions of faith, but also to relativising tendencies or to absolutising particular views;
- the power of sin.

51. One particularly striking experience of human weakness and failure that has afflicted the Christian community in via is the sometimes widespread discrepancy between membership in the church, on the one hand, and vibrant profession and practice of the Christian faith, on the other. Many of our communities face the challenge that some of their members seem to 'belong without believing', while other individuals opt out of Church membership, claiming that they can, with greater authenticity, 'believe without belonging'. The challenge of living our faith as believing communities in such a way that all those who belong are seriously committed Christians, and all who sincerely believe want to belong, is a challenge that we share; it crosses the lines which divide us.

52. The oneness, holiness, catholicity and apostolicity of the Church are God's gifts and are essential attributes of the Church's nature and mission. However, there is a continual tension in the historical life of the Church between that which is already given and that which is not yet fully realised.

53. The essential oneness which belongs to the very nature of the Church, and is already given to it in Jesus Christ, stands in contrast to the actual divisions within and between the churches. Yet in spite of all divisions the unity given to the Church is already manifest in the one Gospel present in all churches, and appears in many features of their lives (cf. Eph. 4.4–5; 1 Tim. 2.5; Acts 4.12). The unfortunate divisions among the churches are due partly to sin, and partly to a sincere attempt of Christians to be faithful to the truth. Working for the unity of

the Church means working for fuller visible embodiment of the oneness that belongs to its nature.

54. The essential holiness of the Church stands in contrast to sin, individual as well as communal. This holiness is witnessed to in every generation in the lives of holy men and women, as well as in the holy words the Church proclaims and the holy acts it performs in the name of God, the All-Holy. Nevertheless, in the course of the Church's history sin has again and again disfigured its witness, and run counter to the Church's true nature and vocation. Therefore in the Church there has been again and again God's ever-new offer of forgiveness, together with the call for repentance, renewal and reform. Responding to this call means fuller visible embodiment of the holiness that belongs to its nature.

55. The essential catholicity of the Church is confronted with divisions between and within the Christian communities regarding their life and preaching of the Gospel. Its catholicity transcends all barriers and proclaims God's word to all peoples:where the whole mystery of Christ is present, there too is the Church catholic. However, the catholicity of the Church is challenged by the fact that the integrity of the Gospel is not adequately preached to all; the fullness of communion is not offered to all. Nevertheless, the Spirit given to the Church is the Spirit of the Lordship of Christ over all creation and all times. The Church is called to remove all obstacles to the full embodiment of what is already its nature by the power of the Holy Spirit.

56. The essential apostolicity of the Church stands in contrast to shortcomings and errors of the churches in their proclamation of the Word of God. Nevertheless, this apostolicity is witnessed to in the many ways in which the Church, under the guidance of the Holy Spirit, has been faithful to the testimony of the apostles concerning Jesus Christ. The Church is called to return continuously to the apostolic truth and to be renewed in its worship and mission stemming from its apostolic origin (cf. Acts 2.42–47). By doing so it makes visible, and does justice to, the apostolic Gospel which is already given to it and works in it in the Spirit, making it the Church.

The Church and Sin

All the churches agree that there is sin, corporate and individual, in the Church's history (cf. Rev. 2.2). Yet they differ as to how this reality should be understood and expressed.

For some, it is impossible to say 'the Church sins' because they see the Church as a gift of God, sharing in God's holiness. The Church is the spotless bride of Christ (cf. Eph. 5.25–27); it is a communion in the Holy Spirit, the holy people of God, justified by grace through faith in Christ (cf. Rom. 3.22; Eph. 2.8–9). As such, the Church cannot sin. The gift is lived out in fragile human beings who are liable to sin, but the sins of the members of the Church are not the sins of the Church. The Church is rather the locus of salvation and healing (cf. Isaiah 53; Lk. 4.18–19). According to this perspective one can, and must, speak only of the sin of the members of the Church and of groups within the Church, a situation described by the parable of the wheat and the chaff (cf. Mt. 13.24–30), and by the Augustinian formula of *corpus permixtum*.

Others, while they too state that the Church, as the creature of God's Word and Spirit, the body of Christ, is holy and without sin, say at the same time that it does sin. They say this because they define the Church as the communion of its members who – although they are justified believers brought to birth by the Spirit, and Christ's own body – in this world are still sinful human beings (cf. 1 Jn 1.8–10).

Yet others believe that while one cannot speak of the sins of the Church, sin in the Church may become systemic and also affect the institution.

While there are these different understandings concerning the Church and sin, we ask whether all churches might not be able to agree on the following proposition:

The relationship between sin and holiness in the Church is not a relationship of two equal realities, because sin and holiness do not exist on the same level. Rather, holiness denotes the Church's nature and God's will for it, while sinfulness is contrary to both (cf. 1 Cor. 15.21–26).

B. In Christ – But Not Yet in Full Communion

57. One blessing of the ecumenical movement has been the gradual and increasing discovery of the many aspects of life in Christ which our still-divided churches share; we all participate in some way in Jesus Christ, although we do not yet live in full communion with each other. Such divisions among the churches hinder the mission of the Church. Not only does mission have as its ultimate goal the koinonia of all; but effective mission is thwarted by the scandal of division: Jesus prayed that all his disciples be one precisely 'so that the world may believe' (Jn 17.21). Thus mission is essentially related to the very being of the Church as koinonia (cf. 1 Jn 1.1–3). This is why the restoration of unity between Christians, brought about through committed dialogue about issues that still divide them as well as through the continual renewal of their lives, is such an urgent task.

58. Growth in communion between our churches unfolds within the setting of that wider communion between Christians which extends back into the past and forward into the future. By the power of the Holy Spirit the Church lives in communion with Christ Jesus, in whom all in heaven and earth are joined in the communion of God the Holy One: this is the communion of the saints. The final destiny of the Church is to be caught up in the intimate relation of Father, Son and Holy Spirit, to praise and to enjoy God forever (cf. Rev. 7.9–10; 22.1–5).

59. There remains by virtue of creation a natural bond between human beings and between humanity and creation. 'So if anyone is in Christ, there is a new creation' (2 Cor. 5.17). The new life of communion builds upon and transforms, but never wholly replaces, what was first given in creation; within history, it never completely overcomes the distortions of the relationship between human beings caused by sin. Sharing in Christ is often restricted and only partially realised. The new life therefore entails the constant need for repentance, mutual forgiveness and restoration. It belongs to the essence of fellowship with God that the members of

Christ's body pray day after day 'Forgive us our sins' (Lk. 11.4; cf. Mt. 6.12). But the Father cleanses us from our sins in the blood of his son Jesus and, if we acknowledge our sins, we will be forgiven (cf. 1 Jn 1.7–10). Nonetheless, there is a genuine enjoyment of new life here and now and a confident anticipation of sharing in the fullness of communion in the life to come.

C. Communion and Diversity

60. Diversity in unity and unity in diversity are gifts of God to the Church. Through the Holy Spirit God bestows diverse and complementary gifts on all the faithful for the common good, for service within the community and to the world (cf. 1 Cor. 12.7 and 2 Cor. 9.13). No one is self-sufficient. The disciples are called to be one, while enriched by their diversities – fully united, while respectful of the diversity of persons and community groups (cf. Acts 2; 15; Eph. 2.15–16).

61. There is a rich diversity of Christian life and witness born out of the diversity of cultural and historical context. The Gospel has to be rooted and lived authentically in each and every place. It has to be proclaimed in language, symbols and images that engage with, and are relevant to, particular times and particular contexts. The communion of the Church demands the constant interplay of cultural expressions of the Gospel if the riches of the Gospel are to be appreciated for the whole people of God.[12] Problems are created

- when one culture seeks to capture the Gospel and claims to be the one and only authentic way of celebrating the Gospel;
- when one culture seeks to impose its expression of the Gospel on others as the only authentic expression of the Gospel;
- when one culture finds it impossible to recognise the Gospel being faithfully proclaimed in another culture.

62. Authentic diversity in the life of communion must not be stifled:authentic unity must not be surrendered. Each local church must be the place where two things are simultaneously guaranteed: the safeguarding of unity and the flourishing of a legitimate diversity. There are limits within which diversity is an enrichment but outside of which diversity is not only unacceptable, but destructive of the gift of unity. Similarly unity, particularly when it tends to be identified with uniformity, can be destructive of authentic diversity and thus can become unacceptable. Through shared faith in Christ, expressed in the proclamation of the Word, celebration of the Sacraments and lives of service and witness, each local Christian community participates in the life and witness of all Christian communities in all places and all times. A pastoral ministry for the service of unity and the upholding of diversity is one of the many charisms given to the Church. It helps to keep those with different gifts and perspectives mutually accountable to each other within the communion.

63. Diversity is not the same as division. Within the Church, divisions (heresies and schisms), as well as political conflicts and expressions of hatred, threaten God's gift of communion. Christians are called to work untiringly to overcome divisions,

to prevent legitimate diversities from becoming causes of division, and to live a life of diversities reconciled.

Limits of Diversity?

While all recognise the wide range of diversity in the Church, there is often a tendency (conscious or unconscious) to give more value to some aspects of this diversity than others. This is especially true with regard to diversity in our position on particular issues, e.g., diversity in our worship.

(a) Diversities in expression of the Gospel, in words and in actions can enrich life in communion. Particular emphases today are carried in the life and witness of different churches. How far are the different emphases conflicting positions, or rather an expression of legitimate diversity? Does the weight placed upon the different emphases obscure the fullness of the Gospel message?

(b) What weight do Christians place on ecclesial and confessional identity? For some the preservation of such identity, for the foreseeable future or even permanently, and even within a life of koinonia, is necessary for safeguarding particular truths and rich legitimate diversities that belong to a life of communion. Others understand the goal of visible communion as beyond particular ecclesial or confessional identities – a communion in which the riches safeguarded by confessional traditions are brought together in the witness and experience of a common faith and life. For others the model of 'reconciled diversity' remains a compelling one. Most, however, agree that an openness is required about the unity to which God calls us; and that as we move by steps, under the guidance of the Holy Spirit (cf. Jn 16.13), the portrait of visible unity will become clearer. Churches understand their relation to the one, holy, catholic and apostolic Church in different ways. This has a bearing upon the way they relate to other churches and their perception of the road to visible unity.

(c) In order for the Churches to move further towards complete mutual recognition and full communion, they need to reflect on how they understand and claim their own ecclesial identity and how they regard the ecclesial status of other churches and other Christians.

One type of Ecclesiology identifies the Church exclusively with one's own community, dismissing other communities or persons which claim churchly status into an ecclesiological void. According to a modified form of this type, other communities may possess elements of the Church which bring those who enjoy them into a real, though imperfect, communion outside of one's own community. Another variant of this type offers a pneumatological account of the existence of Christian life outside the bounds of one's own community – something which is nevertheless, identified as the Church.

A second type of ecclesiology, while claiming for its own community a full place in the Church catholic, allows equal status to some other communities (even though the degree and mode of communion actually existing between it and them may vary). One variant of this approach is the so-called 'branch theory', or *tropoi* theory, used to describe the situation of the different

Churches. Another variant is 'denominationalism', which allows for a quite broad spectrum of churches to coexist in organisational independence while constituting, in aggregate, 'the Church universal'. A further variant is called 'cultural families of churches', each of equal value.

A third type of ecclesiology neither identifies one's own community with the One Church, nor does it speak of elements or different degrees of fullness of the Church; yet it does not place all ecclesial bodies on the same level, either. It states rather that the One Church of Christ exists wherever the Gospel is rightly proclaimed and the sacraments are duly administered, because Christ is present and at work wherever these means of his grace are present. However, according to this position there is a difference between historical church bodies as regards the correspondence between their official practice and teaching, on the one hand, and the Gospel present within them, on the other. Whereas in some churches there is such a correspondence, in other churches the Gospel is enveloped in official teachings and practices that contradict it. According to this view even such contradictions, as long as those means of Christ's grace are recognisably there, cannot prevent his presence; nor do they nullify the belonging to his body, the One Church. But they do establish a difference in rank and status between these historic churches which has to be overcome.

(d) One of the pressing ecumenical questions is whether and how churches, at this stage of the ecumenical movement, can live in mutual accountability so that they can sustain one another in unity and legitimate diversity, and can prevent new issues from becoming causes of division within and between churches.

D. The Church as Communion of Local Churches

64. From the beginning contact was maintained between local churches by collections, exchanges of letters, visits and tangible expressions of solidarity (cf. 1 Corinthians 16; 2 Cor. 8.1–9; Gal. 2.9ff.; etc.). From time to time, during the first centuries, local churches assembled to take counsel together. All of these were ways of nurturing interdependence and maintaining communion.

65. The communion of the Church is expressed in the communion between local churches, in each of which the fullness of the Church resides. The communion of the Church embraces local churches in each place and all places at all times. Local churches are held in the communion of the Church by the one Gospel,[13] the one baptism and the one Lord's Supper, served by a common ministry. This communion of local churches is thus not an optional extra, but is an essential aspect of what it means to be the Church.

66. The communion of local churches is sustained by the living elements of apostolicity and catholicity:Scripture, baptism, communion and the service of a common ministry. As 'bonds of communion' these gifts serve the authentic continuity of the life of the whole Church and help to sustain the local churches in a communion of truth and love. They are given to maintain the Church in

integrity as the one Church of Jesus Christ, the same yesterday, today and tomorrow. The goal of the search for full communion is realised when all the churches are able to recognise in one another the one, holy, catholic and apostolic Church in all its fullness. This full communion will be expressed on the local and universal levels through conciliar forms of life and action. In such a communion of unity and authentic diversities, churches are bound in all aspects of their life together at all levels in confessing the one faith and engaging in worship and witness, deliberation and action.

Local Church

The term 'local church' is used differently by different traditions. For some traditions the 'local' church is the congregation of believers gathered in one place to hear the Word and celebrate the Sacraments. For others, 'local' or 'particular' church refers to the bishop with the people around the bishop, gathered to hear the Word and celebrate the Sacraments. In some churches the term 'local church' is used of both the diocese and of the parish. At another level, 'local church' can refer to several dioceses or to regional churches gathered together in a synodal structure under a presidency.

There are different ecclesiological concepts behind these usages, yet most Churches agree that each local church, however it is defined, is united to every other in the universal Church and contains within it the fullness of what it is to be the Church. There is often a discrepancy between theological description of local church and how the local church is experienced by the faithful.

III. The Life of Communion in and for the World

67. God gives to the Church all the gifts and resources needed for its life and mission in and for the world. God bestows on it the grace of the apostolic faith, baptism and Eucharist as means of grace to create and sustain the koinonia. These and other means serve to animate the people of God in their proclamation of the Kingdom and in their participation in the promises of God.

A. Apostolic Faith

68. The Church is called at all times and in all places to 'continue in the apostles' teaching' (Acts 2.42). The faith 'once for all entrusted to the saints' (Jude v. 3) is the faith of the Church through the ages.

69. The revealed apostolic faith is uniquely witnessed to in Scripture. This faith is articulated in the Nicene-Constantinopolitan Creed (381).[14] The Church is called upon to proclaim the same faith in each generation, in each and every place. Each church in its place is challenged in the power of the Holy Spirit to make that faith relevant and alive in its particular cultural, social, political and religious

context. While the apostolic faith has to be interpreted in the context of changing times and places,[15] it must be in continuity with the original witness of the apostolic community and with the faithful explication of that witness throughout the ages.

70. The apostolic faith does not refer to one fixed formula or to a specific phase in Christian history. The faith transmitted through the living tradition of the Church is the faith evoked by the Word of God, inspired by the Holy Spirit and attested in Scripture. Its content is set forth in the Creeds of the Early Church and also testified to in other forms. It is proclaimed in many Confessions of Faith of the churches. It is preached throughout the world today. It is articulated in Canons and Books of Discipline from many periods and stages in the lives of the churches. Thus the apostolic faith is confessed in worship, in life, service and mission – in the living traditions of the Church.

71. The apostolic tradition of the Church is the continuity in the permanent characteristics of the Church of the apostles:witness to the apostolic faith, proclamation and fresh interpretation of the Gospel, celebration of baptism and Eucharist, the transmission of ministerial responsibilities, communion in prayer, love, joy and suffering, service to the sick and needy, communion among the local churches and sharing the divine gifts which have been given to each.

72. Within the apostolic tradition the Nicene-Constantinopolitan Creed, promulgated by the Early Ecumenical Councils, is a pre-eminent expression of the apostolic faith. Although its language, like that of all texts, is conditioned by time and context, it has been the Creed most widely used by Christians throughout the centuries and remains so today throughout the world. The fact that some churches do not explicitly use this Creed liturgically or catechetically need not be interpreted as a sign of their departure from the apostolic faith. Nevertheless the existence of such differences suggests that churches need to be attentive to the tolerable limits to diversity in confessing one faith.

73. The faith of the Church has to be lived out in active response to the challenges of every age and place. It speaks to personal and social situations, including situations of injustice, of violation of human dignity and of the degradation of creation. For example, when Christians confess that God is creator of all, they recognise the goodness of creation and commit themselves to care for the well-being of humanity and for all that God has made. When Christians confess Christ crucified and risen, they commit themselves to witness to the paschal mystery in word and deed. When Christians confess the Holy Spirit as Lord and Giver of Life, they know themselves to be already citizens of heaven and they commit themselves to discern the Spirit's gift in their lives. When Christians confess the one, holy, catholic and apostolic Church, they commit themselves to manifest and promote the realisation of these attributes.[16]

B. Baptism

74. In the Nicene-Constantinopolitan Creed Christians confess 'one baptism for the remission of sins'. Through Baptism with water in the name of the Triune

God, Father, Son and Holy Spirit, Christians are united with Christ, with each other and with the Church of every time and place. Baptism is thus a basic bond of unity. The recognition of the one baptism into Christ constitutes an urgent call to the churches to overcome their divisions and visibly manifest their communion in faith and through mutual accountability in all aspects of Christian life and witness.

75. Baptism is the celebration of new life through Christ and of participation in the baptism, life, death and resurrection of Jesus Christ (cf. Mt. 3.13–17; Rom. 6.3–5). Baptism involves confession of sin, conversion of heart, pardoning, cleansing and sanctification. It is the gift of the Holy Spirit, incorporation into the Body of Christ, participation in the Kingdom of God and the life of the world to come (cf. Eph. 2.6). Baptism consecrates the believer as a member of 'a chosen race, a royal priesthood, a holy nation' (1 Pet. 2.9).

76. 'Baptism is related not only to momentary experience, but to life-long growth into Christ.'[17] Nourished by the worship, witness and teaching of the Church, the believer grows in his or her relationship with Christ, and with other members of the body of Christ. In this process the faith of the believer – whether he or she was baptised as an infant, or upon personal profession of faith – is nourished by, and tested against, the faith of the Church.[18]

77. All human beings have in common their creation at God's hand, and God's providential care for them; and they share in social, economic and cultural institutions which preserve human life. As people are baptised they are clothed in Christ (cf. Gal. 3.27), they enter into the koinonia of Christ's Body (cf. 1 Cor. 12.13), they receive the Holy Spirit which is the privilege of God's adopted children (cf. Rom. 8.15f.), and so they enjoy, in anticipation, that participation in the divine nature which God promises and wills for humankind (cf. 2 Pet. 1.4). In the present, the solidarity of Christians with the joys and sorrows of their neighbours, and their engagement in the struggle for the dignity of all who suffer, for the excluded and the poor, belongs to their baptismal vocation. It is the way they are brought face to face with Christ in his identification with the victimised and outcast.

Baptism

Although BEM and the churches' responses to it registered a high degree of agreement about baptism, some significant issues remain:[19]

(a) the difference between churches which baptise infants, and those which baptise only those able to offer a personal profession of faith;

(b) the inability of some churches to recognise baptism performed by others, and the related practice of 're'-baptism;

(c) the different starting points and historical development of the terms 'ordinance' and 'Sacrament' (although both are understood as describing the act by which people are brought to new life in Christ);

(d) whether baptism is best understood as effecting the reality of new life in Christ, or as reflecting it;

(e) the difference between the churches which baptise insisting on the Trinitarian formula according to the command of Jesus (Mt. 28.19–20), and those which insist that baptism 'in the name of Jesus Christ' is more consistent with the practice of the apostles (cf. Acts 2.38);

(f) the difference between churches which employ water as the instrument of baptism, and those which believe that Christian baptism does not require any such material instrument;

(g) those communities which believe that baptism with water is necessary, and those which do not celebrate baptism, yet understand themselves as sharing in the spiritual experience of life in Christ.

C. Eucharist

78. Communion established in baptism is focused and brought to expression in the Eucharist. There is a dynamic connection between baptism and Eucharist. Baptismal faith is re-affirmed and grace given for the faithful living out of the Christian calling.

79. The Lord's Supper is the celebration where, gathered around his table, Christians receive the body and blood of Christ. It is a proclamation of the Gospel, a glorification of the Father for everything accomplished in creation, redemption and sanctification (doxologia); a memorial of the death and resurrection of Christ Jesus and what was accomplished once for all on the Cross (anamnesis); an invocation of the Holy Spirit (epiclesis); an intercession; the communion of the faithful and an anticipation and foretaste of the kingdom to come.

80. In 1 Corinthians 10 and 11, Paul highlights the connection between the Lord's Supper and the nature of the Church. 'The cup of blessing that we bless, is it not a sharing in the blood of Christ? The bread that we break, is it not a sharing in the body of Christ? Because there is one bread, we who are many are one body, for we all partake of the one bread' (1 Cor. 10.16–17). He also draws attention to the moral implications of the celebration:'Examine yourselves, and only then eat of the bread and drink of the cup' (1 Cor. 11.28).

81. Just as the confession of faith and baptism are inseparable from a life of service and witness, so too the Mass demands reconciliation and sharing among all those regarded as brothers and sisters in the one family of God and is a constant challenge in the search for appropriate relationships in social, economic and political life (cf. Mt. 5.23ff.; 1 Cor. 10.14; 1 Cor. 11.20–22). Because the Lord's Supper is the Sacrament which builds up community, all kinds of injustice, racism, estrangement, and lack of freedom are radically challenged when we share in the body and blood of Christ. Through Holy Communion the all-renewing grace of God penetrates the human personality and restores human dignity. The Eucharist, therefore, obliges us also to participate actively in the ongoing restoration of the world's situation and the human condition. God's judgement demands that our behaviour be consistent with the reconciling presence of God in human history.

Eucharist

Although BEM and the responses to it from the churches registered a degree of agreement about the Eucharist, significant differences remain:

As regards the understanding and practice of the Eucharist there remains the question whether it is primarily a meal where Christians receive the body and blood of Christ, or primarily a service of thanksgiving.

Among those for whom the Eucharist is primarily a service of thanksgiving, there is growing convergence concerning its sacrificial character. Remaining disagreement centres principally on the questions of how the sacrifice of Jesus Christ on Calvary is made present in the Eucharistic act. A help in reconciling the different approaches has been made by the use of biblical and patristic scholarship to probe more deeply into the meaning of the biblical term anamnesis. However, some maintain that the concept has been made to bear more weight in theological and ecumenical texts than it is capable of bearing.

Churches continue to disagree about the nature and mode of the presence of Christ in the Eucharist. Some important differences remain regarding the role and invocation of the Holy Spirit in the whole eucharistic celebration.

It is a matter of continuing concern that not all Christians share the communion. Some churches believe that eucharistic sharing is both a means of building communion between divided churches as well as its goal; others either do not offer Eucharistic hospitality, or offer it under restricted conditions. Some churches invite all who believe in Jesus Christ to receive communion; other Churches invite only those who believe in Jesus Christ and are baptised and in good standing in their own Churches. Among still other churches eucharistic communion is understood as the ultimate expression of agreement in faith and of a communion in life. Such an understanding would make the sharing of the Lord's Supper with those outside their own tradition an anomaly. As a result, for some churches the practice of 'Eucharistic hospitality' is the antithesis of the commitment to full visible unity.

Behind the variety of practices lie serious theological problems that are at present unresolved. While recent bilateral and multilateral theological dialogues have achieved much in overcoming some of these traditional disagreements, it is evident that there is a continuing need for growth in understanding concerning the actual faith and practice of the divided churches.

D. Ministry of All the Faithful

82. The Church is called at all times and in all places to serve God after the example of the Lord who came to serve rather than to be served. The idea of service is central to any biblical understanding of ministry.

83. Every Christian receives gifts of the Holy Spirit for the upbuilding of the Church, and for his or her part in the mission of Christ. These gifts are given for the common good (cf. 1 Cor. 12.7), and place obligations of responsibility and

mutual accountability on every individual and local community, and indeed on the Church as a whole at every level of its life. Strengthened by the Spirit, Christians are called to live out their discipleship in a variety of forms of service. The teaching of the faith and of its moral implications is entrusted in a special way to parents, although all the faithful are called upon to witness to the Gospel in word and deed. Catechists and theologians provide an invaluable service in handing on and deepening our understanding of the faith. The following of Christ, who came to bring good news to the poor and healing to the sick (cf. Lk. 4.18–19), provides a powerful and specifically Christian motivation for believers to engage in other forms of service:education and health care, charitable assistance to the poor and the promotion of justice, peace and the protection of the environment.

84. Through their participation in Christ, the unique priest of the new covenant (cf. Heb. 9.11), Christians are constituted a royal priesthood called to offer spiritual sacrifices (cf. 1 Peter 2), and indeed their very selves as a living sacrifice (cf. Rom. 12.1) after the example of Jesus himself. This calling underlies the Church's potentially costly witness to justice and the duty of intercession.

85. In this way every Christian, on the basis of the one baptism into Christ, should seek to serve the world by proclaiming good news to the poor, 'release to the captives and recovery of sight to the blind' and setting at liberty those who are oppressed. In short, this is an obligation resting equally on all 'to proclaim the year of the Lord's favour' in all the varied situations of need in the world throughout the ages (Lk. 4.18–19).

E. Ministry of the Ordained

86. In calling and sending the Twelve and his other apostles, Jesus laid foundations for the ongoing proclamation of the Kingdom and the service of the community of his disciples. Faithful to his example, from the earliest times there were those chosen by the community under the guidance of the Spirit, and given specific authority and responsibility. Ordained ministers serve in the building up of the community, in equipping the saints, and in strengthening the Church's witness in the world (cf. Eph. 4.12–13). They may not dispense with the ongoing support and the encouragement of the community – for whom they are chosen, and for whom they are empowered by the Holy Spirit to act as representative persons. Ordained ministers have a special responsibility for the ministry of Word and Sacrament. They have a ministry of pastoral care, teaching and leadership in mission. In all of those ways they strengthen the communion in faith, life and witness of the whole people of God.

87. There is no single pattern of conferring ministry in the New Testament. The Spirit has at different times led the Church to adapt its ministries to contextual needs; various forms of the ordained ministry have been blessed with gifts of the Spirit. The threefold ministry of bishop, presbyter and deacon had become by the third century the generally accepted pattern. It is still retained by many churches today, though subsequently it underwent considerable changes in its practical

exercise and is still changing in most churches today. Other churches have developed different patterns of ministry.

88. The chief responsibility of the ordained ministry is to assemble and build up the Body of Christ by proclaiming and teaching the Word of God, by celebrating baptism and the Eucharist and by guiding the life of the community in its worship, its mission and its service. Essential to its testimony are not merely its words, but the love of its members for one another, the quality of their service to those in need, a just and disciplined life and a fair exercise of power and authority.

89. In the course of history, the Church has developed several means for maintaining its apostolicity through time, in different circumstances and cultural contexts:the scriptural canon, dogma, liturgical order, structures wider than the level of local communities. The ministry of the ordained is to serve in a specific way the apostolic continuity of the Church as a whole. In this context, succession in ministry is a means of serving the apostolic continuity of the Church. This is focused in the act of ordination when the Church as a whole, through its ordained ministers, takes part in the act of ordaining those chosen for the ministry of Word and Sacrament.

Ordained Ministry

Although BEM and the responses to it, multilateral and bilateral dialogues, and church union processes have identified the points of convergence on the subject of ordained ministry there remain issues to be explored further:

(a) the location of the ministry of the ordained in, with, among or over the people of God;

(b) Eucharistic presidency;

(c) the threefold ministry as a means to and expression of unity;

(d) the Sacrament of ordination;

(e) the restriction of ordination to the ministry of Word and Sacrament to men only;

(f) the relationship between the apostolic succession of ministry and the apostolic continuity of the Church as a whole;

(g) the ways in which ordination is considered constitutive of the Church.

F. Oversight:Personal, Communal, Collegial

90. The Church, as the body of Christ and the eschatological people of God, is built up by the Holy Spirit through a diversity of gifts or ministries. This diversity calls for a ministry of co-ordination so that these gifts may enrich the whole Church, its unity and mission. The faithful exercise of the ministry of episkopé under the Gospel is a requirement of fundamental importance for the Church's life and mission. The responsibility of those called to exercise oversight cannot be fulfilled without the collaboration, support and assent of the whole community. At

the same time, the effective and faithful life of the community is served by a ministry of leadership set apart to guide its mission, teaching and common life.

91. In the course of the first centuries, communion between local congregations – which had been maintained by a series of informal links such as visits, letters and collections – became more and more expressed in institutional forms. The purpose was to hold the local congregations in communion, to safeguard and hand on apostolic truth, to give mutual support and to lead in witnessing to the Gospel. All these functions are summed up in the term episkopé.

92. The specific development of structures of episkopé varied in different regions of the Church:this was true of both the collegial expression of episkopé in synods, and its personal embodiment in the individual bishops. The crystallisation of most of the episcopal functions in the hands of one individual (episkopos) came later in some places than in others. What is evident in every case is that episkopé and episcopacy are in the service of maintaining continuity in apostolic truth and unity of life.

93. In the 16th century, oversight came to be exercised in a variety of ways in the churches which took their identity through the continental Reformation. These Reformers, seeking to return to the apostolicity of the Church which they considered to have been corrupted, saw themselves faced with the alternative of either staying within the inherited church structures or remaining faithful to the apostolicity of the Church, and thus accepted a break with the overall structure of the Church, including the ministry of universal primacy. Nevertheless, they continued to see the need for a ministry of episkopé, which the churches which went through the Reformation ordered in different ways. Some exercised episkopé in synodal forms. Others kept or developed ministries of personal episkopé, including, for some, the sign of historic episcopal succession.

Episkopé, Bishops and Apostolic Succession

One of the most difficult issues dividing Christian communities concerns this form of ministry and its relation to the apostolicity of the Church. To focus the question in a very precise way: churches remain divided about whether the historic episcopate – in the sense of bishops ordained in apostolic succession back to the earliest generations of the Church – is a necessary component of ecclesial order as intended by Christ for his community; or is merely one form of church structure which, because it is so traditional, is particularly advantageous for today's community but is not essential. Still other communities see no special reason for privileging episcopal structure, or even believe it is better avoided, for they see it as prone to abuse.

Ecumenical reflection on the more general concept of a ministry of episkopé, as described in the preceding paragraphs, has helped to bring to light hitherto unrecognised parallels between episcopal and non-episcopal churches in the way oversight is exercised. Moreover, both types of churches have been able to acknowledge a degree of apostolicity in one another, even though disagreement about the need for bishops remains.

94. Through the commissioned functions of the ordained ministry, Word, Sacrament and discipline, God not only furthers the announcement of his Kingdom but also discloses its fulfilment. This underlies that aspect of ministry known as episkopé, which means both oversight and visitation. Like every other aspect of ministry, episkopé both belongs to the whole church and is entrusted as a particular charge on specific persons. For this reason it is frequently stressed that, at every level of the Church's life, the ministry must be exercised in personal, communal and collegial ways. It should be remembered that 'personal', 'communal' and 'collegial' refer not only to particular structures and processes, but also describe the informal reality of the bonds of koinonia, the mutual belonging and accountability within the ongoing common life of the Church.

(I) PERSONAL
95. Through the discernment of the community and under the guidance of the Holy Spirit, God calls out persons for the exercise of the ministry of oversight. Episkopé is not to be understood as a function only of these ministers who are in many churches designated bishops. Oversight is always to be exercised within and in relation to the whole Church. The Spirit who empowers those who are entrusted with oversight is the same Spirit who animates the life of all believers. On account of this, those who exercise oversight are inseparably bound to all believers. Those who exercise oversight have a special duty to care for, and recall the community to, the unity, holiness, catholicity and apostolicity of the Church. In discerning vocations and in ordaining others to share in the ministry of Word and Sacrament, they care for the continuity of the life of the Church. An important dimension of their oversight is care for the unity of the community, a unity which involves not only the mutual love of the members, but also their common confession of the apostolic faith, their nourishment by the Word and their life of common service in the world.

(II) COMMUNAL
96. One of the functions of episkopé is to care for the participation of the whole community in what makes for its common life and the discernment of the mind of the faithful. The communal life of the Church is grounded in the Sacrament of baptism. All the baptised share a responsibility for the apostolic faith and witness of the whole Church. The communal dimension of the Church's life refers to the involvement of the whole body of the faithful in common consultation, sometimes through representation and constitutional structures, over the well-being of the Church and their common involvement in the service of God's mission in the world. Communal life sustains all the baptised in a web of belonging, of mutual accountability and support. It implies unity in diversity and is expressed in one heart and one mind (cf. Phil. 2.1–2). It is the way in which Christians are held in unity and travel together as the one Church, and the one Church is manifested in the life of each local church.

(III) COLLEGIAL

97. Enabling the Church to live in conformity to the mission of Christ is a continuous process involving the whole community, but within that the gathering of those with oversight has a special role. Collegiality refers to the corporate, representative exercise in the areas of leadership, consultation, discernment, and decision-making. Collegiality entails the personal and relational nature of leadership and authority. Collegiality is at work wherever those entrusted with oversight gather, discern, speak and act as one on behalf of the whole Church. This implies leading the Church by means of the wisdom gained by corporate prayer, study and reflection, drawing on Scripture, tradition and reason – the wisdom and experience of all church communities throughout the ages. Sustaining collegiality involves preventing premature closure of debate, ensuring that different voices are heard, listening to expert opinion and drawing on appropriate sources of scholarship. Collegial oversight should help the Church to live in communion while the mind of Christ is being discerned. It makes room for those of different opinions, guarding and preaching unity, even calling for restraint while giving spiritual and moral leadership. Speaking collegially can mean reflecting back to the community the legitimate diversity that exists within the life of the Church.

98. Because of the separation of the churches, there has been relatively little collegial exercise of oversight or witness within society on the part of the ministers of our divided communities. The ecumenical movement can serve as a stimulus and invitation to church leaders to explore the possibility of working together in appropriate ways on behalf of their own communities and as an expression of their care for all the churches (cf. 2 Cor. 11.28), and in common witness before society.

G. Conciliarity and Primacy

99. Ministry and oversight, as treated in the previous two sections, are exercised locally and regionally. In addition, ecumenical dialogue has led the churches to ask whether and, if so, how they may function within the church as a communion existing throughout the whole world. Conciliarity and primacy concern the exercise of ministry at every level including this wider context. Conciliarity is an essential feature of the life of the Church, grounded in the common baptism of its members (cf. 1 Pet. 2.9–10; Eph. 4.11–16). Under the guidance of the Holy Spirit, the whole Church, whether dispersed or gathered together, is conciliar. Thus conciliarity characterises all levels of the life of the Church. It is already present in the relations which exist among the members of the smallest local communities; according to Gal. 3.28, 'you are all one in Christ Jesus', excluding divisions, domination, submission and all negative forms of discrimination. In the local Eucharistic community, conciliarity is the profound unity in love and truth between the members among themselves and with their presiding minister. This conciliar dimension is also expressed at wider instances of Christian communion, some more regional and some even seeking to draw in the participation of the whole Christian community. The interconnectedness of the life of the Church is

expressed between Christian communities at different geographic levels, the 'all in each place' linked to the 'all in every place'.

100. In crucial situations synods came and come together to discern the apostolic truth over against particular threats and dangers to the life of the Church, trusting in the guidance of the Holy Spirit, whom Jesus promised to send after his return to the Father (cf. Jn 16.7, 12–14; Acts 15.28). When synods drew together the leaders of the world Christian community, they were called 'ecumenical', provided that their decrees were received by the whole Church. Their reception by the entire Church is an acknowledgement of the important service they have played in fostering and maintaining universal communion.

101. Wherever people, communities or churches come together to take counsel and make important decisions, there is need for someone to summon and preside over the gathering for the sake of good order and to help the process of promoting, discerning and articulating consensus. Those who preside are always to be at the service of those among whom they preside for the edification of the Church of God, in love and truth. It is the duty of the president to respect the integrity of local churches, to give voice to the voiceless and to uphold unity in diversity.

102. The word primacy was used by the Early Ecumenical Councils to refer to the ancient practice whereby the bishops of Alexandria, Rome and Antioch, and later Jerusalem and Constantinople, exercised a personal ministry of oversight over an area much wider than that of their individual ecclesiastical provinces. This suggests that primacy concerns the personal exercise of the ministry of oversight but also, since this exercise was affirmed by the councils, that such oversight is not opposed to conciliarity, which expresses more the communal and collegial service to unity. Historically, forms of primacy have existed at various levels, some wider, such as those of the patriarchates, and some more restricted. According to canon 34 of the Apostolic Canons, the first among the bishops would only make a decision in agreement with the other bishops and the latter would make no important decision without the agreement of the first.

103. Even in the early centuries, primacy in the service of mission and unity became complicated by questions of jurisdiction and even competitiveness between patriarchates. The issues became more polarised as the papacy developed and further claims were made for the direct, immediate and universal jurisdiction of the Bishop of Rome over the whole Church. In recent years, however, both ecumenical rapprochement and globalisation have created a new climate in which a universal primacy can be seen as a gift rather than a threat to other churches and the distinctive features of their witness.

104. Partly because of the progress already recorded in bilateral and multilateral dialogues, the Fifth World Conference on Faith and Order raised the question 'of a universal ministry of Christian unity'. In his Encyclical *Ut Unum Sint*[20] Pope John Paul II quoted this text and invited church leaders and their theologians to 'enter into patient and fraternal dialogue' concerning this ministry. This has led to an increasingly open debate. In subsequent discussion, despite continuing areas of disagreement, there seems to be an increasing openness to discuss a universal ministry in support of mission and unity of the church and agreement that any such personal ministry would need to be exercised in communal and collegial

ways. Given the ecumenical sensitivity of this issue it is important to distinguish between the essence of the primacy and any particular ways in which it has been or is currently exercised.[21]

Conciliarity and Universal Primacy

There is still much work to be done to arrive at a preliminary convergence on this topic. At present Christians do not agree that universal ministry of conciliarity or primacy for the unity and mission of the church is necessary or acceptable. The lack of agreement is not simply between certain families of churches but exists within some churches. The way forward involves coming to a consensus both within each church and among the churches.

There has been significant ecumenical discussion of New Testament evidence about a ministry serving the wider unity of the Church, such as that of Peter or of Paul. Nevertheless, disagreements remain about the significance of their ministries and what they may imply for God's intention for some form of universal ministry in the service of the unity and mission of the Church.

H. Authority

105. Jesus' ministry was characterised with authority and healing which placed itself at the service of human beings. This authority was self-emptying with 'power to lay down' his life (Jn 10.17–18). The vindication of this authority is eschatological (cf. 1 Cor. 15.28).

106. Authority is relational and interdependent. The ecclesiological theme of reception highlights the relation between authority and communion (cf. Jn 1.1–12). Christ's own exercise of authority is shown in his washing of his disciples' feet (cf. Jn 13.1–17). Mt. 28.18–20 witnesses that Jesus gave his disciples the mandate to teach throughout the whole world and to relate their mission to the celebration of Christian initiation in baptism as well as to the faith in the Holy Trinity. In the opening scene of Acts Jesus states that the power of the Holy Spirit will come upon the disciples and will give them authority to witness to the end of the world (Acts 1.7–8):'no one can say "Jesus is Lord" except by the Holy Spirit' (1 Cor. 12.3).

107. All authority in the church comes from God and is marked by God's holiness. This authority is effective when holiness shines from the lives of Christians and the ordered Christian community, faithful to the divine teachings. All the sources of authority recognised in varying degrees by the churches such as Scripture, tradition, worship, synods, also reflect the holiness of the Triune God.

108. One example of the communal aspect of authority in the church is the act of ordination. In ordination both the action of ordaining minister and the assent of the faithful are necessary elements.

IV. In and for the World

109. The reason for the mission of Jesus has been succinctly expressed in the words:'God so loved the world that he gave his only Son' (Jn 3.16). Thus the first and foremost attitude of God toward the world is love to every woman, man and child who has ever been born into human history.[22] The Kingdom of God, which Jesus preached in parables and inaugurated by his mighty deeds, especially by the paschal mystery of his death and resurrection, is the final destiny of the whole universe. One of the convictions which governs our reflections in this text is that the Church was intended by God, not for its own sake, but as an instrument, in God's hands, for the transformation of the world. Thus service (diakonia) belongs to the very being of the Church.[23]

110. One of the greatest services Christians offer to the world is the proclamation of the Gospel to every creature (cf. Mk 16.15). Evangelization is thus the foremost task of the church in obedience to the command of Jesus (Mt. 28.18–20). There is no contradiction between evangelisation and respect for the values present in other faiths.

111. The Church is the community of people called by God who, through the Holy Spirit, are united with Jesus Christ and sent as disciples to bear witness to God's reconciliation, healing and transformation of creation. Discipleship is based on the life and teaching of Jesus of Nazareth testified to in Scripture. Christians are called to respond to the living Word of God by obeying God rather than 'any human truth' (Acts 5.29), by repenting of sinful actions, by forgiving others, and by living sacrificial lives of service. The source of their passion for the transformation of the world lies in their communion with God in Jesus Christ. They believe that God, who is absolute love, mercy and justice, is working through them by the Holy Spirit.

112. In the world which 'God so loved' (Jn 3.16), Christians encounter not only situations of harmony and prosperity, of progress and hope; but also problems and tragedies – sometimes of almost unspeakable magnitude – which demand from them a response as disciples of the One who healed the blind, the lame and the leper, who welcomed the poor and the outcast, and who challenged authorities who showed little regard for human dignity or the will of God. Precisely because of their faith, Christian communities may not stand idly by in the face of major calamities affecting human health, such as famine and starvation, natural disasters and the HIV/AIDS pandemic. Faith impels them to work for a more just social order, in which the goods of this earth, destined for the use of all, may be more justly shared, the suffering of the poor may be eased and absolute destitution may one day be eliminated. As followers of the One whom every Christmas they celebrate as the 'Prince of Peace', Christians must advocate peace, especially by seeking to overcome the causes of war (principal among which are economic injustice, racism, ethnic and religious hatred, nationalism, and the use of violence to resolve differences and oppression). Jesus said that He came so that human beings may have life in abundance (cf. Jn 10.10); his followers must defend human life and dignity. Each context will provide its own clues to discern what is the

appropriate Christian outreach in any particular circumstance. Even now, divided Christian communities can and sometimes have carried out this discernment together and have acted together to bring relief to suffering human beings and to help create a society more in keeping with their dignity and with the will of their loving Father in heaven.

113. The Christian community always lives within the sphere of divine forgiveness and grace. This grace calls forth and shapes the moral life of believers. Discipleship demands moral commitment. Members of the Church rely on God's forgiveness and renewing grace in all moments of their lives, both in faithfulness and infidelity, either in virtue or in sin. The Church does not rest on moral achievement but on justification by grace through faith. It is of no little importance for the unity of the Church that the two communities whose separation marked the beginning of the Reformation have in recent years achieved consensus about the central aspects of the doctrine of justification by faith, the major doctrine at issue in their division.[24] It is on the basis of faith and grace that moral engagement and common action are possible and can even be affirmed as intrinsic to the life and being of the Church.

114. The ethics of Christians as disciples relate both to the Church and to the world.[25] They are rooted in God, the creator and revealer, and take shape as the community seeks to understand God's will within the various circumstances of time and place. The Church does not stand in isolation from the moral struggles of humankind as a whole. Christians both can and should join together with the adherents of other religions, as well as with all persons of good will, in order to promote not only those personal moral choices which they believe essential to the authentic realization of the human person, but also the social goods of justice, peace and the protection of the environment. Thus Christian discipleship requires believers to give serious consideration to the complex ethical questions that touch their personal lives and the public domain of social policy, and to translate their reflections into action. A Church that would want to be invisible would no longer be a church of disciples.

115. Not only must Christians seek to promote the values of the Kingdom of God by working together with adherents of other religions and even with those of no religious belief, but it is also incumbent upon them to witness to the Kingdom in the realms of politics and economics. In particular, despite dangers and distortions the relation between Church and State has been, over the centuries, an arena for Christian advocacy for the transformation of society along the lines which Jesus sketched out in the Gospel. Many historical, cultural and demographic factors condition the relation between Church and State, or between Church and society.[26] One expression of the diversity or catholicity of the Church is the variety of models that these relations to societal structures can take. In each case, the explicit call of Jesus that his disciples be 'salt of the earth' and 'light of the world' (cf. Mt. 5.13–16), and that they preach the Kingdom (the role of which in society is comparable to that of leaven which makes the whole dough rise (cf. Mt. 13.33)), invites Christians to collaborate with political and economic authorities to promote the values of God's Kingdom, and to oppose policies and initiatives

which contradict them. In this way Christians may stand in the tradition of the prophets who proclaimed God's judgement on all injustice.

116. There are occasions when ethical issues challenge the integrity of the Christian community itself and make it necessary to take a common stance to preserve its authenticity and credibility. Koinonia in relation to ethics and morals means that it is in the Church that, along with the confession of the faith and the celebration of the Sacraments (and as an inseparable part of these), the Gospel tradition is probed constantly for moral inspiration and insight. Situations where Christians or churches do not agree on an ethical position demand that dialogue continue in an effort to discover whether such differences can ultimately be overcome – and, if not, whether they are truly church-dividing.

117. Christians and their communities are called to be accountable to each other with respect to their ethical reflections and decisions. This interconnectedness is manifested in their commitment to the reciprocal partnership of giving and receiving (cf. Phil. 4.15). As churches engage in mutual questioning and affirmation, they give expression to what they share in Christ. Christians engage together in service to the world, glorifying and praising God and seeking that full koinonia, where the life which God desires for all people and the whole creation will find fulfilment.

118. 'God did not send the Son into the world to condemn the world, but in order that the world might be saved through him' (Jn 3.17). The New Testament ends with the vision of a new heavens and a new earth, transformed by the grace of God (cf. Rev. 21.1–22:5). This new world is promised for the end of history, but even now the Church, on a pilgrimage of faith and hope marching through time, calls out in worship 'Come, Lord Jesus' (Rev. 22.20). Christ loves the Church as the bridegroom loves his bride (cf. Eph. 5.25) and, until the wedding feast of the lamb in the Kingdom of heaven (cf. Rev. 19.7), shares with it his mission of bringing light and healing to human beings until he comes again in glory.

Conclusion

119. In recent years the ecumenical movement has produced many agreed statements recording converging understandings about the faith and order of the Church. Among the most well known of these is Baptism, Eucharist and Ministry. Such converging understandings have challenged some churches to accept into their life the implications of their common affirmations. Significant proposals for steps towards greater expressions of visible unity have been enacted, or are awaiting decision, by the churches in virtually every part of the world. This ecumenical fact deserves affirmation.

120. Progress has shown itself concretely in the ways by which churches, according to various criteria and to varying degrees, have engaged in processes of reception and thus have advanced towards mutual recognition – or at least towards the recognition of Christian faith and life beyond their preconceived boundaries, as they formally understand them to be. Some have reached a stage of mutual recognition.

121. However, this convergence has not been received everywhere. There has been a significant retrenchment in some areas, expressed in a re-confessionalism or an anti-ecumenical spirit. There are also examples of non-reception which are either the result of deeply held theological convictions, or of the shortcomings of the ecumenical work itself. All the churches, at all levels of their life, are called upon to engage in the task of articulating together a common understanding of Christian identity:the dynamic and pilgrim character of the people of God, constantly called to repentance and renewal.

122. Ultimately the reception of the results of theological convergence will lead us to what the Canberra Statement called for:'The goal of the search for full communion is realised when all the churches are able to recognise in one another the one, holy, catholic and apostolic church in its fullness' and express this in a reconciled common life.

123. Building on the convergence of earlier work, this present document is an attempt to express what the churches might now claim together about the nature and mission of the Church; and, within that perspective, to state the remaining areas of difficulty and disagreement. If the churches were able to agree together to a convergence statement on the Church, this would further significantly the process of mutual recognition on the way to reconciliation and visible unity.

Notes

1. 'Faith and Order By-Laws, 3.1', in *Faith and Order at the Crossroads: The Plenary Commission Meeting, Kuala Lumpur 2004*, Thomas F. Best (ed.), Faith and Order Paper no. 196 (Geneva: WCC, 2005), p. 450.
2. *The Ecumenical Movement: An Anthology of Key Texts and Voices*, Michael Kinnamon and Brian E. Cope (eds) (Geneva and Grand Rapids: WCC and Eerdmans, 1997), pp. 124–5.
3. *Towards a Common Understanding and Vision of the World Council of Churches: A Policy Statement* (Geneva: WCC, Sept. 1997).
4. Faith and Order Paper no. 111 (Geneva: WCC, 1982).
5. Faith and Order Paper no. 153, new rev. version, 4th printing (Geneva: WCC, 1996).
6. Faith and Order Paper no. 151, 2nd rev. printing (Geneva: WCC, 1990).
7. Faith and Order Paper no. 181 (Geneva, WCC, 1998).
8. Cf. 'Towards a Common Understanding of the Church: Reformed–Roman Catholic Dialogue', §96, in *Growth in Agreement II: Reports and Agreed Statements of Ecumenical Conversations on a World Level, 1982–1998*, Faith and Order Paper no. 187, ed. by Jeffrey Gros, Harding Meyer, William G. Rusch (Geneva and Grand Rapids: WCC and Eerdmans, 2000), p. 802.
9. *Confessing the One Faith*, §240.
10. Cf. Report of Section II: 'Multiplicity of Expression of the One Faith', §§13–22, in *On the Way to Fuller Koinonia: Official Report of the Fifth World Conference on Faith and Order*, ed. by Thomas F. Best and Günther Gassman, Faith and Order Paper no. 161 (Geneva: WCC [1994]), pp. 240–2.
11. Cf. §12 of the present study document.
12. Cf. *A Treasure in Earthen Vessels:An Instrument for an Ecumenical Reflection on Hermeneutics*, Faith and Order Paper no. 182 (Geneva: WCC, 1998), §§49ff., and the draft text from the Faith and Order study on *Ethnic Identity, National Identity and the Search for the Unity of the Church*: 'Participation in God's Mission of Reconciliation: An Invitation to the Churches',

FO/2005:11, June 2005, Section II (to be published in revised form as a Faith and Order Paper).

13. *A Treasure in Earthen Vessels*, §38.
14. See *Confessing the One Faith*.
15. *A Treasure in Earthen Vessels*, Section B, 1. (§§38–42).
16. Cf. §12 of the present study document.
17. 'Baptism' section, in *Baptism, Eucharist and Ministry*, §9.
18. Cf. the text-in-process from the Faith and Order study on Baptism: 'One Baptism:Towards Mutual Recognition', FO/2005:06, June 2005, §35.
19. It is hoped that the Faith and Order study on Baptism presently underway will help to resolve these outstanding problems. Cf. the text-in-process from the Faith and Order study on Baptism:'One Baptism: Towards Mutual Recognition', FO/2005:06, June 2005.
20. John Paul II, *Ut Unum Sint: Encyclical Letter of the Holy Father John Paul II on Commitment to Ecumenism* (London: Catholic Truth Society, 1995), §96.
21. Any 'universal ministry of Christian unity' needs to be exercised in a communal and collegial way, resembling Faith and Order's perspective on ministry as expressed in *Baptism, Eucharist and Ministry*, 'Ministry' Section, §26.
22. Cf. the study document from the Faith and Order study on theological anthropology: 'Ecumenical Perspectives on Theological Anthropology', Faith and Order Paper no. 199 (Geneva: WCC, 2005), Section II.
23. Cf. *Church and World*, passim.
24. See *Joint Declaration on the Doctrine of Justification, The Lutheran World Federation and the Roman Catholic Church*, English language edition (Grand Rapids, MI and Cambridge, UK: William B. Eerdmans, 2000); available online at:http://www.elca.org/ ecumenical/ ecumenicaldialogue/romancatholic/jddj/declaration.html.
25. Cf. the text-in-process from the Faith and Order study on Baptism: 'One Baptism:Towards Mutual Recognition', §58, §77.
26. Cf. the draft text from the Faith and Order study on *Ethnic Identity, National Identity and the Search for the Unity of the Church*: 'Participation in God's Mission of Reconciliation: An Invitation to the Churches', Section IV, A.